BEYOND THE CLOUDS

BEYOND THE CLOUDS

The Lifetime Trek of Walter "Matt" Jefferies, Artist and Visionary

To Ben

"Live Long & Prosper"

Richard L. Jefferies

RICHARD L. JEFFERIES

BEYOND THE CLOUDS

The Lifetime Trek of Walter "Matt" Jefferies, Artist and Visionary

Front cover illustration by Matt Jefferies

Back cover illustration by John Amendola

Manufactured in China

For information, please contact:
Brown Books Publishing Group
16200 North Dallas Parkway, Suite 170
Dallas, Texas 75248
www.brownbooks.com
972-381-0009
A New Era in Publishing™

ISBN-13: 978-1-933285-98-6
ISBN-10: 1-933285-98-2
LCCN 2007939784
1 2 3 4 5 6 7 8 9 10

TABLE OF CONTENTS

for

Mary Ann

DEDICATION

This book is dedicated to the loving memory of my brother, Walter Matthews Jefferies Jr.—"Matt," as he was affectionately called by those who knew him. He was a visionary with extraordinary creative ability in aviation and science fiction art. Though he died at the age of eighty-one, his legacy has endured. Predating *Star Trek*, Matt's early life is generally unknown to all except his family, close friends, and associates. On August 2, 2003, I was honored to eulogize Matt at his funeral mass in North Hollywood's St. Charles Borromeo Catholic Church. With admiration for a brother whom I dearly loved, I reached back in time for inspiration and prefaced the narration with these words: "Good gracious," our dear mother would have said in her soft Virginia accent, "How nice of all of you to come today to honor our son." We were a close-knit family. We were taught to honor and respect our parents. Mutual love bound us together. Obedience was mandatory. How well I remember Mother's admonition: "Matt, put that airplane down and eat your breakfast or you will be late for school!" "Yes ma'am," Matt replied as his little red plane was brought in for a perfect three-point landing alongside his plate of pancakes.

—*Richard L. Jefferies*

ACKNOWLEDGMENTS

I acknowledge the divine inspiration of our Heavenly Father in the writing of *Beyond the Clouds*.

The thought of memorializing my brother Matt by writing his biography was shared with only a few following his passing. Foremost in my mind was having the approval of Mary Ann, Matt's devoted wife of fifty-five years. She wholeheartedly approved of the project and assured me of her cooperation in the gathering of pertinent material. Cognizant of the many hours required for researching, writing, and preparing an authentic manuscript for publication, I relied on my wife, Tina, for her patience, participation, and moral support, to which she willingly and enthusiastically acceded. I am particularly grateful to the following individuals and material sources:

For critical reading of the manuscript: John Amendola, Bellevue, WA; Patricia Dickenson and Janice and Bruce Dickenson, Santa Paula, CA; John Jefferies, Granada Hills, CA; Mary Ann Jefferies, Hollywood, CA; Janice Mc Cullum, Dallas, TX; Neil November, Richmond, VA.

For contributions of art work to complement the text: Gerald Asher, Fort Worth, TX; Wendell Dowling, Santa Paula, CA; Daren Dochterman, Sherman Oaks, CA; Doug Drexler, Burbank, CA; Luther Gore, Charlottesville, VA; Mike Okuda, Sherman Oaks, CA; Michael O'Neal, North Bruinswick, NJ; Richard L. Jefferies Jr., Arvada, CO; Robert McCall, Paradise Valley, AZ.

For providing additional background information: John Jefferies, Granada Hills, CA; John Martin, Springfield, VA; Neil November, Richmond, VA; Rick Ruhman, Magalia, CA.

For graphic design and layout: Tina A. Jefferies, Dallas, TX.

For scanning of the graphics and photographs: Flash-Back Lab & Digital Arts, Plano, TX.

Heartfelt gratitude to Milli Brown and her Editorial Staff for their collective expertise in desiging the book. Special thanks to Kathryn Grant, Editorial Director; Tara Nieuwesteeg, Editor, and Ted Ruybal, Creative Director/Designer.

INTRODUCTION

Walter Matthews Jefferies Jr. (1921–2003)

"Where the spirit does not work with the heart, there is no art."

—Leonardo da Vinci

I had the rare privilege of knowing Matt throughout his life. He was a man of high moral character and firm convictions. Many looked to him as a role model—one to be emulated for his passion to achieve high goals and to share his knowledge and experiences with others. His unique artistic talents were complemented by an unwavering determination to seek perfection—in his work, in his art, and in his relationships with others. A Virginian with ancestral ties dating to the American Revolution, he was raised in the lean years of the Great Depression and the uncertain years leading up to World War II. He volunteered for active duty in the Air Corps and served in Europe, defending his country and the freedoms enjoyed by all Americans.

Wisdom suggests that one's character derives in part from those with whom one associates: family, friends, teachers, religious leaders, and counselors all contribute to molding one's inner fiber. In Scripture, Proverbs 19:20 instructs us: "Hear council and receive instruction that you may be wise to the end." In this biography, I wish to share my memories of one who was admired and loved by many. You will perceive the influence of others in encouraging him to learn, to listen, to persevere, and to be grateful to those who guided him along life's arduous path. Walter Matthews Jefferies Jr. I knew him well. He was my brother.

—*Richard L. Jefferies*

GENEALOGY

OF THE SANFORDS AND THE JEFFERIES

The Sanfords   **The Jefferies**

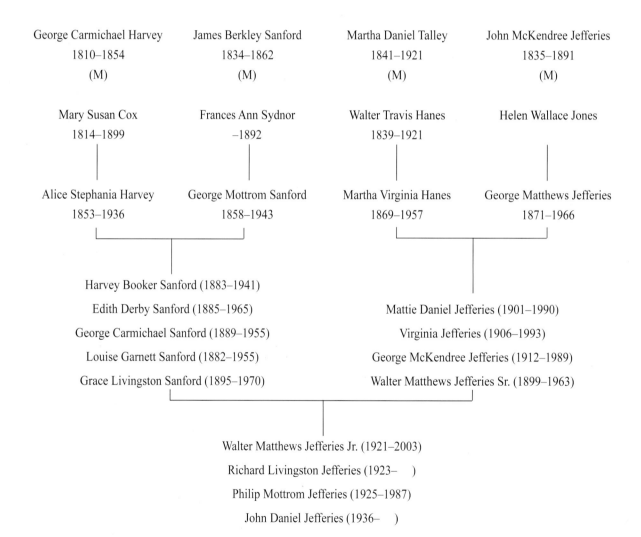

George Carmichael Harvey   James Berkley Sanford   Martha Daniel Talley   John McKendree Jefferies
1810–1854   1834–1862   1841–1921   1835–1891
(M)   (M)   (M)   (M)

Mary Susan Cox   Frances Ann Sydnor   Walter Travis Hanes   Helen Wallace Jones
1814–1899   –1892   1839–1921

Alice Stephania Harvey   George Mottrom Sanford   Martha Virginia Hanes   George Matthews Jefferies
1853–1936   1858–1943   1869–1957   1871–1966

Harvey Booker Sanford (1883–1941)

Edith Derby Sanford (1885–1965)   Mattie Daniel Jefferies (1901–1990)

George Carmichael Sanford (1889–1955)   Virginia Jefferies (1906–1993)

Louise Garnett Sanford (1882–1955)   George McKendree Jefferies (1912–1989)

Grace Livingston Sanford (1895–1970)   Walter Matthews Jefferies Sr. (1899–1963)

Walter Matthews Jefferies Jr. (1921–2003)

Richard Livingston Jefferies (1923–   )

Philip Mottrom Jefferies (1925–1987)

John Daniel Jefferies (1936–   )

Harvey Booker Sanford
1883–1941
(M)

Edith Derby Sanford
1885–1965
(M)

Louise Garnett Sanford
1892–1959
(M)

Katherine Bowie Taylor
1885–1978

Levin Bruce Cottingham
1886–1936

John Howard Snead
1882–1975

Harvey Bowie Sanford
1906–1978

Levin Bruce Cottingham II
1911–1976

Howard Garnett
1911–1994

Catherine Livingston Sanford
1914–

Alice Palmer Cottingham
1912–1982

Elizabeth Harvey
1915–1958

Gordon Taylor Sanford
1921–1990

George Russell Cottingham
1920–

Eugene Chichester
1923–

Edith Harvey Cottingham
1924–1984

George Carmichael Sanford
1889–1955
(M)

Mary Lou Sydnor
1890–1977

Armintrus Caroll Sanford
1915–

Note: These are our aunts and uncles on Mother's side of the family.

These are our first cousins on Mother's side of the family.

Charles Mottrom Sanford
1917–2007

George McKendree Jefferies
1912–1989
(M)
Sarah Edna Wood

Mattie Daniel Jefferies
1901–1990
(M)
Tom Golden

Virginia Jefferies
1906–1993
(M)
Dooley Meadows

George McKendree Jefferies II

Note: These are our aunts and uncles on Dad's side of the family.

These are our first cousins on Dad's side of the family.

Margaret Ann Jefferies

CHAPTER ONE

Walter Matthews Jefferies, my father, was born June 30, 1899, in a house on Clay Street in Richmond, Virginia. His father, George Matthews Jefferies, was a clerk for the T. W. Wood Seed Co. Although born and raised on a farm in Cumberland County, George never "took to farming." Rather, he preferred to work as a merchant. As a young adult, he worked for two of his brothers: John, who owned a lumber business in Richmond, and James, who was a merchant in Kinsale (a small town in Westmoreland County). He had also worked for George Bailey, his sister Lucille's husband, who owned a cannery in Kinsale and produce stores in Kinsale and Baltimore, Maryland. At the time of Walter's birth, George Jefferies was facing a financial crisis. As a result of a serious decline in the seed business, his wages plummeted to as little as a dollar a day. No longer able to provide for his family, he reluctantly returned to farming in Cumberland County.

It was in Cumberland that he courted and married Martha Virginia Hanes—"Jennie," as she was affectionately called by her family and friends. On September 23, 1898, they were married in the parlor of Vue Monte, the antebellum home of Jennie's grandparents, Dr. Edwin Preston and Martha Daniel Talley. Jennie, my grandmother, had often told of their trip from Richmond to Cumberland, a journey of approximately sixty miles. A horse-drawn wagon

Broad St. looking West
Richmond, Va.

Richmond, Virginia, circa 1900

Following the burning of Richmond in 1865 at the close of the War Between the States (the Civil War), phoenix-like, the city quickly rebuilt on the ashes of the former capital of the Confederacy. Electric streetcars were introduced in 1888—the first practical electric street railway system in America. By the turn of the century, the city was a thriving metropolis.

**Cumberland County
Founded 1749**

A middle Virginia county named in honor of William Augustus, Duke of Cumberland and son of King George II. Cumberland County is bordered on the north by the James River and on the south by the Appomattox.

George Matthews Jefferies

(1871–1966)

Martha Virginia Hanes Jefferies

(1869–1957)

Married

September 23, 1898

Vue Monte

From a second-story window on a clear day, one can see Mount Willis near Dillwyn, a distance of fifteen miles, hence the name "Vue Monte" (View of the Mountain). The interior design is unique in that there is no access to the basement from inside the house. Open hearth kitchen, pantry, store rooms, and weaving room were in the basement. Meals were elevated to the *supper room* on the first floor by a rope and pulley dumb waiter. Vue Monte was built by Dr. Edwin Preston Talley (1810–1899). Traditionally, Southern homesteads were often named for their aesthetic settings.

Pennsylvania Avenue

Early streetcars in the District of Columbia received traction power through an electrified "third" rail eliminating the need for overhead power lines

Walter and Mattie

contained all their possessions. "Walter's diapers," Grandma once recalled, "were hung out to dry from the buggy whip." Except to provide food for the table, the farm failed miserably. Corn and hay were sold at a loss. A friend, Phil Turpin, wrote from Washington and encouraged George to give up farming and come to the nation's capital where work was plentiful.

George, Jennie, and their son, Walter, moved to the bustling city. George was hired as a streetcar conductor by the city's transit system. Jennie took in roomers to supplement his pay. Shortly after they had settled in, their good friend Phil Turpin was killed. It was reported that in leaning out of the window of a streetcar, he was struck on the head by a passing streetcar. He died instantly.

On June 16, 1901, George and Jennie became proud parents of a daughter, Mattie Daniel. Disenchanted with life in Washington, George accepted a clerking job in George Bailey's store in Baltimore. Unfortunately, the job was short-lived: George Bailey's partner, the manager of the store, absconded with the profits. The loss culminated in the closing of the store. George accepted his brother-in-law's offer of a clerking job in his Kinsale store. Jennie and George were delighted to return to their beloved state of Virginia. On April 19, 1906, another daughter, Virginia Hanes, was born. George was hard-pressed to provide for a wife and three children on the meager earnings of a store clerk. Ultimately this led to their decision to again return to the farm. Walter, now seven, enthusiastically welcomed the move to the country. He was devoted to his father and worked tirelessly alongside him without complaint: plowing, planting, cultivating, harvesting, milking, wood cutting, feeding the animals, all the many chores associated with farming Cumberland's gray loam and red clay soils. His father taught him to hunt birds, turkey, and deer and to dress out the wild game. He attended classes in a one-room schoolhouse located five miles from home. He walked. Schooling and chores left little time for recreation.

He accompanied his parents to prayer meetings and read the family Bible. Walter understood that parents are to be obeyed and respected. He responded to his parents and elders with "ma'am," "sir," "please," and "thank you." He learned to be a good listener and to think before voicing his opinions. His high moral character developed from the examples that were set by those who loved him. As a member of the family, he understood that his labor on the farm was a responsibility, one to be undertaken in a willing and cheerful manner. He was so appreciative of the trust placed in him to carry out his assigned tasks that he considered it a privilege to work alongside his father.

Dec. 17, 1903, Kitty Hawk, North Carolina—Orville Wright piloted a biplane powered with a twelve horsepower internal combustion engine a distance of 120 feet in twelve seconds. The historic feat marked man's first powered flight.

✳

Clover Lea, or "meadow of clover." A home and land adjacent to the *Vue Monte* estate given by Dr. Edwin Preston Talley to his daughter, Martha Daniel, on the occasion of her marriage to Walter Travis Hanes on November 16, 1865. Martha and Walter Hanes raised five children at *Clover Lea*:

Mary Emeline . . . . born 1866
Martha Virginia . . . . born 1869
Edwin Preston . . . . born 1870
Willie Daniel . . . . born 1873
Walter Travis II . . . . born 1876

Martha Virginia "Jennie" Jefferies was our grandmother.

Willie Daniel was our father's "Aunt Dantie."

Walter Travis II was our father's "Uncle Travis."

Following the death of Dr. Edwin Preston Talley, Willie Daniel and Walter Travis Hanes moved to *Vue Monte*.

Once I asked Grandpa if he had ever had to punish Dad for disobedience. He put a hand to his brow and pondered the question for a time before replying: "Yes, I do recall one occasion when Walter was perhaps ten. I was spring plowing. While I followed the plow, your dad handled the reins. We had worked since sunrise and, except for a brief break for lunch, we continued into the afternoon. I wanted to complete the plowing before sundown, as it looked like rain. Unfortunately, the tip of the plowshare broke, so I sent Walter on foot to purchase a replacement. The blacksmith shop was about three miles away, so I figured he'd be back within a couple hours. However, as he did not return before sundown, I unhitched the mare, fed, watered, and stabled her. We were at the supper table before Walter appeared. I asked what had detained him and he explained that he had stopped by Clover Lea to pay his respects to his Aunt Dantie. He was treated to cool lemonade and something to eat. He was then encouraged to stay for a game of lawn croquet. He enjoyed the game so much that he lost all awareness of time. It was dark before he left Clover Lea. I scolded him and sent him to his attic room without supper."

Walter Travis Hanes

OBITUARY

Walter Travis Hanes, 84, died December 14, 1923, at Vue Monte, his Cumberland County home. He served in the Confederate army under Gen. Fitzhugh Lee as a scout in the cavalry, and suffered several wounds during the conflict. Following the war, he was a deputy clerk in a Richmond court where his father, Garland Hanes, was prominently connected with the city as the first manager of the water department. Walter T. Hanes was an earnest Christian gentleman and won many friends by his sincere sociable nature. He married Martha Talley, the daughter of Dr. E. P. Talley. He is survived by his wife and four children: Mrs. W. L. Lancaster, Mrs. George M. Jefferies, Mrs. W. W. Adams, and Mr. Walter T. Hanes Jr. of Cumberland County. Interment will be at the Presbyterian Church in New Canton, where he and his family are members.

Artist—Wendell Dowling, Santa Paula, CA

"Grandpa," I asked, "is it fair to suggest that the punishment was a little severe for one who had worked in the field for most of the day?"

Grandpa laughed and said: "Hold on, Dick! You haven't heard the rest of my story yet! After your grandmother and I retired and I was certain that she was asleep, I crept out of bed and took a plate of food to your dad. He said he was sorry for stopping by Clover Lea and promised never to disobey again. As I started down the stairs from his attic room, I encountered Jennie coming up with another plate of food. Thinking that I was asleep, she, too, had slipped out of the darkened bedroom to sneak something up to Walter. We've had a lot of laughs over that one!"

"That's quite a story, Grandpa!" I said, joining in on the laughter.

On a property across the road from Clover Lea, Travis Hanes, Jennie's brother, built a house for George and his family. On May 17, 1912, Jennie gave birth to another son, George McKendree. He was affectionately called "Little George."

Two years later, in July of 1914, the residents of Cumberland County, as well as all Americans, learned that war had erupted in Europe, with Germany declaring war on Russia and France. This was followed with Britain declaring war on Germany. All three Allied nations, Britain, France, and Russia, were in dire need of gunpowder. They turned to the United States for help. To meet the growing demand, the Du Pont Chemical Company announced the construction of an immense smokeless powder plant in the little village of Hopewell, Virginia. To provide for up to 28,000 workers, Du Pont constructed houses, schools, medical facilities, and commercial buildings. The new town of Hopewell was provided with electricity, paved streets, running water, and sewers. Workers from throughout the country responded to Du Pont's invitation to come to Hopewell for employment opportunities that were rewarding and served the Allied countries that opposed Germany's aggression. George recognized the announcement as an opportunity to improve his financial condition. In the fall of 1915, he sold the farm in Cumberland and moved to Hopewell. He immediately found work in a lumber yard that supplied Du Pont with building materials. Walter, now sixteen, was hired by Du Pont as an oiler in their newly constructed electric generating plant.

I once asked Aunt Mattie if she remembered Dad's going to work for Du Pont. "Indeed I do!" she recalled. "With his very first paycheck he bought me a lovely gingham dress.

AMERICA'S GREATEST
INDUSTRIAL OPPORTUNITY

HOPEWELL
VIRGINIA

DU PONT CHEMICAL COMPANY
INCORPORATED
WILMINGTON, DELAWARE

DUPONT

Hopewell is located twenty-three miles southeast of Richmond at the confluence of the James and Appomattox rivers. English colonists settled in the area as early as 1613. The city is named for the good ship *Hopewell*, the first ship to sail up the James River after the Indian massacre of 1622. Its mission was to drive the Indians from the village of City Point, now a section of the City of Hopewell.

Walter was a very giving and caring person, always doing for others."

"Aunt Mattie, did Du Pont pay him well?"

"Well enough that he paid Momma and Poppa for his room and board. Then he bought a three-piece suit and a snap-brim hat. He looked mighty handsome in his new duds!"

"Did Dad have time for anything other than his work?"

"Yes indeed, but instead of running with friends he preferred to spend his leisure time with his family. He saved enough money to buy a violin and spent many delightful hours practicing."

"Wasn't it Aunt Dantie who introduced Dad to the violin?"

"It certainly was. Aunt Dantie taught piano, violin, banjo, and zither in her parlor at Clover Lea. She encouraged Walter to try out each instrument. He selected the violin. Whenever he found time from his chores on the farm, he slipped over to Clover Lea for lessons."

At Du Pont, Walter became interested in every aspect of the power plant's operation. He diligently studied the operation and maintenance of boilers, steam turbines, feed-water pumps, electric generators, coal-handling equipment, and electrical switchgear. His acquired knowledge of the mechanical and electrical components that make up a power plant earned him a promotion to the position of operating engineer. For a seventeen-year-old to qualify for such a responsible position was, in itself, a significant accomplishment.

Another interest captured his attention. He became acquainted with Grace Sanford, a lovely brunette who was a billing clerk for the Norfolk & Western Railroad in Hopewell. Grace was born and raised in that part of Virginia known as the "Northern Neck." She was the daughter of George Mottrom and Alice Harvey Sanford. George Sanford was a farmer in Westmoreland County. After graduation from high school, Grace seized the opportunity to leave the farm and seek employment in the progressive city of Hopewell. From their very first meeting, Walter and Grace enjoyed each other's company: they shared the same morals, the same interests, and were both family-oriented. Walter lost no time before having Grace over to meet his parents.

Walter M. Jefferies (SR)

Grace Livingston Sanford was born December 24, 1895, in Westmoreland County.

Downtown Hopewell in the early phases of construction. The Eagle Cafe, the Virginia Cafe, and the Wilmington Barber Shop are doing a thriving business. A law office and a laundry occupy the same building. Housing the workers was the first priority.

Recognizing his competence in all aspects of plant operation, Du Pont transferred Walter to their new shell-loading facility at Penniman, Virginia. He was appointed to the position of supervising engineer and given a raise in pay. His only regret in accepting the position was that he had to leave Hopewell—his family and sweetheart.

America remained neutral in the war being fought in Europe. President Wilson proclaimed that America's neutrality included freedom of the seas. He reminded Berlin that Germany would be held accountable for any loss of American lives or property resulting from belligerent action. Ignoring Wilson's proclamation, on May 7, 1915, a German submarine torpedoed the British liner RMS *Lusitania*, resulting in the loss of 1,200 passengers—128 of which were Americans.

On April 6, 1917, the United States declared war on Germany. On May 18, Congress passed a Selective Service Act requiring all men between the ages of twenty-one and thirty to register for the draft. On June 30, Walter celebrated his eighteenth birthday. Later in the year, Congress broadened the draft from eighteen to forty-five years of age. Because of his work in a major defense plant, Walter was exempt from military service. The Penniman plant was the first of four shell-loading plants built by Du Pont. A sign on the plant's main gate greeted the workers with a challenging slogan: "HELP FILL THE EMPTY SHELL—GIVE THE KAISER_____"

PUSH THE JOB

HELP FILL THE EMPTY SHELL

GIVE THE KAISER

The Northern Neck (peninsula) lies between the Potomac and the Rappahannock rivers. In 1607, following the founding of Jamestown, England's first permanent colony in America, Captain John Smith was taken prisoner by the Algonquian Indians. He was paraded up the peninsula to face Powhatan, the powerful Indian king. He was condemned to death but rescued by Pocahontas, Powhatan's favorite daughter.

Westmoreland County is the birthplace of two presidents: George Washington and James Monroe.

NOTICE!

Travelers intending to embark on the Atlantic voyage are reminded that a state of war exists between Germany and her allies; that the zone of war includes the waters adjacent to the British Isles; that, in accordance with formal notice given by the Imperial German government, vessels flying the flag of Great Britain, or of any of her allies, are liable to destruction in those waters and that travelers sailing in the war zone on ships of Great Britain or her allies do so at their own risk.

IMPERIAL GERMAN EMBASSY
Washington, D. C., April 22, 1915

FWD Model B Army Truck
Circa 1916

Prior to the Great War in Europe, the Four Wheel Drive Auto Company had built only a few trucks. In the fall of 1914, two trucks were shipped to England for testing by the British Army. Impressed with the results, England ordered fifty Model B trucks, followed with orders for 238 more. By the end of 1915, 400 trucks had been shipped to the Allied Nations: England, France, Russia, Spain, and Portugal. In 1916, the United States Quartermaster Corps ordered 147 Model B trucks for the Mexican campaign. Following America's entry into the European conflict, the U.S. Army ordered 3,750 of the three-ton Model B trucks.

Although his position required being on the job for up to ten hours a day, he sought weekend work to earn additional money to purchase his first automobile. "Hey, Walt!" a friend said. "Have you heard that the Four Wheel Drive Company of Clintonville, Wisconsin is looking for drivers to deliver new military trucks from a railhead to the docks in Norfolk?"

"No, but I'm interested!"

"Good! We'll both apply. Have you ever driven a four-wheel drive truck, Walt?"

"No, but I believe I can drive anything that has four wheels. What do you know about the FWD trucks?"

"Not much . . . only that they are a three-ton, all-wheel drive truck powered with a thirty-six-horsepower engine. The two-drive axles are suspended from the steel frame by heavy duty leaf springs. A cab-over-engine design places the driver's seat high up over the front axle. The bed is enclosed on all sides with bulletproof steel plates and covered with a canvas top. Wooden spoke wheels are equipped with solid rubber tires. That's about it, Walt!"

"Thought you said that you knew very little about the truck. Sure you don't have more information?"

"Only that driving one of these monsters is like riding a raging bull! Anything else you'd like to know about the FWD truck, Walt?"

Ottoman—A town located on the Rappahannock River in Lancaster County. For many years, Ottoman's wharf served the steamboats that plied the river carrying passengers, produce, livestock, tobacco, dry goods, and machinery. George and Alice Sanford had left Westmoreland County and bought a farm at Ottoman.

St. Mary's White Chapel Episcopal Church

A Colonial church in Lancaster County, Virginia. Originally known as "Ball's Church." Col. Joseph Ball, a vestryman of St. Mary's White Chapel, owned a plantation called *Epping Forest* located on the left bank of the Rappahannock. Joseph and his wife, Mary Johnson Ball, were the parents of Mary Ball, born in 1708 or 1709. Joseph Ball died when Mary Ball was three years old. Mary Johnson Ball married Capt. Richard Hewes of Northumberland County. After the death of her mother and stepfather, Mary Ball was raised by a guardian, George Eskridge, a well-to-do lawyer in Westmoreland County. Mary Ball married Augustine Washington on March 6, 1730. They became the parents of George Washington on February 22, 1732.

"Yes, how much do they pay to deliver them to the port?" So it was that Walter and his friend devoted weekends to driving the new trucks to the port of embarkation for shipment to France. The money earned coupled with his Du Pont wages enabled Walter to purchase a new Chandler sedan. He frequently drove to Hopewell to visit Grace and his family. On one occasion, Grace was spending a weekend in the Northern Neck. She invited Walter to drive to Ottoman to meet her parents. The wide Rappahannock River was crossed on a ferry. As the flat-decked transport approached the dock on the opposite shore, the Chandler rolled off the deck and landed in four feet of water. It was concluded that some rapscallions had deliberately removed the chocks from beneath the wheels. The ferry operator suggested that the local boys did not approve of outsiders dating their Northern Neck girls. The Chandler suffered no real damage. Walter had it out of the water and running like new within a few hours. When he informed the Sanfords of the event, he laughed it off and said: "I imagine the boys were just being mischievous."

On November 11, 1918, the Great War ended with the formal signing of an armistice. Gunpowder and shells were no longer needed, so Du Pont began to shut down their defense plants. The Penniman plant was the last to close.

Grace accepted Walter's proposal of marriage. Their wedding took place in St. Mary's White Chapel Church in Lancaster County, Virginia, on October 11, 1919. Following a brief honeymoon, Walter drove to Cumberland to visit his parents who, as thousands before them, had left "jobless" Hopewell. Walter was pleased to find that his parents had occupied a new, four-room house located on property deeded to Jennie by her father. Having been raised on a farm, Grace felt quite at *home*.

St. Mary's White Chapel Episcopal Church

In this historic church, Matt and I received the Sacrament of Baptism. As youngsters, we accompanied our grandparents to Sunday services from their farm at Ottoman. The five-mile trip was made by horse-and-buggy. Grandpa was an usher.

Grace L. (Sanford) Jefferies

Walter M. Jefferies

Walter received word that he had been recommended by Du Pont to fill the position of assistant chief engineer for the Hershey Chocolate Company in Hershey, Pennsylvania. He accepted the job. He sold the Chandler, bought a Model T Ford, and reported to work in January 1920. Walter realized that he was indeed fortunate to be gainfully employed as the closing of defense plants had created enormous unemployment throughout the land. Thousands of veterans returned from Europe to join the lines of the jobless. The postwar economy was in shambles with the price of consumer goods inflated to twice that of prewar levels. A dozen eggs sold for sixty-two cents, up from thirty-four cents. A quart of milk was fifteen cents, up from nine cents. Americans no longer had faith in their elected officials. President Wilson suffered a stroke and was barely able to attend to his duties. Presidential hopeful Warren Harding of Ohio proclaimed: "America's present need is not heroics, but healing; not nostrums, but normalcy!" Normalcy to Walter was a job, a loving wife, an automobile, and a house large enough to accommodate a family. They set up housekeeping in a rented bungalow.

HERSHEY

Known worldwide as:
"The sweetest place on earth"

In 1901, Milton Hershey, forty-four years old, chose a large site in central Pennsylvania for his chocolate factory . . . one within a few miles of his birthplace. Conveniently surrounded by dairy farms, his milk chocolate business was a great success. He meticulously mapped out a town and built attractive houses, school, bank, library, shops, an amusement park, and a Community Center. Milton wanted his workers to have pleasant living conditions and to enrich their lives.

The bungalow in Hershey at the time of the births of Walter Matthews, Richard Livingston, and Phillip Mottrom Jefferies. The aroma of chocolate was ever present. Streetlights on the corner of *Chocolate* and *Cocoa Avenue* were in the shape of Hershey's Kisses.

13

Four Generations—Matt, age 1

On December 24, 1920, on her twenty-fifth birthday, Grace informed Walter that by August of 1921, he would become a father. Walter was overjoyed! In preparation for the blessed event, he traded in the Model T Ford for a 1921 Dodge Brothers Model 30 touring car, a two-seater with side curtains. What better way, he reasoned, to take his family on excursions in and around the beautiful city of Hershey. He also became interested in photography and acquired a Graflex camera similar to those used by newspaper photographers. A closet was set aside in the bungalow to serve as a darkroom for developing his pictures. He explained to Grace that he wanted a pictorial record of their family.

On August 12, 1921, Grace gave birth to a son, Walter Matthews Jr. The attending physician said that he was a "happy little fellow!" It was decided to casually call him "Matt"—although his mother often lovingly addressed him as "Matthew."

Twelve months later, Walter was allowed a week's vacation. It was an opportunity to drive to Virginia and introduce Matt to his grandparents. From the time he could talk, Matt expressed a fascination with cars and airplanes. "Wook, Daddy! Airplane!" he shouted at the sight of a biplane landing in an open field.

On their visit to Cumberland County, a four-generation picture was taken. With Matt in his arms, Walter was pictured with his mother and his grandmother, Martha Talley Hanes.

"Walter," Grandpa said, "sure you want this boy to grow up in the North? He looks like a Virginian!"

Richard Livingston Jefferies was named for Dr. Richard H. Jefferies, a brother of George M. Jefferies. "Uncle Dick" was a prominent Richmond dentist. Uncle Dick's namesake, Richard Livingston Jefferies, was also called "Dick" by his family and friends. When Dick was only a boy, his mother often called him "Dickey Byrd," a reference to Richard Byrd, the famed Antarctic explorer.

Walter Sr. & Matt   Grace & Dick

"Can't disagree with you on that, Poppa. Hopefully we will be able to come back to Virginia in the near future. Hershey is a fine place to live. The company has been good to me, but it isn't home."

Matt was baptized at White Chapel Episcopal Church in Lancaster County.

George and Alice Sanford, his maternal grandparents, were his sponsors. Reverend L. R. Combs, Rector of White Chapel, officiated.

It is of some interest to know that at the time, Americans were singing Irving Berlin's "All by Myself." Matt was not to be "all by himself" for long, however, as a brother, Richard Livingston, arrived on February 3, 1923.

Walter took advantage of every opportunity to bundle up his family and take them for long rides. However, Pennsylvania's frigid winter of 1923 restricted their excursions in the breezy touring car, so he traded it in on a 1923 model Dodge Brothers sedan featuring an all-steel body and roll-up windows. Hershey was expanding their production facilities to satisfy the demand of sweet tooth Americans for Hershey Kisses and Hershey Bars. Increased production required a greater kilowatt output, so the power plant's capacity was doubled with the addition of new boilers, steam turbines and electric generators. Walter devoted many long hours to overseeing the installation, testing, and start-up of the new equipment. Following completion, Walter was promoted to chief engineer.

1923 Dodge Brothers Sedan

The town of Hershey expanded along with the growth of the company. Milton Hershey, the founder, developed a huge, landscaped park complete with an athletic field, swimming pool, band shell, theater, and zoo, "for the delight and edification of the children," Milton said. He populated the zoo with wildlife including zebras, elephants, lions, tigers, buffalos, monkeys, and deer. Walter, Grace, and the children spent many enjoyable Sunday afternoons viewing Milton Hershey's menagerie. With the amenities available to Hershey's employees, Walter and Grace felt that there was no better place in America to raise a family. Postwar conditions in America showed little improvement since Warren G. Harding became president in 1921. It was said that Harding's primary qualification for the office of chief executive was that "he looked presidential." Although a man of good intentions, his two years in office were marred by the corrupt actions of those he trusted. Many of his close friends, appointed to high positions in the government, turned out to be swindlers, influence peddlers, confidence men, and other shady characters. In the summer of 1923, President Harding sought to improve his image by undertaking a transcontinental trip. On a stopover in San Francisco, he was taken ill and died. He was succeeded in office by the dour, rigidly honest Calvin Coolidge. A former governor of Massachusetts, "Silent Cal," a man of few words, was once jokingly accused of having been "weaned on a pickle." American consumers were buying automobiles, radios, and home appliances in unprecedented numbers. The demand for chocolate candy increased in direct proportion to the improving economic conditions. Competitive firms vied for Hershey's market share with the introduction of two new candy bars: Milky Way, by Frank Mars and Butterfinger, by the Curtis Candy Co.

Milton Hershey's greatest legacy was the founding in 1918 of an industrial school for orphaned boys (Milton felt that girls were more likely to be adopted). Having no children of his own, Milton transferred all his holdings in Hershey Chocolate Co. to the Hershey Industrial School. Proud of the town which he had founded, Milton Hershey was quoted as saying: "an industrial utopia where the things of modern progress all center in a town that has no poverty, no nuisances, and no evil."

Humorist Will Rogers said of Calvin Coolidge: "Lots of times a man gets in wrong just by an ill-timed remark. That's why Mr. Coolidge never gets in bad. If a man will just stay hushed, he is hard to find out."

On May 31, 1925, Walter handed a cigar to his boss. "What's the occasion, Walt?"

"We now have another son, Philip Mottrom!"

"Congratulations, Walt!"

On May 21, 1927, Walter, Grace, and all Americans were thrilled by the news that Charles A. Lindbergh, the "Lone Eagle," had flown solo across the Atlantic in the *Spirit of St. Louis*. The jubilation resulting from the accomplishment only added to America's optimism. Under President Coolidge's administration, the economy had steadily improved. Near the end of his fourth year in office, on the crest of his popularity, Coolidge announced: "I do not choose to run for president in 1928." The Republican Party nominated his commerce secretary, Herbert Hoover. In the election, Hoover was opposed by the Democratic nominee, Alfred Smith, New York's governor. Smith was a Catholic. No Catholic had ever held the office of president. Few were surprised when Hoover won all forty-eight states. After all, four years of Republican leadership had given Americans more of the good things in life and hope for the future.

Lindbergh euphoria swept the nation. Newborn babies were named "Charles" or "Charles Augustus." The names of schools, towns, streets, and avenues were changed to read LIND-BERGH or CHARLES A. LINDBERGH. The name LINDY LANE had an "appealing ring to it." The Lindy Hop became the latest dance craze. Toy manufacturers turned out replicas of the *Spirit of St. Louis*. Every boy wanted one. Matt and I were no exception.

"Matt, put that airplane down and eat your breakfast or you will be late for school!"

"Yes, ma'am," Matt replied as his little red plane was brought in for a perfect, three-point landing alongside his plate of pancakes.

Walter and Grace became increasingly aware of the isolation from their many loved ones in Virginia. Matt, seven, Dick, five, and Phil, three, were deprived of a meaningful rapport with their grandparents and their many aunts, uncles, and cousins. The Jefferies and Sanford families had always been close-knit with numerous opportunities to spend time together on holidays, weekends, and special occasions.

This void in their lives was of much concern, so Walter explored the possibility of finding work in Virginia. A letter from Walter's mother stated that his father was returning to Hopewell to establish a general merchandise store. This was exciting news to Grace and Walter. Hopewell had a special place in their hearts. They had met in Hopewell and worked there during the war years.

"Oh, if only we could move back to Hopewell!"

"Well, Grace, we'll see about that!"

Matt and Dick

Matt

"Someday I want to fly way way out beyond the clouds"

CHAPTER TWO

Walter lost no time in sending his résumé to industries in the Richmond-Hopewell area. He took advantage of his vacation in June to drive the family to Virginia. After a brief visit in Richmond with Grace's brother, Harvey Sanford, his wife, Katy, and their children, Walter went directly to Hopewell for interviews with several firms which had responded to his application for employment. Hopewell had changed dramatically during his eight-year absence. The manufacturing of guncotton during the war had swelled the population to 35,000. With the close of the war, the city had become a ghost town. Vacant industrial properties stretched all the way to City Point, located at the juncture of the Appomattox and the James rivers. Several large firms recognized the advantages of locating their facilities in Hopewell and had built new plants. The city of Hopewell in 1928 was one of stability and residential charm. Walter was interviewed by the Hummel-Ross Fiber Company and the Atmospheric Nitrogen Company. The latter was increasing the electrical generating capacity of their power plant and required a combustion engineer with experience in plant construction. His years with Hershey Chocolate Company qualified Walter for the position. He accepted their reasonable offer and reported for work on July 1, 1928.

Guncotton or "smokeless powder" was manufactured by saturating the cellulose of cotton fibers with nitric acid. Prior to World War I, nitrates for producing nitric acid came from the mines of Chile. After German submarines cut off the supply, nitrogen was extracted from the atmosphere.

The Hummel-Ross Fiber Company processed cotton fibers for the production of guncotton. The ideal fibers were the short *linters* that adhered to the seeds after the first ginning.

The Atmospheric Nitrogen Company produced pure nitrogen by extracting the gas from the atmosphere. The nitrogen reacted with calcium carbonate (limestone) to produce nitric acid. Both companies were owned by **Du Pont**.

April 2, 1865—General Grant ordered a general assault on Lee's Petersburg lines. Within hours the entire Confederate flank collapsed under the overwhelming attack. Jefferson Davis, president of the Confederacy, was attending church in Richmond when a courier brought a message from this War Department: "General Lee telegraphs he can hold his position no longer." That night, Lee evacuated Petersburg and started his week-long retreat to Appomattox, where he surrendered.

A bungalow was rented at 217 N. 15th Avenue in the heart of Hopewell. The tree-shaded street was lined with neat, wood-framed houses constructed for Du Pont workers during the war. The house was ideally suited for a family of five.

Located two blocks from the residence, a landscaped monument commemorated those who died in the War Between the States, or, the "Civil War," as Northerners refer to the conflict. An antiquated cannon, green with age and flanked by two stone columns topped with iron cannon balls, commanded the site. The imposing monument was a poignant reminder that Hopewell was a Southern city rich in history. In the spring of 1865, the War Between the States was nearing an end. General Robert E. Lee's army was exhausted—the Union forces had twice the number of troops. General Grant asked President Lincoln to visit his battlefield headquarters. Lincoln, his wife, Mary, and son, Tad, boarded the River Queen and arrived at City Point on March 23, 1865. The following morning the president traveled by train to the front at Petersburg where he witnessed the carnage. Meeting with General Grant and General Sherman, they discussed the pursuit of Lee's army and surrender terms.

After abandoning Petersburg and Richmond, Lee moved his army west with plans to turn south and link up with General Johnson's army in North Carolina. However, his escape route was blocked by General Sheridan's troops and his supply train captured. Lee's retreating army continued to fight but were stopped at Appomattox where Lee surrendered to Grant on April 9, 1865.

Home entertainment centered on reading, games, and music. Mom played the piano and we sang our favorite songs and hymns. "Carolina Moon" and "Sweet Sue—Just You" were current hits. Long-time favorites were played on an Edison wind-up phonograph. Dad enjoyed reading the comics aloud to us. A new comic strip, "Popeye," featured a one-eyed sailor who championed honor and gallantry. His girlfriend, Olive Oyl, and pal, Wimpy, a lover of hamburgers, provided Popeye with daily challenges. Books were plentiful and a source of thought provoking discussions at the supper table. Evenings at home were indeed gratifying and a joy for all.

Peter Pan Peanut Butter was introduced by Swift Packing Company. The homogenized peanut butter became a family favorite. A healthy spread of peanut butter between two slices of bread provided a soul-satisfying treat.

Henceforth, the story is best told in the *first person* **as I personally recall the events.**

"Dad," I asked, "did any of your kinfolk serve in the war?" "Yes, my grandfather, Walter Travis Hanes, who was my mother's father, served as a scout in the Confederate army. He was a sergeant in Brigadier General Fitzhugh Lee's Second Brigade. Often as a boy I listened to him tell of his wartime experiences. Also, John McKendree Jefferies, my father's father, was a captain in the Cumberland Troop Cavalry. He suffered a crushed hand when his horse was shot and rolled over on him. He always wore a glove to hide his crippled hand. Both men served proudly for a cause which, at the time, seemed just. However, it turned out to be a *lost cause* that cost thousands of lives on both sides."

"Dad, when you and Mom met here in Hopewell in 1916, how did you know you'd get married?"

Dad smiled at Phil's question and said: "I'll let your mother answer that one!"

"Phil, I fell in love with your handsome father the first time I laid eyes on him. I knew in my heart that he was the man I would someday marry."

"I'm sure glad that you did!" Phil exclaimed.

If ever there was a perfect marriage, our parents were blessed with one. Dad worked hard to support his family and Mom performed her homemaking duties cheerfully. They were always doing little things for one another—a special treat in his lunch box, something he picked up at a store that he knew she would like—just little, thoughtful things to express their mutual love.

Dad plunged into his job at the Atmospheric Nitrogen

Company with much enthusiasm. Although he worked long hours in supervising the plant's expansion and often came home exhausted, he always found time to speak with each of us about our interests.

"Dad, will you take Dick and me on a tour of the plant someday?"

"Sure will, Matt!" As Dad had promised, we spent a fascinating afternoon at the huge Atmospheric Nitrogen plant.

Matt jotted down notes as Dad explained the function of each piece of equipment and when we returned home he drew a schematic diagram of the process. Dad was so impressed with Matt's work that he took the drawing to the plant to show to his coworkers.

We acquired many friends in the neighborhood and at school. One, Pierre Bontecou, lived with his mother at the corner of 15th Avenue and West Broadway. Pierre was a brilliant student and excelled at everything he undertook. He was determined to follow a military career and had his sights set on attending West Point. He had a well-equipped woodworking shop in his garage where he turned out beautifully crafted cars, trucks, and airplanes. Matt and I spent many pleasant hours with Pierre. He willingly shared his interests, his aspirations, and his shop equipment. Our presence was always welcome.

Holidays were always times of great fun for everyone in the city. There was a colorful parade and fireworks on the Fourth of July. On Easter Sunday, the church bells summoned parishioners to attend the joyful services and sing praises to the Risen Christ. Picnics were held in the city park. The local industries sponsored a Halloween cel-

Aviatrix Amelia Earhart, who learned to fly in 1920, was best known for setting a woman's altitude record of 14,000 feet. On June 17, 1928, with pilot Wilmer Stutz, she became the first woman to fly across the Atlantic. The route taken was from Newfoundland to Wales. She was thirty. Thereafter, she devoted her life to aviation.

※

Pierre Bontecou—Following graduation from Hopewell High School in 1938, Pierre attended Virginia Polytechnic Institute in Blacksburg, Virginia, majoring in mechanical engineering. After three years at VPI, he was accepted at West Point. He graduated in June 1944, fifty-eighth in a class of 500, and was commissioned as second lieutenant in the infantry.

※

At VPI, Pierre and I were members of the student chapter of the American Society of Mechanical Engineers.

※

First Lt. Pierre Bontecou, son of Mrs. Eva Archer Bontecou, gave his life in action at Bad Goden, Germany, on April 5, 1945. He served in the Seventh army.

ebration with contests and games for everyone to enjoy. Uncle George Jefferies, now seventeen, volunteered to enter a greased pole contest. The object was to retrieve a fifty dollar bill from atop a tall, wooden pole which was coated with lard. Every man and boy who attempted the climb failed to reach more than halfway up the pole. Uncle George was the last to attempt the climb. He had filled his pants pockets with flour. His strength, coupled with handfuls of flour, enabled him to successfully reach the top. With the fifty dollar bill clenched between his teeth, he slid down the pole to the applause of the crowd. That evening he brought us a large Smithfield ham and an enormous watermelon.

Matt and I attended "B" Village Elementary School, which was located a short distance from our home. Classes were held in barracks-like buildings which were originally built by Du Pont for housing single workers during the Great War. Dad routinely sat with us and reviewed our home-work assignments. He was proficient in mathematics and helped us understand fractions and decimals. There were occasions when our teacher in explaining the solution to a problem left us in complete ignorance. We asked Dad for his help. He would study the problem and rationally arrive at the correct answer while explaining his step-by-step procedure. He was indeed a great teacher!

Our first Christmas in Hopewell was one to be fondly remembered. The Christmas tree, adorned with ornaments and tinsel, and ablaze with colorful lights, was breathtakingly beauti-ful. Dad, seated on the floor before the tree, was surrounded by carefully wrapped presents. Mom, seated in her rocking chair, hands in her

We attended Sunday school at St. John's Episcopal Church in Hopewell. Catechism lessons and The **Ten Commandments** were learned by heart:

I	*I am the Lord thy God: Thou shalt not have strange gods before Me.*
II	*Thou shalt not take the name of the Lord thy God in vain.*
III	*Remember thou keep holy the Sabbath Day.*
IV	*Honor thy father and mother.*
V	*Thou shalt not kill.*
VI	*Thou shalt not commit adultery.*
VII	*Thou shalt not steal.*
VIII	*Thou shalt not bear false witness against thy neighbor.*
IX	*Thou shalt not covet thy neighbor's wife.*
X.	*Thou shalt not covet thy neighbor's goods.*

❋

Graf Zeppelin—Launched July 8, 1928, the German dirigible flew from Friedrichshafen, Germany to Lakehurst, New Jersey arriving October 15th. Thirty passengers paid $3,000 each for the privilege of making history's first commercial transatlantic crossing by air. The flight covered 6,630 miles in 111 hours, 44 minutes. The *Graf Zeppelin* would fly more than a million miles over a period of nine years. It crossed the Atlantic 144 times and made a round-the-world trip in 1929.

❋

Pierre Bontecou, our friend and neighbor, turned out a wooden model of the Graf Zeppelin for each of us. Matt painted the German markings on the airship.

lap, patiently waited for Dad to read out the names on the gifts. In short order, we were engrossed with our toys and the clothes we had received. We laughed when Dad put on Mom's gift of a bow tie, comically placed on his neck over his Adam's apple. It bobbed up and down every time he spoke. Suddenly he stood up and left the room saying that he had just remembered to do something important. Moments later he returned, placed a large bundle of dirty overalls in Mom's lap and said: "Grace, I want you to wash these right away. I realize that it's Christmas, but I'll need them today." As Mom dutifully arose to comply, a box, tied with a bright red ribbon, slipped from amongst the soiled clothing. She gasped in surprise and said: "Walter, pray tell me, what in the world is this?"

"Best way to find out is to open it."

Mom carefully untied the ribbon and opened the gift to reveal a beautiful mother-of-pearl set of combs and brushes in a satin-lined case. She cried with joy and thanked Dad with loving hugs and kisses. Proud of his little ruse, he grinned, retrieved the bundle of soiled clothes, and returned them to the washroom.

On March 4, 1929, we gathered around the radio and listened to President Hoover deliver his inaugural address. His remarks were filled with optimism. He concluded his oratory with these words: "Ours is a land rich in resources, stimulating in its glorious beauty, filled with millions of happy homes, blessed with comfort and opportunity. In no nation is the government more worthy of respect. No country is more loved by its people. I have abiding faith in their capacity, integrity, and high purpose. I have no fears for the future! It is bright with hope!"

Christmas 1929—A Philco cathedral model radio operated on alternating current. Prior to 1929 all radios were battery-operated. One of our favorite programs was *Amos 'n Andy*. White actors impersonated the black co-owners of the *Fresh Air Taxi Company of America*. The comedy show aired daily for fifteen minutes.

Herbert Hoover

The thirty-first president of the United States was elected in 1928. An engineering graduate of Stanford University, Hoover worked in mining in China, Europe, and the United States. By age forty, he was a millionaire and living in London when the Great War broke out in 1914. He became director of the American Relief Commission which helped thousands of stranded Americans secure passage home. In 1915–19 Hoover was chairman of the Commission for Relief in Belgium which distributed food, medicine, and clothing to civilian victims of the war in France and Belgium.

December 19, 1928—Howard Pitcairn introduced the first American made Autogiro, a wingless airplane utilizing unpowered, rotating blades to elevate the machine, sustain it in flight, and allow it to land slowly. Forward motion was provided by a conventional, engine-driven propeller.

"Is Hoover overconfident, Walter?" Mom asked.

"No doubt about it, Grace!" Dad responded with a worried expression on his countenance. "Far too many Americans are gambling every dollar they can spare on Wall Street. They are even mortgaging their homes to acquire extra money to entrust to their brokers. They are blindly buying securities which they hope to sell at enormous profits. The fever of speculation has spread to all classes, from bankers and businessmen to clerks, cooks, and bus drivers. Why, down at the plant, all the guys talk about are their investments and how they will soon be rich and retire early. It's all too good to be true!"

Dad put money aside from each paycheck to purchase a new car. The odometer on the 1923 Dodge Brothers sedan had turned over a hundred-thousand miles and the wear and tear had taken its toll. A competent mechanic, he repaired or replaced whatever component failed. Over the years he acquired a complete set of hand tools which were kept in a sturdy, steel chest. He taught us to recognize each tool and call it by the proper name: open-end wrench, crescent wrench, manifold wrench, feeler gauges, calipers, etc. Tools were handled with care and were wiped clean and oiled before being returned to the chest.

One evening after the supper table was cleared, Dad spread out an assortment of automotive brochures and meticulously studied the specifications of each car. He made a comparative chart, listing vehicle weight, engine horsepower and displacement, type of clutch, transmission, brakes, and other pertinent features. Dodge, Chevrolet, Hupmobile and Ford were evaluated from the specifications.

"Well, Walter, what have you decided?" Mom asked as she fingered through the brochures.

"Well, we've always had good luck with Dodge so I may buy another one. However, before making a decision I'll want to test drive each of them. As a matter of fact, the Hupmobile salesman is driving one here to the house tomorrow. We'll all take a spin in it."

Early the following morning, the sound of a honking horn sent us scurrying outside. Parked at the curb was a shiny, new Hupmobile sedan. A dapper salesman wearing a striped shirt, bow tie, and a straw hat stepped out and greeted us with a winning smile. He shook hands with Dad, tipped his hat when introduced to Mom, and said: "Mrs. Jefferies, you and your sons get in the back, and Walter, you take the wheel."

After we were seated, Dad turned and asked: "Any place in particular you want to go?"

"Let's go to City Point," Matt said, "and show the car to Grandpa and Uncle George."

"Here we go!" Dad said, as he drove away from the curb and proceeded down 15th Avenue. En route to City Point, he expertly checked the operation of the vehicle . . . shifting, accelerating, turning, backing up, and braking. The Hupmobile ran smoothly and performed to perfection. When we arrived at Grandpa's store, Dad parked and honked the horn. Grandpa and Uncle George emerged to inspect the car.

"Sure is a beauty, Walter! You planning on buying it?"

"Don't know yet, Poppa. I'll have to think about it for awhile. It's a good-running car though!"

Recess at "B" Village School—At the sound of the bell, the boys made a mad dash for the playground . . . not to play baseball, but to play marbles. The girls played Jacks, jumped rope, or watched the boys play marbles. A large circle was scratched on the ground and our marbles were brought out for action. Marbles were carried in a chamois bag (one with a draw string), or a cigar box or coffee can. They were our 'crown jewels.' Each one had a distinct personality. A choice was made if playing for *keeps* or playing for *fairs* (*fairs* meaning you got your marbles back). Playing for *keeps* could chance the loss of a favorite *aggie* or *cat's-eye*. Everyone had a prized *shooter*; one that could be counted on for power and accuracy. Marbles were often traded two for one . . . or for a bar of candy. The marbles were beautiful: multicolored spirals and swirls, clearies, cloudies, corkscrews, and, not to be forgotten, the *steelies* . . . slippery little devils, but a sure shot! Marbles were played kneeling, with head bent low for aiming, and the knuckle of the second finger planted firmly on the ground. Marbles became a national craze in the late '20s and early '30s. *Matt and I were crazy about playing marbles!*

Several weeks passed without Dad saying anything further about buying a new car. One day he asked: "Dick, would you like to help replace the piston rings on the Dodge?"

"Yes sir, Dad, but why overhaul the Dodge when you'll be trading it in soon?"

"I've decided against the idea just now. Times are too uncertain and a new car costs a lot of money. I think we should wait."

"But, Dad, I thought President Hoover said that we Americans have nothing to worry about!"

"That's exactly what he said, Dick, but I have a gut feeling that things are not as rosy as everyone seems to believe. I'm afraid that these happy-go-lucky days are the calm before the storm. We'll see how things are later on. The old Dodge will serve us for awhile longer."

We were not overly disappointed as the Dodge was like a member of the family . . . loved and dependable.

Throughout rural America the status of the farmer deteriorated at a disturbing rate. The price of wheat declined from one dollar to as low as fifty cents a bushel. The government loaned millions of dollars to the farm cooperatives to help them through the slump. Agencies were created to conduct large scale market operations to keep farm prices steady.

However, the government's efforts failed to halt the downward slide. Farmers continued to abandon their farms in growing numbers. Grandpa Sanford was no exception. His 1928 crop of corn, beans, and asparagus failed to make a profit. All his life he had farmed in the Northern

---

One cannot be raised in Virginia without acquiring smatterings of colloquialisms:

"Don't have a *conniption fit!*"

"*Fetch* the dog!"

"Dad is all *tuckered out!*"

"Who the *sam hill* are you?"

"She's *right smart.*"

"I took all I could *tote.*"

"He's too *high falutin* for me!"

"I was *fit to be tied.*"

"Such *carryings-on!*"

"Sakes *alive!*"

"I *reckon* he's tellin' the truth."

"Don't be so *ornery!*"

"Chicken *fixings* for dinner."

"*Don't mind if I do!*"

"*Indeed I do!*"

"*Yes indeedy!*"

"*He took off like a blue streak of greased lightning!*"

We were encouraged to avoid these expressions and speak proper English. Our grandparents, and others whom we came in contact with daily, spoke these colorful words as a matter of course.

❋

1929—Ford Motor Company introduced the first station wagon. It was a Model A with a boxy wooden body providing space for passengers and cargo.

❋

1929—Deusenberg introduced the Model J advertised as a "Real Doozie." Built for affluent Americans and Europeans, the costly luxury car, powered with a 265-horsepower engine, had a maximum speed of 116 miles per hour.

Matthew 15:11 "Not that which goeth into the mouth defileth a man; but that which cometh out of the mouth, this defileth a man."

Profanity was forbidden in our family. I **never** heard our parents or grandparents curse! However, we were allowed to utter moderately descriptive swear words when the need arose. Example: Accidentally hitting a thumb with a hammer was justification for exclaiming *"Doggone it!"* or *"Darn it!"* Use of the words *"damn"* or *"hell"* were punishable by an appropriate rap on the head or our being sent to bed without supper. Mom's relevant words were: *"Curse words reveal the condition of a man's heart."*

Wall Street, New York
October 29, 1929

Neck and managed to make a living. However, a solution to the farmer's plight was nowhere in sight and he could not afford to gamble away another year. Although he had no experience as a merchant, he too decided to move to the thriving city of Hopewell and open a grocery store. A vacant store with living quarters in the rear was rented and ready for business in short order. We were present on opening day. I had never seen Grandpa so happy! No longer just another poor, dirt farmer, he was now about to become a respected and profitable merchant. We were delighted to have our grandparents living close by, but knew that we would miss visiting their farm in Ottoman.

Throughout the long, hot summer, most Americans were satisfied that the economy under Hoover was just as healthy as it was during the Coolidge administration. People were buying cars, radios, and home appliances, and continuing to invest heavily in stocks and bonds. They returned from vacation to enroll their children in school and to plan for the holidays. However, on October 29, 1929, economic disaster struck. The stock market crashed! Stock prices had started to slide downward at an alarming rate early in the day. Investors panicked and scrambled to sell their stocks before they would go lower. Even Blue Chip stocks such as GE and AT&T dropped to where they were virtually worthless. Over sixteen million shares were sold on that fateful day.

Thirty billion dollars in capital disappeared overnight; a sum almost equal to the dollar cost of the 1914–1918 war to the United States. Fortunes were wiped out. Many, facing certain bankruptcy, committed suicide. Across the vast nation stunned Americans reacted in utter shock and disbelief. Never in their wildest imaginations did they ever think that their hopes and dreams would be dashed in the blink of an eye.

"Walter, what does this all mean to us and our loved ones?"

"Fortunately we have no money invested in stocks. We won't have to grieve over something we didn't have in the first place."

"That's some consolation. However, I'm worried about how this crisis will affect our parents. They were just getting established and now the future of their business is in doubt."

"We'll just have to take it a day at a time. As long as the plant keeps producing nitrogen, my job should be secure. The plant depends on electricity to operate. It's our job in the power house to provide it. If a reduced demand for nitrogen results in a drastic reduction in production, or should the plant close, we'll be in the same boat as thousands of others. As for our parents, I seriously doubt if they can remain in business very long. Their unemployed customers will move elsewhere."

"At least, Walter, our parents can return to their farms."

The following day President Hoover addressed the nation and assured the American people that prosperity was "just around the corner" and that the panic was merely "psychological." He was wrong! In the weeks and months that followed, wages were cut, mortgages foreclosed, and hundreds of banks failed. FOR SALE signs appeared on houses and business establishments across the land. The unemployed stood in endless bread lines for handouts to feed their families. Men who had lost their fortunes stood on street corners and sold apples for five cents apiece. Americans had lost confidence in their government and in themselves.

As though Mom didn't have enough to worry her, Matt and I inadvertently gave her an alarming scare. We had placed our little brother, Phil, into the circular opening of an old truck tire and told him to grip the edges of the sidewalls with his fingertips. We took turns in rolling the tire in circles in front of our North 15th Avenue residence. As Phil got the hang of holding on securely, he asked that we push the tire a little faster. Somehow the tire got away from us and headed downhill at a fast clip. Phil continued to hold on even as the tire's speed increased—his doubled-up form now only a spinning blur. Unable to catch the runaway tire, we could only watch in abject horror as it approached a busy intersection at the bottom of the hill. To our supreme relief, the tire, with its passenger intact, crossed the dangerous intersection without mishap and rolled to a wobbly stop in a vacant field.

Artist—Wendell Dowling, Santa Paula, CA

Emerging from the tire, Phil was too dizzy to stand. When his equilibrium returned, he asked if he could do it again! Our shouts brought Mom and several neighbors outside to see what the commotion was all about. Needless to say, Mom was relieved to see that Phil had survived the downhill ride. She scolded us for placing Phil's life in jeopardy and told us that Dad would be duly informed. That evening when we told Dad what had occurred, he patiently listened to our explanation. Then he censured us firmly for not considering the consequences that could have resulted from our actions. He concluded by saying: "Boys, your mother has enough to worry her. Be careful not to upset her as you did today! Next time I'll give you a lesson you will not soon forget. Now run along and help your mother with the dishes." I thought I detected an amused look on Dad's face when he added: "And tell Phil I want to have a little talk with him."

During the cold, winter months of 1929–1930, it became painfully evident that a return to prosperity was not "just around the corner" as Hoover had assured the nation. The depression only worsened. Factory closures continued, throwing thousands more into the ranks of the unemployed. Fearful of losing their savings, depositors withdrew their funds and hid them under their mattresses or in their backyards. Hundreds of banks were forced out of business. Apple peddlers set up their stands on the streets of every town and city across the nation. All sense of job security vanished. Optimism quickly faded to abject pessimism. Never, not even in wartime, had so many Americans been so adversely affected. People reached out for anything to take their minds off of their problems. The radio was one source of diversion. A new drama captured their imaginations. It began with the announcer saying: "A fiery horse with the speed of light, a cloud of dust and a hearty 'Hi-ho Silver,' the Lone Ranger rides again!" The hero, a masked

Apple Peddlers

"Hoovervilles"—Ramshackle communities housing the homeless sprang up in every city. Constructed of packing cases, rusty sheet metal, and discarded lumber, the shanties occupied vacant lots, garbage dumps, and swamplands. Thousands of hobos roamed across the land seeking food, shelter, and employment.

※

"The Lord was wise to the world, and He just wanted to show 'em that after all, He was running things, in spite of what The New York Stock Exchange thought. Well, that was a terrible blow to finance, to learn that the Lord not only closed the stock market on Sundays, but that He could practically close it any day of the week."
—Will Rogers

In 1929, 71 percent of American families had annual incomes below $2,500 which was considered the minimum necessary for a decent living.

※

Automobiles manufactured in 1929 totaled 4.5 million. In 1930 the output would be reduced to only 2.7 million. Unable to sell their inventories, the factories closed down, idling thousands of workers.

※

Coca-Cola introduced a catchy theme in their advertising: *"The Pause that Refreshes."*

※

Our next door neighbor, Mr. Mays, owner of the Texaco station, kept us supplied with used tires and inner tubes as they were needed. We had a particular need for inner tubes which were cut into bands for use in our homemade *rubber guns*. Pierre Bontecou turned out finely crafted rifles in his woodworking shop. The rifles were fitted with clothes pin arming devices (the spring clamp type). The running battles we had with other kids in the neighborhood were easily won thanks to the high velocity rubber band projectiles which were cut from the inner tubes provided by Mr. Mays.

Western Electric Company introduced the Orthophonic phonograph, an improved gramophone that would eventually replace wind-up record players.

❋

Agricultural depression sent cotton from thirty-five cents to fifteen cents a pound and wheat from $2.16 a bushel to $1.03.

❋

In the summer of 1930, nature contributed to the Depression. An unprecedented drought covered virtually the entire South and Central Plains. High temperatures, deficient rainfall, high winds, and massive insect infestations damaged crops on millions of acres. Lakes, ponds, streams, and rivers dried up creating critical water shortages. Livestock and wildlife perished. Billowing clouds of dust often obliterated the sun. Unable to live on the land, the desperate people moved away from the drought-stricken area. The year 1938 marked the beginning of a steady migration to the West. The physical and emotional hardships endured by these people are legendary.

Lone Ranger, and his sidekick, Tonto, were the topic of discussion following every episode. One day we entered Grandpa Jefferies's store to find him all excited about something as he greeted us. "I want you to see this!" he said, as he reached for a loaf of Wonder Bread. "See, it's sliced! Can you imagine that? Sliced bread in a waxed paper package! "We knew only too well that Grandpa's grocery business was failing. Yet, he found it in himself to be fascinated by something new: *sliced bread!*

Our parents realized that at our young ages, it was difficult for us to fully comprehend the gravity of the deepening depression. To impress upon us that we must each do our part to economize, they asked us to sit with them one evening for a family discussion. After explaining the seriousness of the depression and how we must be frugal, Dad questioned us to make certain that we understood what was expected of us.

"Matt, what will you do to help out?"

"I'll eat everything on my plate!"

"Good, son! And, Dick, what about you?"

"I'll write on both sides of my school papers."

"Phil, what will you do?" Five-year-old Philip was absorbed in trying to stay within the lines of a coloring book. He apparently did not hear Dad's question. "Phil, pay attention! I asked you what you will do to help during the Depression."

"Yes, sir! Well, I'll save hot water by taking my bath in Matt or Dick's bath water . . . but, if the water is too dirty, I just won't take a bath!"

In July the Hummel-Ross Fibre Company shut down and

President Hoover invited Great Britain, France, Italy, Germany, and Japan to Washington for a conference to propose limiting the construction of naval vessels. The conference produced a treaty which fixed limits on warships ranging from cruisers and destroyers to submarines.

Complying with the terms of the treaty, the modernization of British and American fleets was virtually placed *on hold*. However, Germany, Italy and Japan quickly forged ahead with ambitious building programs. There were those in America who voiced concern about our lagging behind in the construction of warships, but their voices were drowned out by the cries of the unemployed, the hungry, and the homeless.

May 15, 1930—Registered nurse Ellen Church became the first airline stewardess. On a Boeing Air Transport flight between San Francisco, California and Cheyenne, Wyoming, she introduced the in-flight service which became the norm for passenger planes. The plane was a Boeing Model 80-A Trimotor having a maximum speed of 138 mph. Aboard were twelve passengers and a crew of three.

terminated hundreds of employees including several of our neighbors. Many defaulted on their mortgages and the banks foreclosed on their homes. Within a short time, numerous houses on our block had FOR SALE signs in their yards. As a result of the Hummel-Ross closure, Grandpa Sanford lost most of his customers. He was forced to close his store and return to the Northern Neck. It was a sad day for us all when we saw them depart.

"Grandma, when will we see you and Grandpa again?" Phil tearfully asked.

"Don't cry, little one. You'll be coming down to visit with us on the farm in Ottoman."

One evening, Mom packed a picnic basket and we drove to City Point and parked next to the docks. We sat on the running board of the Dodge, ate our sandwiches, and watched the activity in the bustling harbor.

"Boys, look there . . . to your left . . . see that old, rusty freighter being loaded with scrap iron?"

"Yes, sir!"

"Well, that's one of the many freighters that have been sold to the Japanese who must import all their iron to make steel. Our factories are being scrapped and sold piece by piece. Even that old freighter will probably be melted down in their blast furnaces. Can't figure out why they need so much scrap iron."

One day, Dad told us that the engine in the old Dodge Brothers sedan was sluggish and beginning to burn oil. "I can't put it off any longer," he said. "The engine needs a ring job and the valves may have to be ground. I could use two extra pairs of hands. Any volunteers?"

"Yes sir!" we responded in unison. Early the following Saturday, Dad jacked up the front of the car and set it down on wooden blocks. He crawled under the engine, drained the crankcase and asked me to pass him a 3/8" open-end wrench for removal of the oil pan. This accomplished, he emerged from beneath the car, raised the hood, and removed the bolts that clamped the cylinder head to the engine block. After lifting the head, he showed us how to remove the carbon deposits that had accumulated on the underside of the head. While we were occupied with this chore he crawled back under the car to remove the nuts that retained the connecting rod caps. Calling up to me, he said: "Son, now I want you to climb up on the fender. I'll push the piston and connecting rod assemblies up to you. When the rings clear the cylinder, grasp the piston firmly and pass the assembly to Matt to place on the work bench. Any questions?"

"No, sir!"

We did as instructed. Dad crawled out from under the car and carefully scrutinized each component: cylinder walls for possible scoring, and rod bearings, pistons, and rings for wear. "Cylinder walls look good, boys! Now, Matt, I want you to hand crank the engine . . . slowly . . . so I can inspect the valve faces."

"OK, Dad."

As the intake and exhaust valves opened, Dad determined that they would have to be ground. Mom appeared carrying a tray of sandwiches and cold lemonade. She smiled as she looked us over and said: "How are you grease monkeys coming along?"

"Good, Mom! We've got the engine apart. Next we'll grind the valves."

"Well now, Dick, that's really something! Gracious, your trousers are filthy! How did you manage to get so much grease on them?"

"Gee, Mom, I don't know. They're my old, ragged ones anyway."

Dad glanced at my trousers, laughed, and said: "Son, let me show you something. You've been using your oily hands to hitch up your trousers. An experienced mechanic never does. Watch and I'll show you how a mechanic does it." Dad pressed his elbows to his hips and hoisted up his trousers without the use of his hands.

"Thanks, Dad. I'll try and remember that!"

As we sat atop his tool chest to eat lunch, Dad explained the workings of a four-cycle, internal combustion engine, "like this Dodge Brothers engine," he said. We admitted that the extent of our knowledge was that "gasoline was burnt in the engine to make the car run."

"We have a lot of work ahead of us, so let's get to it. Hand me the pliers."

It was almost sundown when we finished the overhaul. It had been an eventful day and we were eager to find out how well the engine would perform. Dad started the engine, listened to it run for a few minutes, and observed the exhaust smoke when he revved it up. Satisfied that all was in order, he closed the hood and slid into the driver's seat.

"OK, boys, hop in. We'll take her for a trial run."

"Dad, let's drive over to Grandpa's so we can tell him what we did today."

As we drove to City Point, Dad said that the engine was no longer lacking in power and the exhaust was clear of black smoke. He was pleased!

"Good gracious, Dick," Grandpa exclaimed once we had arrived, "how did you get your trousers so dirty?"

"Matt and I helped Dad do a ring and valve job on the car."

"Guess that explains it. Dick, I think you'd better pull your trousers up before they fall off!"

"Yes, sir!" I responded as I pressed my elbows to my hips and hoisted up the trousers.

"How'd you learn to pick up your trousers like that, Dick?"

"All mechanics do it that way, Grandpa."

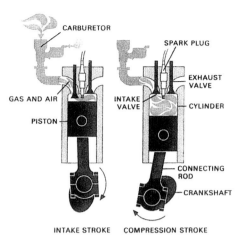

The four stroke-cycle internal combustion engine does its work in a sequence of four strokes of the piston in its cylinder. *First*, the piston moves down, drawing a mixture of air and fuel from the carburetor into the cylinder through the open intake valve. *Second*, the valve closes and the piston moves up, compressing the air-and-fuel vapor to as little as one-fourteenth its original volume.

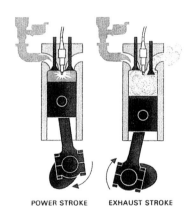

Third, an electric spark from the spark plug ignites the compressed vapor, producing an explosion which pushes the piston down. The connecting rod transforms the piston's vertical movement into the crankshaft's rotary motion. *Fourth*, the exhaust valve opens; the piston moves up, forcing the burned gases from the cylinder to prepare it for the next cycle.

Artist—Wendell Dowling, Santa Paula, CA

"You going to be a mechanic when you grow up?"

"Don't know, but someday when I have my own car, I'll know how to replace the rings and grind the valves."

"Matt, what about you?"

"I want to be a pilot like the 'Lone Eagle' and have my own plane."

That said, Matt extended his arms and took off running, swooping, diving, circling, and mimicking the roar of an airplane engine.

"Walter, I do believe that boy is determined to fly someday!"

"It's all he talks about, Poppa."

I glanced about the store. It had changed dramatically since our visit a month ago. Previously it had been crammed with produce and canned goods. Now only a few baskets of potatoes, apples, and corn were on display. Many shelves were bare. Dad made the same observation and said: "Poppa, what's happening to your business?"

The Otto Cycle Engine—The internal combustion engine in the 1923 Dodge Brothers sedan operates on the same principle as today's automotive engines. Named for its inventor, German engineer, Nicolas August Otto, the engine is a four-stroke cycle reciprocating piston engine. Dr. Otto exhibited his first four-cycle gas engine at the World's Fair at Paris in 1867.

"There isn't any, Walter! Most of my customers have little money or have moved away. I can't continue losing money. I'll have to close the store and move back to Cumberland. I see no end in sight to this terrible depression."

"I agree that you haven't a choice, Poppa, but we sure hate for you and Momma to leave here. By the way, how's Momma taking all this?"

"Well, as you know, this is not the first time we've had to return to Cumberland because of adverse conditions. Your mother welcomes a return home . . . always has. Had it been left solely to her, she would have never left Cumberland County."

I listened to this exchange in silence. I wondered how long it would be before Dad came home one day to say that he too had been laid off.

Throughout the summer and fall we continued to economize and to save for "a rainy day," as Mom expressed it. Frequently we drove to the farmers' markets in Richmond and Petersburg to purchase fresh produce for canning. We all pitched in to help in the preparation of the fruits and vegetables for the cooking kettles. Dad erected shelves in the basement for storage of the Mason jars. Tomatoes, corn, snap beans, butter beans, beets, apple sauce, pears, and peaches—colorful jars, labeled and aligned on the shelving for the day when food could not be purchased from a grocery store.

The year 1931 brought no relief from the depression. On the contrary, it only worsened. Detroit laid off another one-hundred thousand workers. President Hoover recommended public works projects and Congress began to allocate funds. One of the first projects to be considered was the construction of a huge dam in a deep canyon on the Colorado River in Nevada. It would employ thousands of workers and take at least seven years to build. Plans for the dam were already on the tables of the Bureau of Reclamation in Washington. When the approval of the project was announced, men and entire families began to migrate to the vicinity of the dam site in hopes of being hired for a job that would pay good wages. Some of our jobless neighbors quickly decided to leave Hopewell and travel to Nevada. A few months later they wrote to inform us that they were bitterly disappointed. The start of construction was many months away, as the Bureau had not yet selected a contractor to build the dam. There was no place for the newcomers to live. The nearest town, Las Vegas, was little more than a settlement of prospectors, cowboys, and gamblers. Saloons lined the streets and served hard liquor in defiance of Prohibition. Every night was one of wild drinking, shouts, and gun shots. Las Vegas was obviously no place for a family, so many camped along the banks of the Colorado River.

Some slept in tents or under their cars. They cooked on open fires and carried water from the river. In spite of these disturbing reports, a flood of workers continued to pour into the area. Many of the newcomers had no experience in construction. Unemployed factory workers, students, farmers, store clerks, and waiters gambled all they owned to join the potential work force with dreams of fat paychecks and rewarding futures. Arriving in Las Vegas, they were shocked to see long lines of men, many with their families, lined up at the town's soup kitchens. Newspapers described the situation as "pitiful and pathetic!" Although the Bureau of Reclamation admonished potential workers not to go to Las Vegas unless they were assured employment, people continued to arrive in caravans and by Union Pacific Railroad.

One day Dad returned from work with a worried look on his face.

"What is it, Walter?" Mom asked as she poured him a cup of hot coffee.

"Atmospheric Nitrogen passed out pink slips to seventy employees. Production has been cut in half."

"You don't think they will close the plant, do you?"

"Hard to say, Grace. At least my job should be secure for awhile unless they bring in electrical power from the outside. Anyway, we'll just have to wait and see what happens."

"Were any of your men laid off, Walter?"

"Yes, five . . . three were helpers and the other two were Joe Roberts and Charles Huneke, my best oilers. Joe and Charley are talking about driving to the Boulder Dam project where there are good paying jobs. Charley will sell his old Model T coupe and they'll go together in Joe's Chevrolet flatbed truck."

"Will it take them all the way to Nevada?"

"Charley is a pretty good mechanic. He'll patch it up as they go along. They'll make it all right."

"I hope they're not planning on taking their families with them."

"They are taking everyone . . . Charley's wife and daughter, Joe's wife, her mother, and their three kids. He's planning on pitching a tent on the bed of the truck. It'll look something like a covered wagon."

"Good gracious! I feel sorry for them! Nevada is two thousand miles away. They'll have to cross the Alleghenies, the Great Plains, the Rockies, and the vast deserts of the West. When they arrive . . . that is, if they get there at all . . . there will be no housing, no schools for the children, nor medical facilities. Why don't they wait until these things are available for the workers?"

"They are well aware of the reasons why they should not go, but they need jobs to survive. As for the trip to Nevada, Joe said that if the pioneers could cross the continent in an ox-drawn covered wagon, there's no reason why they can't make the same crossing in a truck."

Dad commented that it would certainly be exciting to work on a project of that magnitude. We wondered what was going

---

Displayed on the wall of one of the markets was a hand-lettered sign which read:

**IF A DOG COULD TALK,
HE'D TELL YOU
THAT HE BURIES HIS BONES
SO HE'LL HAVE THEM
WHEN THERE ARE NONE**

Boulder City—A town to house the workers and their families was constructed on a ridge seven miles from the dam site. Up to 6,000 workers occupied a thousand homes and a dozen dormitories. The community included four churches, a grade school, shops, restaurants, a 700-seat theater, a dining hall seating 1,300, recreation halls, and a sixty-bed hospital.

Hoover Dam—Originally called *Boulder Dam*. Name changed to Hoover Dam when construction began in 1931. The dam is 725 feet high and 1,244 feet long. The base is 660 feet thick. Construction entailed excavating three-and-a half million cubic yards of rock, pouring four-and-a-half million cubic yards of concrete, and utilizing forty-five million pounds of pipe and structural steel. The scope of the project was mind-bending. A writer referred to the Hoover Dam as "The Great Pyramid of the American Desert." The project was completed in 1936. Lake Mead, the reservoir created by the dam, is 115 miles long and 500 feet deep. The hydroelectric power plant generates 1,345,000 kilowatts of electrical power serving the needs of portions of Nevada, Arizona, and Southern California.

1931—Unemployment in the United States exceeded eight million. Jobless citizens staged a hunger march to the White House in Washington, D. C. They demanded a guarantee of employment at a minimum wage. All were turned away.

❄

Each of us were avid collectors of pictures and printed material related to our particular interests. Matt saved and catalogued pictures of airplanes and automobiles. I saved pictures of automobiles and submarines. Phil collected pictures of Hollywood stars.

❄

I particularly remember Matt's attention to his collection. He recognized each aircraft on sight and memorized its configuration and specifications. His '20s collection included:

Curtiss JN-4 Jenny

American DH-4 De Havilland Gypsy Moth

Sopwith Pup

Sopwith Snipe

Ford Tri-motor

Fokker F-10 Trimotor

Vickers Vimy

Swallow biplane

through his mind. Was he also thinking of possibly going to the Boulder Dam project to find work should he lose his job? Matt and I had overheard everything that was said and the whole idea of driving to Nevada sounded exciting. We'd surely see cowboys and Indians and the thought of crossing the Rockies was pretty fascinating! We said nothing of this to Mom as she stood over the stove preparing supper. She was crying softly. We sensed that she was worried about Dad and about our future. It saddened us to see our good mother so distressed.

Weeks prior to Atmospheric Nitrogen's massive layoff, Dad had been apprehensive about the company's ability to maintain their level of production during the worsening economic crisis. Fearing a shutdown of the facility, he began to look elsewhere for employment. Every evening after the supper dishes had been cleared, he sat at the table and wrote to various firms and utilities. Only two responses were received: one from New Jersey and one from Ohio. Neither appeared very promising. Although he had no desire to again leave Virginia, he realized that he might have no choice. No replies had been received from the Virginia firms he had approached. It was very discouraging, but he continued to search trade papers and newspaper advertisements for leads.

On June 10, Dad returned from work and informed us that his last day on the job would be on June 15. The plant had drastically cut production and ordered the powerhouse to shut down two of their three units. We were stunned with the realization that the depression had finally reached out to threaten our way of life. Dad remained optimistic, however, and assured us that he believed he would soon find employment elsewhere.

Lincoln Memorial—Dedicated on Memorial Day in 1922. President Warren G. Harding accepted the memorial on behalf of the American people. Engraved above the solemn figure of the Great Emancipator are these words:

IN THIS TEMPLE AS IN THE HEARTS OF THE PEOPLE FOR WHOM HE SAVED THE UNION THE MEMORY OF ABRAHAM LINCOLN IS ENSHRINED FOREVER

Lincoln Memorial

A few days later, Dad received a letter from the Research Department of the Mathieson Alkali Works in Niagara Falls, New York, requesting his résumé. He immediately responded, stating that he would welcome an interview. They replied with the information that a representative would be in Richmond to meet with job applicants and, if interested, he should be present at the appointed time and place. Dad felt that the interview went well. Four days later he received notification that his application had been approved. He was instructed to report to work on June 30, coincidentally, his thirty-second birthday! We had mixed feelings about our pending move to New York. Our three years in Hopewell had been happy ones. Yet we were curious and excited about the new adventures that awaited us in Niagara Falls. Mom showed us pictures of the great waterfalls, colorfully illuminated at night. She told us that people could go to the base of the falls in a little boat called the *Maid of the Mist* and look up at the spectacular falls through a billowing mist. Also, she said, one could cross over a high bridge spanning the Niagara River gorge and enter Canada. As if all this wasn't enough to raise our spirits, Dad added that we would stop in Washington, D.C. to see the Capitol,

Washington Monument

White House

the Washington Monument, and the Lincoln Memorial. "Daddy, will we get to see President Hoover?"

"Probably not, Phil, but we'll see the White House where he lives."

"I don't think I like President Hoover!"

"Why, Phil?"

"Because he made the depression."

"Who told you that?"

"I heard it on the radio."

With less than two weeks to pack and drive to Niagara Falls, we put playing aside and pitched in to help with the packing. Our furniture, Dad's tool chest, the Edison phonograph, and a number of Mom's Mason jars were taken to Ottoman for storage at Grandpa Sanford's. Dad explained that we would probably live in a furnished apartment until he was settled in his new job. In time, he said, we would search for a house similar to our Hopewell home.

In 1930, Hoover signed a trade bill which imposed a stiff tariff on goods imported to America. Our manufacturers could not compete with those countries that pay their workers very little and sell the same product for less money. In retaliation, the foreign countries punished America by increasing the tariffs on goods sold to them. As a result, we were unable to buy from them and could no longer sell to them. Large quantities of goods filled American warehouses and our plants shut down.

We arrived in Washington on a hot, sunny day. The city was more beautiful than we had imagined. We were impressed with all the sites: the great dome of the Capitol, the five-hundred-and-fifty-five-foot Washington Monument, the magnificent Lincoln Memorial, and the White House. As we drove along tree-lined Pennsylvania Avenue, we observed many protesters pacing in front of the White House. Others jammed Lafayette Park across the street. They displayed large placards and chanted: "*DOWN WITH THE TARIFF!... DOWN WITH HOOVER!*" Most were shabbily dressed and their faces reflected their desperation.

"Dad, what are they shouting about?" Matt asked.

"They are blaming the depression on President Hoover."

"See, I told you so!" Phil chimed in.

"Hoover honestly thought the import tariff would help our economy, but it only made matters worse," Dad explained.

"It seems that no matter how hard he tries, Hoover's policies fail."

"True, Grace, but placing all the blame for the depression on Hoover is not entirely fair. It's something like throwing a wild party and leaving the mess for someone else to clean up. During the Coolidge Administration, America was enjoying the good life. The crash of '29 ended the party. Hoover is expected to perform miracles."

Two blocks from the White House, we observed a long line of destitute men, perhaps numbering several hundred, patiently waiting for the daily distribution of bread. On virtually every street corner, the apple vendors were ubiquitous. Crudely lettered signs read: *HELP THE UNEMPLOYED. BUY AN APPLE A DAY AND EAT THE DEPRESSION AWAY.* The long bread lines and the apple peddlers were stark reminders of the severity of the depression that had gripped the nation since the crash of '29.

Matt (10), Phil (6), and Dick (8)

Departing Washington, we traveled north to Frederick, Maryland, and west to Harrisburg, the capital of Pennsylvania, where we crossed the wide Susquehanna River. After following the course of the river for many miles, we approached the foothills of the Appalachian Mountains. It was here that Dad turned off the highway and parked. We climbed out and moved about to stretch our legs while Mom brought out something for us to eat. Dad lit a can of Sterno canned heat to boil water for coffee and hot chocolate. We sat on the running board and each ate a sandwich and a boiled egg.

Dad could not have selected a more beautiful place. The rippling waters of the river reflected a backdrop of mountains. The golden rays of sunset filtered through a canopy of tall trees blanketing the mountain slopes.

"Beautiful, isn't it, Walter?"

"Indeed it is, Grace."

"Wish we could camp out right here!" Matt said.

"Not this time, son. We've only come halfway and must get to Niagara Falls as soon as we can. I'll bed you boys down in the back and you can get some sleep. It'll be dark in a little while so you'll no longer be able to see anything."

"How's the car running, Dad?"

"OK, Matt! The ring and valve job we did really paid off. The engine is running well and I

Dick, Matt, and Phil

While traveling, we were never bored! There was always something of interest to see and comment on. A favorite diversion was identifying the make and model of cars . . . Ford, Chevrolet, Buick, Cadillac, Packard, Oldsmobile, and an occasional Auburn or Franklin. Reading aloud the humorous Burma-Shave signs which frequently appeared alongside the roadway was great fun.

THE ANSWER TO A MAIDEN'S PRAYER

IS NOT A CHIN

OF STUBBY HAIR

BURMA-SHAVE

PITY ALL THE MIGHTY CAESARS

THEY PULLED

EACH WHISKER OUT

WITH TWEEZERS

BURMA-SHAVE

HIS FACE WAS SMOOTH

AND COOL AS ICE

AND OH LOUISE!

HE SMELLED SO NICE.

BURMA-SHAVE

Roosevelt Highway is named for Theodore Roosevelt, America's twenty-sixth president. It is the State of Pennsylvania's section of U.S. Route 6, the Grand Army of the Republic Highway, honoring the Union forces of the Civil War. U.S. Route 6 was America's first transcontinental highway. Each of the fourteen states own and maintain their section of the highway.

haven't had to add any oil. We'll soon see how it performs climbing the mountains ahead."

"Walter, are you planning to drive all night?"

"Don't mind in the least! As a matter of fact, I like driving at night."

Dad removed some luggage from the running board and placed it level with the back seat, forming a pallet for us to sleep on. We were soon bedded down. The steady drone of the engine quickly lulled us to sleep. Awakened hours later by the realization that we were no longer in motion, we sat up to see why Dad had stopped.

"We're in a very thick fog and I can't see to drive." Dad explained. "We'll stop here until the fog lifts. Sunrise is only a couple hours away. Hopefully we will then be able to continue on. Lie down now, boys. Your mother and I will try and get a little shut-eye."

Daylight revealed that we were parked atop a mountain. The morning sun was pleasantly warm and inviting.

"Boys, before we leave, we'll have some breakfast, and then your father will take your picture. While he's getting his camera ready, I want you to straighten out your clothes and comb your hair. We want to send some pictures back to your grandparents and I don't want you to look like ragamuffins. Hurry now!"

While we were enjoying an oatmeal breakfast, a Pennsylvania highway patrol car pulled up beside us. A smartly uniformed trooper stepped out and asked if we needed any assistance. Dad explained that he had stopped several hours ago because of the thick fog.

"That was the smart thing to do," the trooper said. "It's burning off now, so you should be able to proceed OK."

CHAPTER THREE

Never in our wildest imaginations did we expect the waterfalls on the Niagara River to be so spectacular. Our first sighting of the famed Natural Wonder of the World was shortly after our arrival in the city.

American Falls

Although Dad was exhausted from the long trip and eager to get settled before reporting for work the next day, he wanted us to see the phenomenon. After all, he reasoned, we had come far from our home in Virginia to resettle in a distant city of which we knew nothing except that it was famous for its waterfalls.

From a scenic promenade we had an unobstructed view of the rushing waters plunging from the precipice in a thundering display of power. A billowing mist obscured the fallen rocks at the base of the falls.

"Look," Phil shouted above the roar of the falls, "I see a boat down there!" We all peered through the mist to where Phil pointed and saw a small, sightseeing boat bucking the currents toward a wild, churning maelstrom.

At that moment a friendly park ranger approached,

The earliest inhabitants of the area were the Seneca Indians who referred to the falls as the "Thundering Waters."

LaSalle, the French explorer, visited the area in the late 1600s. He was accompanied by a priest, Father Hennepin, who wrote of his impressions:
"Betwixt the Lake Ontario and Erie there is a vast and prodigious cadence of water which falls down after a surprising and astonishing manner, insomuch that the universe does not afford a parallel."

The approximate distance from Hopewell, Virginia, to Niagara Falls, New York, was 650 miles.

The *American Falls* are 1,100 feet wide and 182 feet high.
The *Horseshoe Falls* are 3,000 feet long and 176 feet high.

Canadians prefer to refer to the "Horse-shoe Falls" as the "Canadian Falls."

The water that flows into the Niagara River drains from four of the Great Lakes: Superior, Huron, Michigan, and Erie. In the summer, 700,000 gallons a second flow over the Niagara cataracts.

Horseshoe Falls

glanced at our car, and said: "Hi, folks! See from your plates that you're from Virginia. Just get here?"

"Yes, we arrived in the city only minutes ago," Dad replied.

"Your son sees the *Maid of the Mist*. That's the name of a sightseeing boat. Would you like to know the legend behind the name?"

"Sure would," Dad said.

"Well, it's been said that two braves fought over the affection of a beautiful Indian maiden. When her favorite brave was slain, she joined him in death by pitching herself over the falls in a canoe. Many say they have seen her spirit rising from the mist and reaching to the heavens for the one she loved."

"There she is! I can see her now!" Phil exclaimed.

"Where? I don't see the Indian maiden!"

"No, Matt—not the Indian maiden! I'm talking about the *Maid of the Mist*. It's coming out from beneath the falls!"

"These are the American Falls. I suggest you cross over to Goat Island for a better view of the Horseshoe Falls," the ranger said.

Abraham Lincoln was quoted as saying: "The thing that struck me most forcibly when I saw the falls was where in the world did all that water come from."

Charles Dickens wrote: "When I felt how near to my Creator I was standing, the first effect, and the enduring one, instant and lasting, of the tremendous spectacle was Peace. Peace of Mind: Tranquillity: Calm recollections of the Dead: Great Thoughts of Eternal Rest and Happiness: Nothing of Gloom and Terror. Niagara was at once stamped upon my heart, an Image of Beauty."

H.G. Wells said: "The real interest of Niagara for me was not in the waterfall, but in the human accumulations about it. They stood for the future, threats and promises, and the waterfall was just a vast reiteration of falling water. The note of growth in human accomplishment rose clear and triumphant above the elemental thunder."

"Thanks," Dad responded. "I understand they are even more impressive!"

"Yes, they are twice as wide as the American Falls. It's the horseshoe shape that makes them so beautiful. They are certainly one of the most inspiring sights in the world. Well, it's been nice talking with you folks!"

We crossed a stone bridge spanning the river from the mainland to tree-covered Goat Island. Our view of the Horseshoe Falls was breathtaking. Brilliant sunbeams, slanting into the wide sweep of cascading water, spawned numerous rainbows that arched skyward. From our vantage point the view was supernatural.

Our visit to the falls was a delightful way to begin our life in the city. We knew that in the months ahead we would have many opportunities to visit the site. In our fascination with the waterfalls, we thought of little else. However, in driving around the city's commercial area, we saw numerous reminders that Niagara Falls was also suffering from the deep depression. FOR SALE, FOR RENT, and VACANCY signs were displayed in many store windows. The unemployed lined up for bread and the ever-present apple peddlers were seen on virtually every street corner.

Dad registered at a small hotel located only a few blocks from the falls. Our second-story room fronted on a narrow street lined with small shops, a delicatessen, bakery, shoe repair shop, haberdashery, and a drugstore. Vacant buildings were occupied by artists who could be seen working at their easels in the storefront windows.

Leaving Dad to soak in a hot bath, we accompanied Mom to shop for groceries. At the bakery she treated us to hot cinnamon rolls. She gave the baker specific instructions for a cake for Dad's thirty-second birthday. Apparently it was not the first time the baker had been asked to make a frosted cake reproduction of the waterfalls, for he acknowledged that he understood what she wanted and would have it ready the following day.

"Not a word to your father, boys! Remember, we want to surprise him when he returns from work tomorrow."

We returned to the hotel to find Dad sleeping soundly. Mom unpacked an electric hot plate to heat chicken soup and hot chocolate. For dessert we enjoyed home-canned pears.

We spread blankets on the floor and welcomed the opportunity to settle down for a night's sleep.

The following morning we were awakened by a booming rendition of "Onward, Christian Soldiers." We rose from our pallets to peer out at the street below. Beneath our window, a Salvation Army quartet had attracted an attentive crowd.

"Good morning!"

"Good morning, Mom," we replied in unison.

The classified section of a newspaper and a large map were spread out on the bed.

"What are you doing, Mom?" Matt asked.

"I'm marking the locations of vacant apartments on a city map."

"We're not going to live in a house like the one we had in Hopewell?"

"No, Phil. Your dad and I think it may be best to rent a nice apartment close to downtown. We want you boys to have all the advantages a big city has to offer."

"Like what, Mom?" Matt asked.

"Like being within walking distance to school . . . to the large park we saw yesterday . . . and the falls. We think it would also be nice if we could live close to the YMCA where you and Dick can learn to swim and to play in the gym when it's too cold outdoors."

"Boys, it's a beautiful, sunny day, so let's go outside and enjoy it." As we emerged from the hotel, the Salvation Army was playing Mom's favorite hymn, "The Old Rugged Cross."

Illuminated American Falls

Strolling about the downtown area, we observed many well-dressed couples walking hand-in-hand among the local shoppers. They appeared to be exceptionally happy and without a care. Their demeanors were in sharp contrast with those of the needy and the drifters. "Those happy couples are newlyweds," Mom explained. "They come to Niagara Falls for their honeymoon. This is considered the honeymoon capital of the world."

"Why Niagara Falls, Mom?"

"Because it's so beautiful and romantic. They say that the falls on a moonlit night is a sight they will cherish all their married life. Many believe that viewing the falls will bring them good luck."

We paused often to watch artists at work in the store fronts. Most of their paintings were of the falls, scenes of the translucent, plunging waters in brilliant sunlight, scenes of the falls bathed in soft moonlight, winter scenes of the falls crusted over with ice, and pictures of a beautiful Indian maiden paddling a canoe to the brink of the falls.

Niagara—Hollywood, in 1952, released a Technicolor film starring Marilyn Monroe, Joseph Cotten, and Jean Peters. *Niagara* was Marilyn's first starring role. The story line is that of a faithless wife plotting to kill her husband while visiting Niagara Falls. However, in the end, he has the last word. A *New York Times* review of the film stated: "Seen from any angle, the falls and Miss Monroe leave little to be desired." Marilyn Monroe's impression of Niagara Falls was along different lines. With a wink, and smiling demurely, she said: "The falls produce a lot of electricity, but the honeymooners don't use very much of it at night."

1932—Amelia Earhart, flying a Lockheed Vega monoplane, became the first woman to make a solo flight across the Atlantic. From Harbor Grace, Newfoundland, to Londonberry, Northern Ireland, the nonstop flight lasted fifteen hours and eighteen minutes.

Matt, Phil, and Dick

Over time, hundreds of artists have painted Niagara Falls. George Catlin, the famed Plains Indian artist, created a masterpiece in 1847 depicting Father Hennepin and his Seneca Indian friends gathered along the banks of the cataract.

Frederic Church, the brilliant Landscape artist, painted the Horseshoe Falls as viewed from the precipice. Seven-and-one-half feet long, the large canvas, completed in 1857, was viewed in London and New York by thousands. It is considered the finest painting of the falls ever produced.

—Corcoran Gallery, Washington, D.C.

We guessed that the artists had spent many hours viewing the falls for they were painting from memory. They appeared to be doing a brisk business. The honeymooners were their best customers.

"Anyone hungry for a hotdog and a soda pop?" Mom asked.

We crossed over to the large park that parallels the Niagara River. From a street vendor, Mom bought each of us a hotdog and a Nehi. The tree-shaded grounds were spacious and inviting. Our beautiful, natural surroundings were enhanced by the roar of the mighty falls. While Mom relaxed, we found great pleasure in running and frolicking in the great outdoors.

"Where are we going next, Mom?" Phil asked.

"To the YMCA. It's important that we get Matt and Dick signed up for swimming lessons."

Following our visit to the YMCA, we returned to the bakery to pick up Dad's birthday cake. It was the most beautiful cake we had ever seen. The American Falls, the

Horseshoe Falls, and Goat Island were artistically duplicated in form and color. Appreciating our favorable response to his artistry, the baker gave each of us a jelly-filled bun and urged us to return.

We greeted Dad enthusiastically when he arrived back at the hotel. His wide grin was a clear indication that things had gone well for him on his first day on the job. Wanting to know all that he had experienced at the plant, we plied him with questions.

Mom had accomplished a miracle on the hot plate: vegetable soup, corned beef hash, lima beans, and boiled potatoes. Sliced peaches, bread, butter, and strawberry jam rounded out the meal.

"Grace, everything is sure delicious! The limas are almost as good as those we had in Virginia."

"They are the same," Mom said, smiling. "I opened one of the jars we canned in Hopewell."

No mention was made of it being Dad's birthday. We had agreed to say nothing about his special day until Mom surprised him with the cake. We were excited in anticipation of the moment. Mom rose, gathered up the dishes, and said: "Walter, you and the boys stay put. I'll just clear away the table while you tell us about your job."

"OK, boys, what is it you want to know about my work at Mathieson Alkali Works? I'm in the research department. My job is to develop specialized equipment for processing alkali metals. After the equipment is designed it has to be fabricated and assembled."

"What's an alkali metal, Dad? Is it something like iron or copper or gold?"

"No, Matt, not at all. Alkali metals are so soft they can be cut with a knife. They are white in color and have a brilliant luster. One alkali metal, sodium, combines with chlorine to make sodium chloride, or salt, as we all know it. Sodium can also be combined with carbon dioxide to produce sodium bicarbonate, commonly called baking soda. This plant produces sodium bicarbonate."

"Does it cost a lot to make baking soda, Dad?"

"Not as much here as it would if the plant was located in Virginia. You see, the process uses a tremendous amount of electricity and electricity is much cheaper here in Niagara Falls."

"Why, Dad?"

"Because part of the Niagara River bypasses the falls. The water is piped to a hydroelectric plant at the lower river level. Electricity produced by water power costs much less than that produced by burning coal or gas."

Although we were following Dad's every word, subconsciously we were eagerly awaiting Mom's return with the birthday cake.

"HAPPY BIRTHDAY, WALTER!" Mom exclaimed as she crossed the room with the cake.

Dad's expression was one of complete surprise. For a moment he was speechless. We all joined in singing "Happy Birthday" at the top of our voices. Dad smiled in appreciation as he admired the scenic cake.

"Well now, this is indeed a surprise!" he exclaimed. Mom kissed Dad affectionately and handed him a knife.

"Well," he said, "this is almost too beautiful to cut! Anyone in favor of leaving it as it is? . . . No? Matt, do you want a slice of the American or the Horseshoe Falls?"

"The Horseshoe Falls, please, Dad."

"And you, Dick . . . American or Horseshoe?"

"American, please."

"And Phil, what's your choice?"

"I think I'd like a slice of Goat Island."

"Anything you say." We watched as Dad cut a slice of the American Falls for Mom and one for himself. He then put his arm around Mom and kissed her. We ate in silence, content and thankful for our good parents. Their eyes reflected the love they had for us and for one another.

Other industries requiring cheap electrical power located in the Niagara Falls-Buffalo area. One, the **National Biscuit Company's Shredded Wheat Bakery**, continuously baked two-million biscuits daily in their electric ovens. Their motto: "Made of the whole wheat with nothing added and nothing taken away."

The Carborundum Company manufactured silicon carbide abrasives and refractories. Huge electric furnaces heat a mixture of sand and powdered coke to 3,000 degrees F. The crystals of carborundum are almost as hard as diamonds.

Mom and Dad accompanied us on tours of these plants. We also visited **Niagara's hydroelectric plant** below the falls. The plant manager escorted us through the huge facility. He traced the flow of the river water from its intake at the upper level, its one-hundred-seventy-foot vertical drop through the penstocks, to its discharge into the spinning blades of the huge turbines which powered the electric generators. High voltage lines supported on tall skeletal towers snaked away from the plant towards the rim of the Niagara River gorge.

The following morning we were abruptly awakened by a newsboy shouting at the top of his voice:

"EXTRA! EXTRA! READ ALL ABOUT IT! JAPANESE INVADE MANCHURIA!"

"Mom, where is Manchuria?"

"It's part of China, Matt."

"Can the Chinese defend themselves and drive them out of the country?"

"I don't think so. China is a huge country but very poor. Their army is no match for the Japanese. It's a sad state of affairs and may lead to a broader war."

En route to the hotel, Dad had bought a copy of the newspaper at a corner newsstand. He read the feature article in silence. Then, folding the paper and laying it aside, he shrugged his shoulders and said: "Just as I feared! The Japanese generals are gradually taking control of the country. Manchuria is only the beginning. In time, more aggression will surely follow! The sad fact is that America is helping Japan become militarily strong by selling them our factories and machinery. Unfortunately, no country is capable of helping China resist the Japanese. The depression has weakened America and all of Europe. Why, we can barely help ourselves!"

"Then who will eventually stop Japan's aggression?"

"No one at present, Grace, but I fear that the day will come when it will be up to America! Think about it. Where would we be if we had not come to the aid of our allies in 1917 when they were on the verge of defeat? Germany would be ruling all of Europe and possibly our country as well."

We all have in our cache of memories special moments or events that are readily and vividly recalled with a deep sense of appreciation for having experienced the occasion. The recollection of that evening in a cozy room in a small hotel on a narrow street in Niagara Falls is one I will always remember and cherish.

Many people were concerned that Japan would someday invade China. Japan, a small country, needed more space for their people. They also needed food, coal, and lumber . . . things that China had in great abundance.

Dad's decision to attend night school was to acquire technical expertise for designing process equipment for the laboratory. His previous experience in power generation included such devices as pumps, valves, piping, electric motors, and instrumentation. However, to combine these devices into new equipment required further knowledge.

YMCA—Frank Wakley, the YMCA youth director, took a keen interest in nurturing young men mentally and physically. A world traveler, and one interested in all things, he opened our minds to new horizons. He was British and proud to inform us that the Young Men's Christian Association was founded in London in 1844. He stressed character-building through education, recreation, and spiritual practices. In scheduling recreational activities, he made certain that every boy participated. Exercise drills using wooden dumbbells and heavy medicine balls, swimming, and hiking were mandatory. Volunteer instructors taught us swimming and wrestling. After every session, Mr. Wakley welcomed us into his study for discussions and story telling. Frank Wakley was indeed a valued educator, advisor, and mentor.

Seeing Mom's worried look, Dad abruptly changed the subject. He said that he had given it a great deal of thought and decided to attend night school to take courses in machine design. "That's a wonderful idea, Walter! I'll accompany you and take courses in shorthand and typing."

"Boys, what do you think of your mother and me going back to school?"

"Great, Dad! Now, with Phil starting kindergarten in the fall, we'll all be in school."

"Boys, I'd like to hear about what you did today."

"Well, Dad," Matt replied, "we visited the 'Y' and met with the director, Mr. Frank Wakley. He's British and a very interesting person. In his office, there is a huge world globe, and all sorts of other objects he has collected on his trips around the world. He has hundreds of books and *National Geographic* magazines which he shares with anyone who is interested. He signed Dick and me up for swimming and a hiking trip along the rim of the Niagara River gorge."

"Good! Dick, what do you think of Mr. Wakley?"

"I liked him, Dad. He's an avid stamp collector and offered to help me get started with spare stamps from his collection. I think I've found a very interesting hobby!"

Early Saturday morning we started our search for an apartment. Following Mom's list of rental units, we drove from one to the other until we found one that best suited our needs: a second-story apartment on 3rd Street.

Although small in comparison to our home in Hopewell, it served our purpose well enough. We could not have wished for a better location. The 5th Street Elementary School was only three blocks away and the YMCA a distance of eight blocks. We were to reside within earshot of the falls!

The months of July and August were ones of profound activity. Mom and Dad attended night school three nights a week. Matt and I visited the "Y" on a regular basis. Our hike along the rim of the Niagara River gorge was an exciting event. On weekends, Dad drove us to see many interesting sites in and around the city. Several times we crossed the Rainbow Bridge to Ontario to view the Horseshoe Falls from the Canadian side. We drove to Buffalo on an occasional Saturday evening to see a vaudeville show and a movie. We visited Old Fort Niagara which was built by American patriots prior to the Revolutionary War.

Knowing that Dad had been concerned about his lack of engineering design experience, I asked about his work at the lab. To this he replied: "I respect the engineering director and his staff and they, in turn, have told me that my practical approach to solving problems is a great help to them."

Clearly, the director was pleased with Dad's performance for he was awarded a three-hundred dollar bonus. "Now," Dad said, "I can buy a new car! The old Dodge has seen better days. I don't think we should attempt to drive it to Virginia."

"Are we going to Virginia for Christmas, Dad?"

"Only if I can get a good deal on a new car."

"Will you buy another Dodge?"

Although the Revolutionary War ended in 1776 with the defeat of the British, America's problems with the "mother country" were far from over. British sea captains seized American ships and impressed seamen at an alarming rate. On June 12, 1812, the United States declared war on Britain. The British responded by capturing Detroit. In retaliation, American forces captured and burned York (Toronto). In 1813, the British captured **Fort Niagara** and burned Buffalo. The tide turned, however, in July 1814 with the American forces defeating the British near Chippewa Creek upstream from the falls.

Phil atop a 1931 Pontiac

"No, I don't think so . . . but only because the new model Dodge is still powered with a four-cylinder engine. General Motors has introduced a fifty-horsepower, six-cylinder engine in their new Pontiacs. They call it the 'Big Six.' We need the extra horsepower for driving through the mountains of Pennsylvania."

"How much will it cost?"

"About seven hundred dollars, son."

Two weeks later, Dad arrived home in a brand new, 1931 Pontiac sedan. We went for a long drive along the Niagara River. Dad was noticeably pleased. The three of us registered to start school in September.

We shopped at Sears & Roebuck for new clothes and school supplies. We concluded the day's activity by stopping at an ice cream parlor where double-dip cones were sold for five cents. We had a choice of many flavors. Matt asked for vanilla and I asked for chocolate. Phil, on the other hand, asked Dad to read the menu. Starting from the top of a large wall-posted menu, he read: "DAILY FLAVORS: VANILLA, CHOCOLATE, STRAWBERRY, PEACH, BUTTERSCOTCH." "Which flavor do you want, Phil?" Phil couldn't decide. After a few moments he said: "I'll take the DAILY FLAVORS!"

On a Sunday outing, we visited Buffalo's Museum of Science where the astronomy exhibits captivated our interest. An animated model of the solar system illustrated the relative positions of the planets orbiting the sun. Matt and I recalled that Buck Rogers and Wilma never visited Mercury or Venus as they were too close to the sun. Rather they traveled through space to Mars, Jupiter, and Saturn. Matt remembered Wilma saying: "To think that no other person from Earth has ever seen Saturn and its rings so close! I wonder what Saturn's moon, Titan, will be like?"

Many afternoons were spent flying kites. Balmy skies and a strong wind compelled us to seek open spaces in the

Competition among the ice cream parlors was fierce. The "single-dip" for a nickle was soon replaced with the "double-dip" for the same price. Ultimately, to lure customers, vendors offered "three for five," i.e. three scoops for five cents!

park to send our kites high over the Niagara River banks. The tug on the string of a high-flying kite was a thrilling sensation. Matt was particularly adept at experimenting with various lengths of trailing kite tails to attain the most favorable flight control.

With the waning of summer, autumn arrived in a blaze of color. We often visited Goat Island and the American Falls promenade to enjoy the beauty of the changing seasons. In late October, cold, northerly winds scattered the falling leaves and sent the mercury plunging to record lows. A hard freeze was predicted by the weather forecasters. Wagers were made of the date the falls would be completely crusted over with ice. When the day arrived, viewers flocked to the falls to witness the wintry scene. Dad brought his camera to record the phenomenon. The frozen panorama was unlike anything we had ever witnessed. Although beautiful in its total whiteness, the ice-shrouded falls were bleak and desolate in contrast to the furious cascading falls as we knew them. Frozen mist embraced everything in the surrounding area—trees, shrubbery, walkways, park benches—all coated with a thick layer of ice. Missing from the dazzling spectacle was the roar of the mighty falls and the colorful rainbows. Although bone-chillingly cold, we were so caught up in the wintry scene that we found it difficult to walk away. That evening after supper, Dad entered his closet-size darkroom and developed his pictures, taking great care to select the proper chemicals and to accurately time each step of the process for optimum results. The resulting photographs were spectacular!

The rigid airship (dirigible) *Graf Zeppelin* is named for its inventor, Count Ferdinand Zeppelin. During World War I German dirigibles were used for observation and bombing missions. Beginning in 1915 over fifty bombing raids were carried out over England.

In the 1930s the *Graf Zeppelin* flew regularly scheduled passenger service from Germany to Rio de Janiero, Brazil, and Lakehurst, New Jersey, in the United States. It was the only airship to circle the globe. In 1929 the *Graf Zeppelin* flew around-the-world from Lakehurst, New Jersey, in twenty-one days, seven hours, and thirty-four minutes.

ATLANTIC OCEAN BALLOON CROSSING ATTEMPT

April, 1861—American aeronaut Thaddeus Lowe ascended from a field in Cincinnati, Ohio, in a large balloon, *"Enterprise."* Taking advantage of the prevailing westerly winds, his objective was to cross the Atlantic Ocean to Europe. After drifting for nine hours, the balloon came down near Unionville, South Carolina.

"That reminds me, boys, I heard on the radio that the German airship, *Graf Zeppelin*, is expected to fly over Niagara Falls next Saturday. It will be quite a sight for us to see. It's scheduled to lift off from the Naval Airship Station at Lakehurst, New Jersey, at an early hour. It cruises at fifty miles an hour so hopefully we'll see it pass over before dark. I'm told that it is 800-feet long and powered with five Diesel engines. It's on another trip around the world. It must be quite an experience to fly in a Zeppelin but I don't like the idea of using hydrogen gas to keep it aloft."

"Why, Dad?" Matt asked.

"Because hydrogen is highly explosive . . . one spark and the airship would blow up. So far, the *Graf Zeppelin* has performed extremely well. It's been flying since 1929 without a mishap. That's a pretty good safety record. Germany has every reason to be proud." Saturday morning we arose early to listen to the radio for news of the airship's departure. At eight o'clock we learned that with fifty passengers aboard, the *Graf Zeppelin* had cast off from the mooring mast at the Naval Airship Station. Throughout the day we received reports of its progress across the State of New York. Finally, shortly after sundown, it was announced that the *Graf Zeppelin* was approaching Niagara Falls. We rushed outdoors to scan the sky for the airship. The drone of the engines reached our ears before we sighted it. Suddenly, directly above us, the giant *Graf Zeppelin* appeared, slowly moving towards the Canadian border. The cabin, mounted under the huge cigar-shaped fuselage, was brightly illuminated. Passengers could be seen at every window. "Look!" Matt shouted. "They're waving at us! Wow! What a sight!"

During the spring of '32, the economy sounded the depths. Thousands of Americans faced starvation. Families existed on stale bread and thin soup. Unable to afford to heat their homes, many people dismantled vacant houses to use the wood as fuel. Landlords gave up trying to collect rent and allowed the tenants to remain free of charge in order to prevent the destruction of their houses. President Hoover, in his statements to the nation, no longer spoke of "prosperity around the corner." As the end of his term approached, he seemed to have grown dour and pessimistic. The terrible depression had climaxed twelve years of Republican rule and there was no sign of any improvement in the offing. Americans were eager for a change!

Although Hoover faced certain defeat, he agreed to run for a second term. His opponent in the forthcoming election was the governor of New York, Franklin D. Roosevelt. In his acceptance speech to the Democratic Convention in Chicago, Roosevelt's words had an electrifying effect on the people of America. In a forceful and convincing voice he declared: "I pledge to you and I pledge to myself a NEW DEAL for all Americans!" There was something in his delivery that conveyed a sense of confidence and optimism. As a resounding applause erupted in the convention hall, Dad turned off the radio and said: "I hope Roosevelt wins the election in November. He sounds like a man who will turn things around. We'll learn much more about Franklin Roosevelt during the campaign. No doubt about it, our economy cannot continue to go from bad to worse. Americans are ready for a change!"

"Will you and Mom vote for Roosevelt?"

"Yes, indeed we will, Matt."

Throughout the long summer and fall months, Governor Roosevelt toured the country by train. From coast to coast the campaign train made brief "whistle stops" for the public to see the Democratic candidate and to hear his message. He was eloquent and persuasive. His wide smile imparted a feeling of confidence. After listening to Roosevelt speak from the rear platform of his coach, Americans sensed that here was a man who could lead the nation out of the depression. On November 8, 1932, Roosevelt won an overwhelming victory.

As the excitement of the election waned, we thought of little else except our lessons, our activities at the "Y" and our forthcoming Christmas trip to Virginia. A typical evening found the entire family engrossed with studying. Dad practiced the use of his K&E slide rule. Mom practiced her typing and shorthand. Matt, Phil, and I had homework and reading assignments. The weeks passed and before we realized it, our day of departure arrived.

In May, a Bonus Expeditionary Force of over fifteen thousand veterans of the Great War marched on the nation's capital. They camped on the banks of the Potomac River while their leaders lobbied Congress for payment of bonus certificates which were not scheduled to mature for another thirteen years. Congress voted against paying the bonus. Most of the veterans returned home. However, about two thousand of the men, many with families, established a shantytown on the flats of the Anacosta River within view of the Capitol. President Hoover ordered the U.S. Army to disperse the bonus seekers. Troops under the command of Chief of Staff General Douglas MacArthur attacked the encampment with tear gas and riot weapons. They set fire to the shacks and drove everyone from the site. The use of troops against their former comrades-in-arms resulted in severe criticism of Hoover throughout the country.

U.S. Route 66 linking Chicago and Los Angeles was completed. The highway was to become the "Main Street of America." Merchants were quick to meet the needs of the travelers with motor courts, filling stations, curio shops, and roadside cafes. St. Louis, Oklahoma City, Amarillo, Gallop, Flagstaff, and San Bernardino were among the many cities through which Route 66 passed.

Wiley Post, 1931—The famed aviator and his navigator, Harold Gatty, circled the globe in the *Winnie Mae*, setting a world record of eight days, fifteen hours, and fifty-one minutes.

In 1933, Post would fly around the world solo in seven days, eighteen hours and forty-nine minutes.

Roosevelt's 1932 victory was of landslide proportions. It was estimated that twenty-three million citizens voted for him in contrast to sixteen million for Hoover. In the Electoral College the count was 472 to 59 with Hoover carrying only six states.

CHAPTER FOUR

We left Niagara Falls at a very early hour in a blinding snowstorm. The weatherman had predicted that the entire Eastern Seaboard could expect heavy snow for perhaps the next twenty-four hours. Dad's driving skills enabled us to progress along the snow covered highway at a steady rate.

As we penetrated the mountains of Pennsylvania, Dad installed chains in order to negotiate the steep grades. Except for stopping for gas and an occasional rest stop, we continued, mile after mile, until at long last we approached the outskirts of Frederick, Maryland. Suddenly we were startled by a metallic grinding sound from beneath the car and a loss of traction. Dad steered to the shoulder of the highway and coasted to a stop.

"What is it, Walter? What was that noise?"

"I'll know in a second, Grace," he replied as he proceeded to engage the clutch and shift into low gear. As he released the clutch, the car remained motionless.

"That's it! Just as I suspected . . . we have a broken rear axle!"

"What can we do, Walter? It's Christmas Eve . . . nearly five o'clock. I imagine the garages are closing early. Do you think we can get someone to tow us into the city so we can find a hotel?"

"I'll see what I can do. I'm going out to look for a phone and will be back as soon as I possibly can. I'll leave the engine running . . . the heater will keep everyone warm enough."

"Please be careful, Walter. It's snowing so hard you won't be able to see where you're going!"

Matt kept a logbook, faithfully recording odometer readings when we stopped for gas. The gallons were accurately noted. In New York and Pennsylvania, Dad bought Ethyl Gasoline. In Maryland and Virginia, Texaco. A honk of the car's horn would bring an attendant scurrying out of the filling station to pump the gas, check the oil, wash the windshield, and check the tires. Road maps were free for the asking. Sometimes we were treated to a Nehi with a choice of orange, lime, lemon, grape, chocolate, and strawberry, or a Dr Pepper 10~2~4. All soda pop cost a nickel. Gas and soda pop were paid in cash. City and town parks frequently provided us with an opportunity to get out of the car for a brief stretching, use of a picnic table and "necessary room," or to replenish our supply of water. Roadside stops were made for chocolate and coffee, heated over Sterno's Canned Heat.

The realization that Dad was trudging through deep snow in rapidly fading daylight and had no visible destination gave us cause for worry. As the minutes slowly ticked away, we became more and more anxious for his safety. At last, after an interminable wait, Dad returned in a tow truck. The driver of the truck proceeded to attach a chain to the rear of the Pontiac and hoist it up to raise the wheels off the ground.

"Mister," he barked, "get back in the car and we'll get rolling!"

"Walter, I don't like the way that man is acting. Has he been drinking?"

"Yes, but he's not drunk! I spotted his tow truck parked in front of a tin shed where he and a few friends were starting off the Holidays with some homemade brew. He agreed to tow us into town for twenty-five dollars. I wouldn't have hired him if I thought he wasn't sober."

"Where is he taking us?"

"He called the Pontiac agency in Frederick and asked the owner to remain until we arrive."

Suddenly, our immobilized car, tilted at an angle behind the tow truck, was jerked into motion. We were in for a wild ride! Dad made an effort to control the steering as we rounded the curves but was unable to prevent the car from swerving from side to side. We truly believed we were in imminent danger as we sped along the streets of the city. Miraculously, we arrived at the agency without mishap. I'm sure that Dad wanted to give the driver a piece of his mind for his wanton recklessness, but nothing was said except: "How much do I owe you?"

The driver hesitated, glanced into the car to peer at each of us, and replied: "Nothing, mister! Merry Christmas!" He jumped into his truck and sped away.

Dad talked briefly with Mr. Johnson, owner of the agency, and informed him of the broken axle. Mr. Johnson stated that he had a replacement axle for a '31 Pontiac but all his mechanics had left the premises. He offered to drive us to the nearest hotel.

"We'd like to get to Richmond tonight. If you'll trust me to remain in your garage I can install the axle. I should be able to finish the job in a couple of hours. How about it, Mr. Johnson?"

"You've got a deal, Mr. Jefferies. Just trip the lock on the door when you leave. I'll leave the heat on. Your wife and youngsters can wait in the office up front. There's a hot plate up there if you want hot coffee or to heat something for the boys. Help yourself to any tools you may need."

"How much for the axle and the use of your garage?"

"Twenty dollars for the axle . . . that's it! Glad I could be of assistance. I hope you make it to your destination without any further trouble. Have a Merry Christmas!"

"Thanks, Mr. Johnson! Merry Christmas!"

As Dad started to work replacing the axle, we retired to a comfortable waiting room. A brightly-decorated Christmas tree and a Nativity scene occupied a corner. Mr.

Johnson had left the tree lights on. Christmas carols emanated from a small radio. Mom let each of us open one present, which she had brought from the car. We were so excited with our new toys that we momentarily forgot that we were still miles away from Richmond and celebrating Christmas Eve in a garage in Frederick, Maryland. Mom reminded us that we had much to be thankful for. "I have a treat for each of you," Mom said, "a Hershey Bar."

Two hours later Matt asked: "May Dick and I see how Dad is coming along?"

"By all means, Matt."

"Thanks Mom!"

As we reentered the garage Dad looked up and said: "I'm about finished, boys. Only thing left is to tighten the lug nuts. We'll soon be on our way."

We arrived at the Sanford residence in Richmond around four o'clock in the morning. Responding to our knocking, Uncle Harvey, in his bathrobe, opened the door and switched on the porch light. "Good gracious," he exclaimed. "Look what Santa has brought! We gave up on you when you failed to arrive before midnight. Come on in out of the cold!"

"Sorry to awaken you, Harvey," Mom said as she kissed her brother. "Now just show us where you want us to sleep and you can go back to bed."

We were awakened at noon by the jingling of bells. Aunt Katy appeared with a tray of orange juice, hot chocolate, and coffee. "Merry Christmas, everyone!" she sang out. "Come down when you are ready. Dinner will be served in about an hour. I know you must be famished!" We were enthusiastically welcomed by all. Aunt Katy smothered us with hugs and kisses. Everyone wanted to hear about our experiences in Niagara Falls. When we told of our seeing the *Graf Zeppelin*, Cousin Gordon pressed us for details. Cousin Catherine was more interested in hearing about Niagara Falls, saying that someday she would like to go there for her honeymoon.

Cousin Harvey Bowie laughed until his sides ached when we told him of how Matt had searched for the Indian maiden in the misty falls. Uncle Harvey was curious about what had happened to the Pontiac. "We worried about you folks," he said. "Thought you might be stranded somewhere in a snowdrift in the Pennsylvania mountains."

"Well, Harvey," Dad said, "we are very fortunate to be here for Christmas! If the Pontiac garage had not had a spare axle, we'd be celebrating Christmas in a hotel room in Frederick, Maryland."

"Yes, Walter, but having the axle is one thing; being able to install it is another! It's not everyone who can do a job like that. And, it was certainly kind of the owner to let you use his garage. I guess there are still some decent people around."

"Harvey, how's your business coming along?"

"As well as can be expected, Walter. I've been with Toledo Scales too long to consider anything else. Many of our potential customers have gone out of business so there's quite a glut of used scales in the marketplace at prices much lower than new. To meet my sales quotas I have to travel more than I did before the crash of '29, but, as they say, It goes with the territory! What about you, Walter? Any chance you will find a job in Virginia? We sure miss having you folks closer. Our family get-togethers are not the same without you."

"Not any time soon, Harvey, as much as I'd like to. Hopefully, jobs will become more plentiful after Roosevelt is inaugurated and his New Deal brings about some positive changes in the nation's economy. Hoover's programs have failed miserably. At least Roosevelt is adventurous enough to try something new!"

"Now, Walter," Aunt Katy interjected, "politics can wait, but dinner cannot—and it's on the table!"

We did not have to be asked a second time to take our places. Servings of Virginia ham, turkey, potatoes, string beans, tomatoes, cranberry sauce, hot biscuits, and gravy were passed around. We were encouraged to take generous helpings. Laughter and the sounds and sighs of anticipation filled the room.

The Toledo Scale Company was founded in 1901 in Toledo, Ohio. The company slogan was adopted in 1904 and appeared on every Toledo scale.

"NO SPRINGS HONEST WEIGHT"

Their product line comprised a wide variety of scales with each model designed for a specific purpose. Grocery stores and meat markets were among Uncle Harvey's best customers for the counter top models. A very popular floor model bore the welcome message:

"YOUR WEIGHT FREE"

Cousin Harvey Bowie followed in his father's footsteps by devoting his working career to selling Toledo Scales.

The early Indians who lived along the river banks were the **Rappahannocks,** an Indian word for "the people of the quick-rising stream," an allusion to the rapid rise and quick flowing ebb of the tides. The Atlantic Ocean tides reach the Chesapeake Bay and also penetrate the rivers that drain into the bay. The town of Tappahannock is as far as the tides generally reach. Local fishermen claim that they catch salt water fish from the downstream side of the bridge and fresh water fish from the upstream side. The original name of the town was New Plymouth. Established in 1780 as a place for loading vessels, the port became an important center for river commerce when a customs house was erected.

"Quiet, everyone!" Uncle Harvey announced. "Time to say the blessing . . . we thank the Good Lord for this food, and for this day, and for the Jefferies family, whom You watched over . . . along the snowy way! AMEN! MERRY CHRISTMAS EVERYONE!"

"Katy, I didn't know my brother could come up with such a poetic blessing."

"Grace, Harvey has many talents! Wait until you sample his homemade peanut brittle! He's making it in batches and selling it to his customers. I would not be surprised if he gives away more than he sells!"

"I'll never tell!" Uncle Harvey said. "Now, who wants a drumstick?"

The following morning, we departed from Richmond for our visit to the Northern Neck. In addition to Uncle Harvey, Mom had another brother, George Sanford, and two married sisters, Louise Snead and Edith Cottingham. The Sneads, Cottinghams, and Sanfords lived in the Northern Neck. En route to visit with them and with Grandma and Grandpa Sanford in Ottoman, we crossed the Rappahannock River at the little town of Tappahannock and stopped briefly to watch the fishermen casting their lines over the bridge rail.

"Judging from what they are pulling in, Dad, fishing must be great!"

"Matt, the Rappahannock is considered a fisherman's paradise."

We left the bridge and entered the Northern Neck peninsula. A birth registered in the courthouse at Montross

Richmond County—The county is named for Richmond in Surry County, England. It is bordered on the west by the Rappahannock River and on the east by Westmoreland County. At the county seat of Warsaw, the will of Francis Lightfoot Lee, signer of the Declaration of Independence, is recorded.

Richard Henry Lee (1732–94) presented to the Continental Congress the motion that resulted in the Declaration of Independence in 1776. His brother, Francis Lightfoot Lee, was a fellow delegate from Virginia.

is that of one Grace Livingston Sanford, born December 24, 1895—our mother. As we drove through the historic countryside, Mom told us of her childhood days in Westmoreland County. Our drive to the little town of Ottoman in Lancaster County routed us through Warsaw, the county seat of Richmond County. Here, Mom explained, is recorded the will of Francis Lightfoot Lee, signer of the Declaration of Independence. Within a half-hour, we arrived in the town of Lively, where we stopped to briefly visit with Mom's sister, Louise Snead. As we pulled into the driveway, Dad honked the horn. Uncle Howard and Aunt Louise rushed out of the house followed by cousins Elizabeth, Garnet, and Gene. We were warmly greeted with an abundance of hugs, kisses, laughter, and joyful banter: "Grace, the north must suit you . . . you're prettier than ever!" Uncle Howard exclaimed as he embraced Mom. "Walter, will you folks stay for lunch?"

"Thanks, Howard," Dad replied. "We'll only stay a few minutes, as Mr. and Mrs. Sanford are expecting us. You and your family will join us in Ottoman tomorrow as planned, right?"

"You can count on it, Walter! We never miss an opportunity to attend a family reunion!"

As we neared Ottoman, the familiar landmarks were called out. A roadside marker stated that we were nearing St. Mary's White Chapel Church, the church where Mom and Dad were married. We stopped at the ivy-covered church only long enough to enter and pray for our loved ones and for an end to the depression. Another five miles and we rounded the final curve to catch sight of our grandparents' farm. The trees were bare and the fields fallow. Set well back from the road, the two-story house was a welcome sight. A sprawling blue spruce and an arched arbor were the only signs of greenery. The scene was in sharp contrast to that of our memories of the farm in summer when the grass, nourished by rain and sunshine, blanketed the

landscape in hues of green and rows of tall corn stretched endlessly across the fields. The sweet fragrance of honeysuckle permeating the air and the orchard laden with apples, peaches, and pears were fond memories. We were lovingly welcomed by Grandma and Grandpa and made to feel that we were indeed back home in Virginia. Matt, Phil and I lost no time in rushing outside to get acquainted with the chickens, the hogs, and Hampton, our favorite horse. Silvery clouds skidded across a slate-colored sky, obliterating the sun. A cold wind whipped wisps of straw and grass into whirling dervishes. A storm was brewing, and we sensed that it would bring snow to the Northern Neck. Chilled by the penetrating wind, Matt and I sought refuge in the barn. Entering through a wicket in the large door, we paused to examine our surroundings. Hampton, in his stall munching hay, was oblivious to our presence. It was as though we had never been away. We paid our respects by reaching over to stroke his neck and ask if he would like some corn added to his hay. He must have understood our offer for he swished his tail and nodded his head in a most friendly manner. "Follow me," Matt said. "We'll climb he loft and throw some corn down to Hampton."

The house in Ottoman was a typical, weather-boarded frame building having an **L**-shaped floor plan. Gingerbread moldings graced the eaves line and the front porch railings and posts. From the entrance, a long hall bordering a parlor, stairs to the second floor, and two bedrooms extended to the most imposing room in the house, a large dining room. An immense, masonry fireplace in the dining room and a wood-burning stove in the kitchen were the sole sources of heat. The kitchen occupied the **L** of the structure. The second floor contained three bedrooms and a large storage room. Lightning rods at each corner of the roof provided protection from the damaging electrical storms so common in the area. The house had no electricity or inside plumbing. *Never was a house loved more!*

Loose hay filled every corner of the spacious loft. Through gaps in the wall boards, pale shafts of light filtered into the darkened interior.

"Look, Dick!" Matt said, as he peered through a large knothole. "From here we can see the entire farm . . . the house, orchard, corn crib, the well, Dad's car . . . even the outhouse!"

We flopped down on the hay and talked of how we wished to someday spend an entire summer on the farm. Grandma had often told us that we were always welcome.

"Matt, Dick, come on down! Dinner is about ready and you can help set the table."

"We're coming, Dad!" we replied.

"Boys, you can wash up in the basin on the back porch. When you're finished I want you to refill the pail from the well. Be sure to get the hay out of your hair . . . and brush off your clothes."

"Yes sir!"

We were soon seated at the table waiting for Grandpa to say the blessing.

"Now, Alice," he said, "everything is on the table so take your apron off and sit down!"

"Lord, bless this food which we are about to receive from thy bounty. Amen." Grandpa's blessing was brief but spoken piously.

As platters of fried chicken, mashed potatoes, butter beans, carrots, and tomatoes were passed around, Grandpa explained that everything on the table had been grown on

George Mottrom Sanford farmed eighty acres of Lancaster County's sandy loam soil. Corn and asparagus were the income-producing crops. Tomatoes, potatoes, lima beans, cabbage, carrots, peas, lettuce, turnips, and spinach were grown for home consumption.

A large barn, chicken coop, corn crib, and hog pens were located a respectable distance from the house. The ground floor of the barn provided a large area for the storage of farm implements: buggy, corn grinder, harness, and hand tools. A walled-in stall accommodated Hampton, Grandpa's only horse. Hay and corn were stored in a large loft. Adjacent to the barn, a corral was Hampton's playground.

An orchard contained a large variety of fruits: apples, pears, peaches, cherries, and plums. Watermelons and cantaloupes were grown in a melon patch.

A well was located adjacent to the house. Water was drawn by a hand-operated pump. Last, but certainly worthy of mention, a white-washed outhouse was conveniently positioned within a short distance from the house.

"IN A LITTLE SPANISH TOWN,
'TWAS ON A NIGHT LIKE THIS,
STARS WERE
PEEK-A-BOO-ING DOWN,
'TWAS ON A NIGHT LIKE THIS,
I WHISPERED "BE TRUE TO ME,"
AND SHE SIGHED "SI, SI."
MANY SKIES HAVE TURNED TO GRAY
BECAUSE WE'RE FAR APART,
MANY MOONS HAVE PASSED AWAY
AND SHE'S STILL IN MY HEART.
WE MADE A PROMISE AND
SEALED IT WITH A KISS,
IN A LITTLE SPANISH TOWN,
'TWAS ON A NIGHT LIKE THIS."

❄

"K-K-K KATY, BEAUTIFUL
KATY, YOU'RE THE MOST
BEAUTIFUL GIRL THAT
I ADORE. WHEN THE M-M-M
MOON SHINES OVER THE
COW SHED,
I'LL BE WAITING AT THE
K-K-K KITCHEN DOOR."

❄

"RED SAILS IN THE SUNSET,
WAY OUT ON THE SEA.
OH, CARRY MY LOVED ONE
HOME SAFELY TO ME.
SHE SAILED AT THE
DAWNING,
ALL DAY I'VE BEEN BLUE.
RED SAILS IN THE SUNSET,
I'M TRUSTING IN YOU.
SWIFT WINGS YOU MUST
BORROW.
MAKE STRAIGHT FOR THE SHORE.
WE WILL MARRY
TOMORROW
AND SHE GOES SAILING
NO MORE
RED SAILS IN THE SUNSET,
WAY OUT ON THE SEA.
OH, CARRY MY LOVED ONE
HOME SAFELY TO ME."

Matt's all-time favorite song.

the farm—including the two chickens he had fattened up for the occasion.

"Walter, I know how much you like butter beans, so please take more,"

"Thanks, Mrs. Sanford, I will."

"And, Matt, you love tomatoes, so help yourself."

"Thanks, Grandma." We enjoyed a sumptuous meal and listened to Grandpa's commentary on the crops, the animals, local politics, and the weather. "Anyone for more chicken?" he asked.

"I'm saving room for a piece of Grandma's apple pie!" Phil responded.

"Phil, you're like the preacher who had dinner with us last Sunday. He said that your grandmother's apple pie is the best in Lancaster County, and he has tasted everyone's. Naturally, I agreed with the good reverend, but I suspect he was hinting for another invitation."

We were excused from the table and at liberty to explore the spacious old home. In the front parlor, we played records on the Edison phonograph which we had left with our grandparents when we moved to Niagara Falls.

Matt selected "Red Sails in the Sunset" and we sang along with the lyrics.

"Dick, see if you can find 'In a Little Spanish Town' in that stack of records. It was Dad's favorite when we were in Hopewell. I'll go and get him after we've heard 'K-K-K Katy' one more time." Dad was noticeably pleased that we had remembered his favorite song. We roamed throughout the house, looking into every nook and cranny with the exception of our grandparents' bedroom (Grandma had told

Fourteen first cousins under one roof was almost more than Grandma and Grandpa had bargained for. We were encouraged to play outdoors. However, the girls decided to remain indoors and play records on the Edison, that is, except for Edith Harvey, who said that she would rather be with us. Our favorite activity was playing "Cowboys and Indians." No one wanted to be an Indian, so half became cowboys and the other half, robbers. To keep it fair, we drew straws and chose up sides. Each of us had a favorite cowboy movie star although there were plenty to go around: Tom Mix, Hoot Gibson, Buck Jones, Ken Maynard, Tim McCoy, Gene Autry, Rex Bell and Roy Rogers. [Edith Harvey played Dale Evans and stayed alongside Roy]. In short order we were running, hiding behind the barn, trees, the corn crib and the watering trough, and blasting away with our cap pistols. Shouts of "I got you first!" or "No, I got you first, you're dead!" mingled with the explosive cracks of our shootin' irons. It was all great fun! Years later, when we were grown and together again, it was to be expected that one of us would shout: "I got you first!"

us that their bedroom was private). As there was no heat in any of the rooms except the kitchen and the dining room, we soon settled down in the kitchen where a large, cast iron, wood stove made the room quite comfortable. Grandpa challenged Matt and me to games of checkers. Phil proceeded to paint in his coloring book. Grandpa beat us at every game until finally, both of us won several times. I guessed that he had purposely allowed us to win.

At bedtime, Grandma provided us with a kerosene lamp and asked us to be very careful in carrying it upstairs. Our bedroom was extremely cold and drafty. In the soft glow of the lamp, we quickly undressed and dived under the covers. It had been an eventful day. Normally we would lie in bed and talk for hours. This night, however, we both covered our heads and dropped off to sleep. Early the following morning, we were awakened by the crowing of a rooster. We remained under the quilts; they were too warm and comfortable for us to even think about getting up. Responding to a light tapping on the door, Matt said: "Come on in!" Grandma entered carrying a large ceramic pitcher. She smiled as she observed our huddled forms and said: "Good gracious! I thought there were three boys in this room, but I must be mistaken."

"We're here, Grandma!"

"Well, so you are! Now, who wants pancakes for breakfast?"

"We do!"

"They'll be on the stove in ten minutes so why don't you get up, get dressed, and wash your faces. I've brought you a pitcher of water. Hurry now! We are all waiting for you in the dining room. Your grandpa has a nice fire going in the fireplace."

Grandpa and Dad were discussing president-elect Roosevelt when we entered the dining room. Mom was helping Grandma in the kitchen. We quickly took our places. The pleasant smell of the wood-burning fireplace coupled with the aroma emanating from the kitchen stimulated our appetites. Presently we were helping ourselves to platters of delicious hot cakes. Country sausage, hot biscuits, golden honey, and orange marmalade rounded out the feast. As we were about to ask permission to leave the table, the honking of a car horn brought us to our feet. We quickly rushed outdoors to encounter Uncle Bruce Cottingham, Aunt Edith, and cousins Alice, George, and Edith Harvey emerging from their car. A little later Uncle Howard Snead and his family arrived, followed by the arrival of Mom's brother, our Uncle George Sanford, Aunt Mary Lou, and cousins Charles Mottrom and Armintrus. As Grandpa observed the gathering of the clan, he announced that everyone was present except Harvey, Katy, and their children. With the words barely out of his mouth, they, too, drove up. The final count of all gathered under one roof was twelve adults and fifteen children. Everyone brought food and Christmas candies. Uncle Harvey even brought a generous supply of his homemade peanut brittle. It was indeed a gala affair. As the last family departed, we realized how much we missed living closer to those we loved so much.

"Boys, rise and shine! We must start early for Cumberland. Get up now and dress. You know where the outhouse is. Breakfast is ready."

Again, as in Hopewell, we regretted having to leave our grandparents. Mom promised us that sometime in the future we could spend an entire summer on the farm. We sadly waved good-bye as Dad turned from the driveway to follow the road towards Tappahannock.

"When will we arrive at Grandpa Jefferies' farm in Cumberland, Dad?"

"Hopefully we'll be there early this afternoon, Phil."

Dad made good progress, and by noon, we were passing through Richmond. Half an hour later, Dad pulled into a filling station to buy gas. A bearded attendant in faded overalls emerged from the station and greeted us with a toothless smile. "Afternoon, Mister! Fill 'er up?"

"Yes, please . . . and let's have a look at the dipstick."

"Yes sir!"

"Interesting town you have here . . . Short Pump . . . often wondered why it's called Short Pump."

"Old folks here say that it was named after an early tavern called Short Pump Tavern. Seems the well was beneath the porch where only a short-handled pump would fit, so they named the place Short Pump Tavern. The town was named after the tavern. Sounds farfetched to me, but it's the only name we've ever had, so we're used to people askin'. Outhouse in the back if you folks have need of it."

We traveled alongside the muddy James River to the town of Columbia where we crossed the river into Cumberland County. Rolling farmland, white clapboard houses, barns and silos, haystacks and fences flashed by in a moving panorama all too familiar to us. "Now we're back in the country where you lived as a boy, right, Dad?"

"Indeed we are, son."

As we approached Grandpa's farm, we had a distant view of the country store he had built on the front of the property. Its barn's red paint reflected the rays of the afternoon sun. The house was as we remembered it: a one-story, clapboard structure topped with a steep, slate roof. A plume of smoke spiraled skyward from a red brick chimney.

Against a backdrop of tall pines and hardwoods, the little house appeared as a refuge from the stark, wintry countryside.

Dad pulled into the driveway and parked under a walnut tree. A honk of the horn brought Grandpa rushing outside to greet us. "Goodness gracious, Walter, sure glad you made

The original name of this home was *The Refuge.* Following the death of our grandparents, George and Jennie Jefferies, Aunt Virginia Meadows and Aunt Mattie Golden renamed the house ***Golden Meadows.***

Prior to 1840, the James River provided the most efficient means of commerce between Richmond and Columbia. Large, flat-bottomed boats (*bateaux*) hauled tobacco, flour, coal, lumber, molasses, and whiskey to the docks in Richmond. A bateau was forty-six feet long and pointed at both ends. It was designed to navigate the shallow waters and rapids of the James. Fully loaded, it could operate in one foot of water. A trip down the river was not difficult. However the trip up the river was another matter. Three pole men were required to man a bateau. Two, one on each side, poled the boat. The third steered with a long oar called a *sweep.* In 1840, the James River Kanawha Canal, alongside the river, was completed. Mules towed packet boats hauling freight and passengers in both directions.

it OK! Grace, you look wonderful . . . and boys, you're growing like Johnson grass! Come on in where it's warm. Your grandma is in the kitchen making cornbread. Anybody hungry?"

Travis

"Poppa, I've never known these boys not to be hungry!"

"You were no different, Walter."

"We're all looking forward to Momma's cornbread," Mom said as she embraced Grandpa.

"Where's Little George?"

"He's staying over at Vue Monte with Travis. He promised to be here first thing in the morning. He and Travis have gone on horseback to Sports Lake."

"How is Uncle Travis, Poppa?"

"The same. You know how he is . . . loves his moonshine!"

"Is he working?"

"He works when he needs the money. Folks around here have plenty of carpentry work for him. He's good at what he does . . . built this place, you know. Thought he'd never get it done. Some days he never showed up, or when he did, he was hung over, and I had to send him back home. Don't know how he survives. Little George takes good care of him."

Grandma wiped her hands on a flowered apron as she emerged from the kitchen. "Thank the Lord you're here . . . safe and sound! Now come here, boys . . . give your grandma a hug. Then make yourselves at home. I'll make some hot chocolate for you. Grace and Walter, coffee's on the stove. I've just put cornbread in the oven . . . must have sensed you were coming."

"It's sure nice and cozy in here." Mom said.

"Yes, Grace, that old wood stove heats the house quite well. Of course, it's terribly hot in the kitchen when I'm cooking, but I'm used to it."

"Any plans to have the house wired for electricity, Poppa?"

"Little George has worked with a contractor and learned quite a bit about electricity. Says he'll have the house wired before summer."

"That reminds me, Poppa, how's your supply of firewood?"

"I have plenty cut up . . . mostly pine. Wish I had more hardwood but it's really tough to cut by hand. Pine burns pretty fast, you know . . . and it soots up the chimney." "One of these days, Poppa, when we move back to Virginia, I'll put together a powered saw. Should have no trouble picking up a good Model T engine."

Long after retiring, we lay awake and listened to the muted voices of our elders who were gathered in the warm kitchen. They were discussing the terrible depression and expressing the hope that Roosevelt could turn the economy around with his New Deal.

"Walter, have another cup of coffee."

"Don't mind if I do, Poppa . . . thanks!"

"The depression has certainly separated thousands of families," Mom remarked. "So many of our friends have been displaced."

"Indeed it has, Grace," Grandpa responded. "Husbands have had to leave their wives and families for wherever they can find employment. Which reminds me, did you ever hear from your friends who left Hopewell for the Boulder Dam project?"

"No, not a word! Sure hope it turned out well for them."

"At least their families accompanied them. You were also fortunate in that respect, Walter. You took your family with you to Niagara Falls."

"Yes, Momma, I am fortunate. We've had to make some sacrifices . . . living in a small apartment as opposed to having our own home, for example. Of course, I miss working in electrical power generation . . . and having to be so far away from Virginia has been especially trying for us."

"Have you asked Virginia Electric and Power Co. if they have any openings?"

"Yes, Poppa. I've written to them several times. They responded stating that I would be considered for any future openings."

"I have a good reason for asking, Walter. The manager of VEPCO's Bremo Bluff plant often stops by the store on his way to Sports Lake. He's an avid fisherman. I've told him of your experience in electrical power generation. He said they may have an opening for an operating engineer sometime next year. Seems that their present engineer will retire and there is no one qualified to fill his shoes . . . at least no one in the Bremo plant."

"My, my, Walter, wouldn't that be wonderful! Bremo is right across the James River, only ten miles from here. We'd all be together again!"

"Yes, Momma, it would indeed. I'll drive over to Bremo tomorrow and visit the power plant. What's the manager's name, Poppa?"

"George McCullough. You'll like him . . . a fine fellow."

George Matthews Jefferies, our grandfather, called on **Martha Virginia Hanes** at her home, Clover Lea. Over time, a courtship evolved with George urging Jennie to marry him. However, she was reluctant to move too quickly on his proposal. On August 26, 1886, Jennie, age seventeen, wrote to George, age fifteen, these words:
"To say that I do not like you would not be true for I believe there is no one that I like better. But to say more than this would not be true and I know you would not have me guilty of a falsehood. Are you not satisfied to know that I care no more for any other than I care for you?"
George and Jennie married on September 23, 1898.

❊

In another letter to George, Jennie told him to promise to destroy all her letters. Either he did not promise to do so, or he broke his promise, as he saved every letter written to him. None of his letters to her have survived.

❊

"Good morning, Miss Jennie. How are you this morning?"
"Tolerably well, George."

"Good morning, George. How are you feeling today?
"Fair to middling, Jennie."

Early the next morning as we were eating breakfast, Uncle George arrived and enthusiastically greeted us: "Well, look what the wind blew in! Sure is good to see you folks!"

"Sit down, Little George, and have some ham and eggs with us."

"I'll do just that, Momma. I only hope that these boys haven't eaten all the biscuits! Just kidding!"

"George," Mom said, "you sure turned out to be a real handsome fellow. How old are you now?"

"Thanks, Grace. I'll be twenty-one next May."

"How's your Uncle Travis, Little George?"

"Well, he's off the moonshine . . . at least for now. Today he's a little under the weather so he asked me to give all of you his regards."

"Enough about my worthless brother, Little George!" Grandma said. "He knows how I feel about hard liquor."

"OK, Momma, but I've got to tell what Uncle Travis said to you last summer."

"Well, go ahead, son, and tell your little story."

"I will, Momma. Well, one evening last summer, Uncle Travis was walking along the road with a jug on his shoulder. Momma was sitting on the porch in her rocker and saw him passing by. Realizing that his sister was watching him, he shouted: 'Molasses, Jennie, molasses!'"

"Really, Little George, you ought to be ashamed talking about Travis that way."

"Well, Grace, it's the truth, but we all love him anyway."

Ratified in 1919, the Eighteenth Amendment to the US Constitution prohibited the manufacturing or sale of liquor in the United States. Illegal stills in the backwoods of Virginia satisfied the demands for *moonshine*, so named as the night is the most undetectable time for making it. Crudely made stills consisted of a large oaken barrel for making *mash*, a black pot for cooking the *mash*, a copper distillation vessel, and another barrel for collecting the liquor as it drips from a copper condensing coil. Corn whiskey *mash* is made by stirring up a mixture of corn meal, sugar, yeast, and spring water in a barrel. The *mash* is allowed to *work* for three days. It is then cooked in a kettle, brought to a boil and vaporized. The vapor is condensed in a copper coil and the drippings collected in another barrel. Matt and I were cautioned about staying clear of known stills as the moonshiners might think that we were *Revenuers* coming to arrest them and destroy their stills. They were known to always have shotguns to ward off raids by the hated *Revenuers*.

Scattered amongst towering pines in the forest behind *The Refuge* were a wide variety of hardwoods: hickory, black walnut, cherry, chestnut oaks, red cedar, white ash, holly, and hemlock. A canopy of branches cast skeletal shadows on the leaf-covered forest floor. With our approach, squirrels hurriedly scampered up the trees to seek refuge in nests cradled high overhead.

Goldsborough, Dec. 11, 1894—Cumberland, poor abused Cumberland, is still alive, and as fox hunting seems to be the popular amusement of the season, a crowd of her young people met at Clover Lea,the residence of Mr. Walter Hanes, for the purpose on Friday, the 7th. Regardless of the cry raised by some of the old people in the neighborhood, that fox hunting was not intended for ladies, Saturday at 7 o'clock Misses Jennie and Dantie Hanes, Mrs. Willie Lancaster, Mrs. Lacy Hudgens, and Mrs. Sallie Anderson, accompanied by Messrs Lancaster, Coleman, Hanes, Jefferies, Brown, Allen, Guthrie, Leitch, Wilkinson, Gary, Hudgens, White, and Tally were mounted and ready for the chase. They started down the river road and were joined by other friends untill, it is said, the riders numbered forty-five or fifty. Mr. W. White, who had been employed to manage the dogs, met with them at an early hour with his famous hounds. A fox was soon roused and an exciting chase commenced in which the girls joined with enthusiasm, caring naught for ditches, fences, etc. After six hours of reckless riding, the chase was broken up by rain and the tired hunters went home feeling that "into each life some rain must fall." By the way, that is not the only thing that fell, Mr. T. Leitch's horse fell with him, rolled over him twice, and if the dust of which he is made had not been of good quality, he would have ridden after no more foxes. Mr. Phillips' horse turned a "somersault" with such ease and grace that we are forced to believe he has done the like before. However, no one was hurt and the merry party arrived at Clover Lea about 2 o'clock and declared they were ready for the next hunt which takes place December 25th.

—D.H.

"Matt, Dick," Uncle George said. "bundle up good, put your boots on and come with me. I have to go into the back woods . . . promised Poppa I'd repair the fence down by the creek."

"Dad, are you coming, too?"

"No, Dick, I want to drive over to Bremo Bluff and visit the power plant. You boys go ahead with your uncle George."

It was a cold, wintry day with skies overcast and a stiff wind blowing across the dark, fallow fields. We hurried past the corn crib, chicken yard, pig pen, and barn and entered the forest. The thick stand of trees offered some relief from the penetrating wind. Other than the crunching of our boots on the frozen path and the whisper of the wind assailing the tall tree tops, the forest was deathly silent. As Uncle George repaired the barbed wire fence, Matt and I sat on a log and watched. At our feet, the clear, trickling waters of a little creek meandered along an ice-crusted course.

"How was the fence damaged, Uncle George?"

"A whitetail buck used this cedar post to rub the velvet from his antlers. See, here, where all the bark has been scraped off. He probably got his legs tangled in the wire and pulled it loose in his struggles to get free."

"What other wild animals are in these woods?"

"Squirrels, porcupines, raccoons, skunks, foxes . . . can't forget the foxes! For many years Cumberland County was noted for the sport of fox hunting. Even before they were married, your grandparents rode the hunt. Often as many

The adventuresome riders included Jennie Hanes, our grandmother, and her sisters, Willie Daniel (Aunt Dantie), and Aunt Mary (Mrs. Willie Lancaster). Jennie, who was twenty-five and single, was being courted by George Matthews Jefferies (our grandfather).

This newspaper account was submitted by Dantie Hanes.

as fifty mounted hunters and their dogs would gather together to hunt a lone fox. It was a popular pastime."

Having completed the repair, Uncle George sat with us on the log and we talked. "Uncle George, as far back as I can remember you've always carried a book with you . . . like the one in your back pocket. You must really like to read."

"I do indeed, Matt, and let me tell you something. I've never been anywhere further than Richmond but reading has allowed me to travel all over the world. . . to visit exotic places and to meet interesting people including many of the most famous. I've sailed the oceans and climbed mountains. I've crossed the Sahara on camelback and explored underground caverns. I've fought alongside our troops, hunted whales, and witnessed natural disasters. All of this is available to us in the written word. I encourage you and Dick to read."

"What are you are reading now, Uncle George?

"Ernest Hemingway's *A Farewell to Arms* . . . a story of an American ambulance driver at the Italian front in the Great War. Hemingway is a great author . . . one you should read."

On returning to the house we were greeted by Aunt Virginia who had driven up from State Farm, Virginia.

"Boys, come on in and warm up beside the stove. You must be chilled to the bone. Little George, you should be ashamed . . . keeping Matt and Dick out in the cold so long!"

"We don't mind the cold, Aunt Virginia. Remember, we live in Niagara Falls where sometimes it is so cold that even the falls freeze over."

"That's amazing, Matt! I want to hear all about it. Come now. I'll make you some hot cocoa."

"Aunt Virginia, have you read *A Farewell to Arms?*"

"Yes, indeed I have, Dick . . . many times, why?"

"Well, Uncle George is reading it now. He says that Ernest Hemingway is a great author. I think I'd like to read it when we are back home." Aunt Virginia proceeded to quote the opening paragraph of the book from memory. Speaking softly and enunciating every word, she said: "*In the late summer of that year we lived in a house in a village that looked across the river and the plain to the mountains. In the bed of the river there were pebbles and boulders, dry and white in the sun, and the water was clear and swiftly moving and blue in the channels. Troops went by the house and down the road and the dust they raised powdered the leaves of the trees . . .*"

Matt and I were amazed that Aunt Virginia could remember Hemingway's words and quote them verbatim. We asked her to explain. "Boys, beautifully written words are like precious jewels . . . to be retained and cherished for a lifetime."

"Walter, when you pass through Pennsylvania on the way to Niagara Falls, will you be able to stop by the hospital to see your sister?"

"Yes, Momma, we'll visit Mattie, if only for a few hours."

"Wish you didn't have to leave in the morning, Walter, but I realize you must get back to work."

We departed at the crack of dawn. It had rained during the night, so our progress was slowed. However, as we crossed

Virginia Hanes Jefferies graduated from Radford State Teachers College. She taught school for several years in North Carolina and Richmond, Virginia. She married Dooley Meadows, a career soldier in the United States army. Following World War II, Virginia was a counselor for the Virginia Department of Corrections' State Farm for Women.

※

Aunt Virginia's home library occupied shelves and bookcases in three of the four rooms of *The Refuge*. Numbering over five hundred, the collection of books comprised biographies, historical novels, fiction, poetry, and the classics. Well-known authors included Jane Austen, Jack London, Charles Dickens, Thomas Hardy, Mark Twain, Bret Harte, Washington Irving, Scott Fitzgerald, James Joyce, Ernest Hemingway, Zane Grey, John Steinbeck, and Pearl Buck. The Holy Bible and a collection of Shakespeare's plays lay atop a drop-leaf table. Aunt Virginia impressed on us that the best way to improve one's vocabulary is to read and to understand the meaning of words. She urged us to look up words in the dictionary. Her love of words inspired her to work crossword puzzles and to memorize the definitions. "Dick," she asked, "What is a four-letter word for a tailless cat?
Minx?"
"No, Dick, it's a *manx*. A *minx* is an impudent woman. You must never confuse those two words!"
"Yes, ma'am."

into Pennsylvania, the weather cleared and Dad made good progress. Again we were entertained by the many Burma Shave signs along the roadway. Dad told us that the jaunty little jingles were so popular with travelers that the brushless shaving cream firm placed them all across America. The signs offered the viewing public a refreshing approach to advertising. During the depression, humor in advertising was rare.

"We're here to see my sister, Mattie Jefferies," Dad informed the hospital's receptionist upon our arrival.

"Oh, yes, Mr. Jefferies. She's talked of nothing else for days! I'll summon her at once!"

Moments later, Aunt Mattie arrived and quickly crossed the floor to where we were waiting. Attired in an immaculate nurse's uniform, she was the personification of "an angel of mercy." She smiled, opened her arms to us and said, "I'm so happy to see you!"

Aunt Mattie, a woman of great beauty, radiated warmth and love. In her presence, one felt that somehow, the world was a better place. With her natural gifts of compassion and tenderness, she was ideally suited for her profession. "Come, my dears, we'll find it to be more comfortable in the solarium. I've arranged to be off-duty for the rest of the day. We'll have an hour to relax and talk before supper. I want to hear all about your visit with Momma and Poppa."

Mattie Daniel Jefferies, our Aunt Mattie, received her nursing degree from the Medical College of Virginia in Richmond. As a very young girl she was determined to become a registered nurse and care for the sick and dying. In order to raise money to help towards her tuition, she made rock candy and sold it in Grandpa's store. On July 26, 1940, Mattie married Tom Golden, son of Robert Golden, a writer for the *Richmond Times Dispatch*.

"Mattie, how do you like living here in the mountains of Pennsylvania?"

"I love it, Walter! Of course, it isn't Virginia, but I find the mountain air to be refreshing . . . and the people here are absolutely wonderful."

Aunt Mattie gave us an extensive tour of the hospital. Doctors, nurses, and orderlies alike greeted her affectionately as we passed them in the hallways. She introduced us to several of her patients. Upon seeing her enter, their countenances brightened and they smiled.

"Mr. Jefferies, I must confess that I don't care if I'm ever released from this hospital. I'm in love with your lovely sister. If she'll have me, I'd like to marry her!"

"Mr. Peterson, if you don't behave, I'll have to call an orderly. I'm here to help you get well," she scolded. "When you are up and back on your feet again, I'll seriously consider your proposal."

As the door closed behind us, Mom whispered: "Mattie, what is Mr. Peterson's condition?"

"Poor dear! He's ninety-three years old and dying of cancer. He never complains, but every night, he refuses to go to sleep until I have tucked him in."

We enjoyed a fine dinner in a private dining room reserved for the medical staff. It gave Dad and Aunt Mattie the opportunity to talk.

"Now, tell me Mattie, is there any truth to your becoming engaged?"

"Yes, Walter, I casually mentioned it to Momma in a letter several months ago but much has happened since then. I did indeed fall in love with a very wonderful intern here at the hospital. We discussed marriage but felt we should wait until he completed his internship. Tragically, he died in a car accident. It was a devastating experience for me and his parents. I didn't want to worry Momma and Poppa about the matter."

"Mattie, I'm sorry for your loss."

"Thank you, Walter. God works in mysterious ways. However, He gives us the strength to go on with our lives and do what is expected of us. Walter, you've been driving all day. Surely you can spend the night."

"No, Mattie. I have to return to work on Monday."

Five years later, January 1938, a similar ice flow destroyed the abutments and the Rainbow Bridge collapsed into the ice choked river.

❋

Rainbow Bridge was known popularly as the "Honeymoon Bridge."

❋

March 4, 1933: Franklin D. Roosevelt was sworn in as the thirty-second President of the United States. In his inaugural address he called for faith and courage, saying to all Americans: *"This great nation will endure as it has endured; will revive and prosper. So, first of all, let me assert my firm belief that the only thing we have to fear is fear itself!"*

As we drove away, Aunt Mattie, standing under a porch light, waved.

During our absence from Niagara Falls, the temperature had plummeted to well below zero. The extreme cold had persisted for days. As time passed, alternating days of freezing and warming temperatures generated immense chunks of ice which fell to the rocks below the falls. Gradually, the giant mass of ice began to break up and flow downstream. The Rainbow Bridge was in danger of its abutments being dislodged. Crews used dynamite to break up the ice pack in an effort to relieve the pressure on the abutments. For days it appeared that they were fighting a losing battle. The massive ice flow ground against the concrete abutments sending shock waves to the bridge structure. The crashing of the ice as it sheared away from the precipice of the falls and the grinding of the ice pack were frightening sounds. More blasting was ordered. The crews worked around the clock to save the bridge. Onlookers prayed. The bridge was saved!

During the crisis, Matt and I were drawn to the site to watch the supreme efforts made to prevent the loss of the famed Rainbow Bridge.

Every Saturday, we took swimming lessons at the "Y." After leaving the pool, it was customary for us to visit Mr. Wakley in his study. On one such occasion, we found him at his desk studying a map. Upon hearing us enter he looked up, smiled, and said: "Come in, boys, and sit down. You've arrived at an appropriate time. You see, I've been reading up on the Civil War. I am trying to determine where the Battle of Manassas was fought. As you are Virginians, perhaps you can help me."

"Yes, sir, but Virginians call it the War Between the States."

Mr. Wakley laughed. "I stand corrected," he said. "As you say, it was a war between the Northern and Southern states. We can only hope and pray never again will America have to suffer such a tragedy."

That evening we told Mom and Dad of our conversation with Mr. Wakley regarding the War Between the States and of his fervent wish that America would never again have to go to war.

"I don't believe that we'll ever again see America divided with brother against brother," Dad said, "but I fear that we will eventually have to stand up and fight in order to preserve world peace. If the worldwide depression continues, wars will most assuredly erupt in many parts of the globe, particularly in Europe."

"Why Europe?" Matt asked.

"Because the chancellor of Germany, Adolf Hitler, is a ruthless dictator. He vows to use whatever means are necessary to restore Germany's power and prestige in Europe and, for that matter, throughout the world. He has declared that no country is strong enough to oppose him."

"One would think that Germany's defeat in 1918 would have convinced the German people to want to live in peace and harmony with their neighbors."

"No doubt about that, Grace! The people of Germany want peace as much as we do. However the Depression has left them in despair . . . no longer trusting their elected officials to come up with economic solutions. Radical factions, first the Communist Party, and now the Nazi Party, have easily won over the people with promises of a "New Germany," a Germany that will be strong economically and militarily."

"Let's pray that the problems in Europe will be solved without America getting involved," Mom said.

"I fear that America will have no alternative," Dad said. "As in the last war, we cannot sit idly by and watch Germany gobble up all of Europe. Tonight we'll listen to what President Roosevelt has to say on the radio. He has promised to keep Americans informed of his *New Deal* programs and world developments with informal 'Fireside Chats' from the White House."

On an occasional Saturday afternoon, we would go to a movie theater to see a Western. Then, for an exceptional treat, we drove to Buffalo to attend a vaudeville performance with singing, dancing, gymnastic exhibitions, comedy skits, and other theatrical acts.

On weekdays, our evenings were spent doing homework assignments, studying, reading, and, if time permitted, working on our hobbies. One evening, upon seeing us filling out a questionnaire, Dad asked what we were doing.

"We're enlisting as Buck Rogers Solar Scouts," Matt replied.

"Buck Rogers Solar Scouts, huh?"

"Yes, sir."

"What is required for you boys to become Solar Scouts?"

"We must fill out an enlistment form asking for the following information: name, age, height, weight, color of eyes, color of hair, school grade, favorite sports, previous rocket ship experience (if any), and finally, favorite newspaper adventure strip."

"Where will you send the questionnaires?"

"Hdq. Buck Rogers Interplanetary Solar Scouts, Earth Division, Scout Patrol Unit, G. H. Q., Niagara."

Matt and I were familiar with the science fiction writings of Jules Verne and H. G. Wells, but the "Buck Rogers" strip captured our imaginations as none other. We had been reading it since it first appeared in 1929. Each episode depicting adventures in space in a "world of tomorrow" was exciting and thought-provoking. The "Buck Rogers" strip was the first thing we turned to in the newspaper.

The weeks and months passed swiftly. With the coming of spring, the cold, wintry days were but a memory. Soon, school was out and we were enthusiastically planning our sum-

Anthony Rogers, nicknamed *Buck*, was a fictional character in the publication *Amazing Stories,* which appeared in 1928. Rogers was a former US Air Service pilot in the Great War in France. After leaving the service he worked in Pennsylvania where he was trapped in a mine cave-in. He was overcome by a strange radioactive gas that put him in a state of suspended animation for 500 years. It was then that Buck Rogers began his life in the twenty-fifth century. The first person he encounters is Wilma. She tells him of a Mongol plot to dominate the world. With Wilma as his companion and the brilliant Dr. Huer as his advisor, Buck battles the Red Mongols and Killer Kane.

❋

The imaginary view of the twenty-fifth century as illustrated in the Buck Rogers comic strip foretold rocket ship travel in outer space, laser guns, and jet-propelled back packs. Amazing as it seems, each of these things became a reality in the twentieth century. Buck Rogers and his beautiful companion, Wilma, successfully defeated the Red Mongols and the despised Killer Kane.

mer activities. One afternoon we arrived home to find Mom and Dad eager to tell us something of importance.

"We have wonderful news," Mom said. "You tell them, Walter."

"I have accepted a job with Virginia Electric & Power Company at their Bremo Bluff plant. I'm to start to work on July 10."

"Wow! That means we'll be moving back to Virginia!"

"That's right, Matt."

We were overjoyed with the turn of events. Our two-year stay in Niagara Falls had been exciting and rewarding. We had never ceased to be fascinated by the majestic falls. Our activities at the "Y" and our friendship with

Mr. Wakley would be sorely missed, but we knew that Bremo would open up a whole new world of discovery.

"I guess we'll have to hang up our roller skates."

"You're right, Dick," Mom responded. "There are no sidewalks in Bremo. We'll have to see what can be done about getting bicycles for you boys."

"Dad, will we have our own home?"

"Sure will, Phil! VEPCO will rent us one of their houses. I drove by their row of houses when I visited the plant and I remember that they are quite nice. There's also a large plot of land behind each house where we can have a garden and perhaps some chickens."

"What about school, Dad, will we have to ride a bus?"

"Probably. We'll just have to wait and see. However, you will be able to walk to the Episcopal Church for your Sunday School lessons. Enough questions for now, Boys. I want each of you to help your mother with the packing. We have only two weeks before we must leave."

CHAPTER FIVE

As soon as we were settled in our new home, Matt and I took every opportunity to venture out and explore the countryside. The post office, dry goods store, grocery store, and other commercial establishments were located in Lower Bremo along the banks of the James River. The VEPCO power plant was a quarter of a mile downstream.

Upper Bremo was a residential community situated atop a high bluff rising some six-hundred feet above the river. Our home was one of six aligned alongside a narrow, paved road which extended a half-mile across a tree-covered plateau. From Upper Bremo the road descended to Lower Bremo via a series of serpentine curves. When viewed from Lower Bremo, the outcropping of jagged rock atop the high bluff was a striking sight. It was said that in earlier times the rocky bluff was considered a prominent landmark by those who traveled on the James River and the James River Kanawha Canal.

Dad was obviously delighted to be again working in a power plant. As an operating engineer, he was responsible for the entire plant. He generally worked 3 p.m. to 11 p.m. but was always "on call" should any emergency arise. When not on duty, he could be summoned

Bremo Bluff is located in Fluvanna County. Formed in 1777, Fluvanna County was named by the colonists for "Good Queen Anne," daughter of King James II of England.

❋

The Bremo plant consisted of two turbo generators rated at 15,000 kilowatts each. Steam produced by the boilers had a temperature of 830-degrees F and a pressure of 525 pounds per square inch.

❋

The **HIGH VOLTAGE** signs warned of the danger of coming into contact with 2400 volts.

❋

When Dad worked the 3 p.m. to 11 p.m. shift, Matt and I often took turns taking him a hot dinner. Although climbing Bremo hill on our return home was arduous, we derived great pleasure from the experience. In the beginning we hiked the distance. However, when we had our bicycles, the downhill ride at night was thrilling.

by five consecutive blasts of the plant's steam whistle. It was said that everyone within a five mile radius would stop what they were doing when they heard the blasts and say: "There goes Walter Jefferies again! Sure hope he can keep our lights burning!"

One day Matt and I accompanied Dad for a tour of the power house. The towering brick plant was an imposing structure. Twin stacks emitted billowing clouds of black smoke in sharp contrast to the clear, blue sky. Earthen dikes protected the plant from potential flooding of the river. A string of Norfolk & Western Railroad gondola cars, laden with coal from the mines of western Virginia, awaited unloading. A bank of electrical transformers, enclosed within a protective, chain link fence displayed signs which read: "HIGH VOLTAGE, KEEP OUT!"

"Boys, before we go inside the plant, I want to explain something." As we approached the rail siding, Dad stooped to pick up a lump of coal. "Here, boys, look at this. Locked within this lump of coal is an energy source . . . energy that is released by combustion. The heat energy generated by burning coal is used to produce high pressure steam in the boiler. The steam is then put to work turning the turbines which are direct-connected to the electric generators. What occurs is rather remarkable: heat energy transformed to mechanical energy which in turn is transformed into electrical energy."

Dad proceeded to guide us through the plant and explain the function of every component. Particularly impressive were the high pressure steam boilers. Seen through a smoked glass, the white hot fire inside the brick-lined fire boxes was supernatural. We concluded our tour in the generator room. In sharp contrast to the noise and smoke of the boiler room, the turbo generators were in an environment that was quiet and pristine. Only the hum of the turbo generators greeted our ears. Standing before a giant switchboard resplendent with red, green, and yellow lights, Dad explained the purpose of each switch and indicator light. He told us how it was possible to control the plant's electrical output and to monitor the performance of every major component in the plant. The entire operation, he said, could be "fine-tuned like a violin." As we drove away from the plant we looked back. Smoke plumes from the smokestacks spiraled skyward. Electrical transmission lines strung on skeletal, steel towers, snaked away from the plant and disappeared from view. We readily understood why Dad so loved his work. The magic of generating electricity from a lump of coal was, in itself, fascinating.

We were overjoyed with our home in Upper Bremo. It was, in fact, very much like our home in Hopewell. The ground floor contained a living room, dining room, kitchen, and a bedroom for Mom and Dad. The three of us boys occupied a large bedroom in the attic, one complete with dormer windows from which we could have a clear view of the great outdoors. A coal-fired furnace in the basement provided heat for the entire house.

Our view from the house was a forest of tall pines. Deer were often seen browsing among the outer edges of the dense forest. Rabbits, porcupines, squirrels, and skunks were prevalent. Deep in the woods were several springs, perpetually running with clear, cool water.

A screened-in side porch was our favorite place of enjoyment on hot summer evenings. Flowers, shrubbery, oak trees, and a spacious lawn complemented the cream-colored, stucco house. On a large plot of land behind the house, we planted vegetables, berries, and melons.

We frequently crossed the James River to visit Grandma and Grandpa in Cumberland. Grandma insisted that we looked undernourished, so at mealtime, we were served generous helpings. The savoring of home grown victuals coupled with spontaneous table banter made mealtime an enjoyable occasion.

"Matt and Dick, what will you do this afternoon?"

"We're hiking to Sports Lake, Grandpa."

"And, Phil, what about you?"

"I'd like to go too!"

"Good! Now you boys be careful if you take a boat out on the pond. Stay close to the dam where you can be seen and heard!" Mom admonished. "Yes, ma'am."

One of our favorite pastimes was to walk the two miles to Sports Lake and explore the old grist mill.

Trenton Mill (*Sports Lake*) was built on or about 1750. Prior to the construction of the grist mill on Randolf Creek, there was a large settlement at the site. Several dwellings, coopers shop, blacksmith shop, wheelwright, and a sassafras mill comprised the Randolf Creek Settlement. Sassafras, an American tree of the laurel family, is common throughout central Virginia. The aromatic bark of the root is brewed as a tea and used medicinally as a stimulant and a diuretic. Sassafras oil is distilled from the root and used as a flavoring and in perfumery. The trees were sawn into boards for use in trunks and chests of drawers. It is said that no insects will be harbored by a bedstead made of the wood.

The mill had long ago ceased to process grain.

The ground floor served as a store where fishermen and the local gentry could purchase anything from a loaf of bread to canned ham, chewing tobacco and fish bait. The second floor had been cleared of milling machinery to provide an open space for Saturday night square dancing. Always present was the sound of the lake water cascading over the dam. We found Uncle George chatting with his many friends. Outgoing and interested in all things, he enjoyed the lively discussions ranging from politics, the crops, hunting and fishing, to cars and world affairs. No subject lacked for his commentary. He acquired his knowledge from avid reading and listening to the stories and opinions of others.

"George, is it true that Roosevelt has announced the formation of a Civilian Conservation Corps?"

"You're right, Henry, the CCC will put up to three million men to work planting trees, clearing brush and tackling ground erosion problems. They'll live in barracks like those of the army and get three squares a day."

"How much will it pay, George?"

"A dollar a day."

"Guess that's better than loafing. Are you thinking about signing up?"

"I'm thinking about it, Henry . . . maybe I will. What about you?"

"Well there's no work around here, so maybe I'll consider the CCC."

"Charlie," George said, "I heard that you attended the Chicago World's Fair. How was it?"

Some of FDR's political enemies suggested that the real purpose of the CCC was to create a pool of young men for military service should war erupt in Europe. Hardened by their labors in the forests and parks, they would be physically fit, conditioned to camp life, and easily trained for combat.
Over its eight year existence, three million young men were members of the CCC. The twofold purpose of the Corps was to provide useful work for the unemployed and to control soil erosion by reforestation. Over two billion trees were planted by the CCC.

The 1933 Chicago World's Fair commemorated 100 years of the incorporation of the City of Chicago. The theme of the fair was "A Century of Progress." To hold such an ambitious affair in the midst of the Great Depression was a bold under-taking. Attendance fell far short of expectations and the fair closed after running only six months. It was widely reported that the fair would have closed sooner had it not been for Sally Rand, an exotic dancer. Her fan dance performance attracted many thousands of visitors to the fair. Considered naughty, Sally Rand's ostrich feather fan dance was choreographed to excite illusions of fantasy and sensuality.

"It was great, George! Saw the very latest in science and industry. The exhibits were out of this world! I guess you know that Sally Rand, the fan dancer, was the star attraction at the fair."

"Charlie," Henry asked, "did you see Sally Rand do her fan dance?"

"Nope . . . wanted to . . . a man's got to have something to take his mind off the Depression! Martha said we couldn't afford to see her show . . . and it was only a half-dollar. The newspapers say that Sally Rand has received the most credit for the fair's success."

"OK, fellows, enough about Sally Rand," George said. "You shouldn't be discussing her in front of these youngsters anyway."

"Uncle George, is it OK for us to borrow one of those row boats?"

"Sure, Matt, but I don't want you to venture too far out on the lake."

We left Uncle George and his friends and walked to the shoreline of the lake where several row boats were tied up. Phil sat in the bow while Matt and I pushed the boat away from the bank and jumped in. We took turns at rowing. The lake was placid and the reflection of the distant trees on the surface was beautiful. Beneath the clear waters of the lake we could see many fish. Shallow areas were covered with floating lily pads.

Following one of our visits to Sports Lake, Matt and I returned to the farm to find Dad and Grandpa busy at the wood pile. Grandpa was sawing a log cradled in a saw horse and Dad was splitting wood on the stump of a tree.

Both were wet with perspiration. Judging from the pile of wood, they had been working for some hours. As we approached, Dad laid the ax aside, wiped his brow on his shirt sleeve, and said: "Remember, Poppa, I once promised that when we returned to Virginia I'd make you a circular saw. Well, I've located an old hearse behind a lumber yard in Bremo. It hasn't been used in years and the owner of the yard said he'd like to be rid of it. He said I could have it. With a little work, I could dismantle it and fabricate a sturdy frame for mounting the saw. The engine is no good, so I'll rig up a pulley to belt drive the saw from the jacked up, rear wheel of your Model A Ford. Either that or I'll locate a good, used engine."

"That would be a real blessing, Walter. The stoves eat a lot of wood; sure you can find time for such a project?"

"I'll make time, Poppa. Matt and Dick will lend a hand . . . won't you, boys?"

"Yes, sir!"

"I smell Grandma's cornbread! Must be almost supper time!" Matt said. "Wonder what Grandma's cooking . . . chicken, pork chops, ham hocks? It makes no difference! I'm mighty hungry!"

The following Saturday, Matt and I accompanied Dad to the lumber yard in Bremo. Mr. Smith, the owner, repeated what he had previously told Dad: that he could have the old hearse, or what was left of it, at no charge. He was more than glad to get it out of his lumber yard! We followed Mr. Smith through a maze of stacked lumber to the far side of the yard. What remained of the hearse was all but hidden from view in tall weeds. The body had been removed and was used as a tool storage shed. The engine, clutch and gear box had also been removed. Only the chassis, driver's seat, wheels, and steering wheel remained.

"How do you plan on towing it out of here, Walt?"

"The Pontiac should pull it OK once we get it up to the road. Would you consider towing it to level ground with your truck?"

"Sure, Walt! Glad to oblige!"

Mr. Smith soon returned with his truck and linked the two vehicles with a long, stout chain.

"OK, Walt, climb aboard and we'll get rolling!"

With all four tires flat and firmly sunk in the hard ground, the old relic resisted moving and remained in place. Mr. Smith backed up and tried again. With the throttle wide open, the truck moved forward and snapped the chain taut. A cloud of dirt and dust kicked up by the truck's spinning rear wheels showered Dad as he gripped the steering wheel. Once dislodged, the hearse followed obediently to a level spot on the road. The Pontiac was then linked to the hearse and we were on our way. Matt and I gripped the steering wheel and followed in the tracks of the Pontiac. Within a short time, we turned into our driveway and came to a crunching halt. Mom emerged from the house and gazed in awe at the skeletal monstrosity.

"Boys, when we finish the job, your grandpa will be able to cut up his logs in nothing flat. Now, let's get to it!"

"What's first, Dad?"

"We'll jack it up and set it down on blocks. We can then remove the wheels, axles, springs, and steering gear." The removal of these parts was not easily accomplished. Nuts and bolts, rusted in place, resisted all attempts to loosen them. Not having a cutting torch, Dad had to make good use of a hammer and chisel to cut them off. The work was difficult and time consuming, but eventually only the bare frame remained on the blocks. Dad made some measurements and set to work with a hacksaw to shorten the frame. He was careful to allow sufficient space for mounting a circular saw. Hours of labor and countless saw blades were consumed in cutting the frame members. Cross braces and other structural components were fabricated from the cutoff portions of the frame. Holes were hand drilled for bolting the assembly together. Matt and I became quite proficient in assisting Dad with the challenging work. Finally, the project was complete, except for the mounting of pillow block bearings to support the blade shaft, a flat-faced pulley for driving the saw, and the installation of a 24-inch circular saw blade. Dad had acquired these parts and they were properly installed.

"How will Grandpa power the saw, Dad?"

"He'll jack up one wheel of his Model A Ford and belt drive the saw. I've fashioned a drive pulley from an old Model A wheel. All he has to do is to remove the wheel that's jacked up, replace it with the drive pulley, and connect the two pulleys with a flat belt. He'll then be ready to cut wood."

No words can accurately describe the elation we experienced on the day the saw was put to work. The shrill scream of the blade as it sliced into stout, hardwood logs, accompanied by the muffled bark of the Model A engine as it lugged down under the power demand, was indeed a thrilling experience. Within a short time, a pyramid of firewood was accumulated.

"Thanks, Walter!" Grandpa said as he shut off the engine. "This will save me many hours of work! I'm amazed at how well it performed!"

"Much obliged, Poppa. I couldn't have done it without the boys' help!"

"You men have done enough for one day," Grandma said, "so let's all go to the front yard and sit in the shade. I've made you some cold lemonade."

Germany, 1933—Adolf Hitler vowed to increase Germany's Aryan population. His absurd description of an Aryan was a Caucasian of non-Jewish descent. To encourage marriage, he offered financial incentives. For each new baby, he awarded the parents a cash bonus.

❋

The Luftwaffe, 1933–1945— Early planes manufactured in Germany for the *Luftwaffe* were the Junkers Stuka dive bomber, the *Heinkel He 111*, and the *Dornier D017* bomber. During the invasion of Poland in 1938, the *Luftwaffe* used 1750 bombers and 1200 fighter planes. In 1940 Germany built 10,800 planes, 11,800 in 1941, 15,600 in 1942, 25,500 in 1943 and 39,800 in 1944. Too late to be effective in World War II, The *Luftwaffe* began flying jet aircraft including the *Messerschmitt Me 262* and the *Heinkel He 162*.

"Good idea, Momma! I'll be along in a few minutes. I have to get something from the car." Dad returned with a six-volt battery and a small radio. The radio was set atop a fence post. We relaxed and enjoyed lemonade while listening to music and news reports.

"Walter, what did the announcer say about Hitler?"

"He said that Hitler has organized an air force called the *Luftwaffe*. It will give Germany air superiority. It is to be commanded by one of Germany's flying aces from the Great War, Hermann Goering."

"Hitler is up to no good! While America and most European countries are in a deep depression, Hitler is arming for another war. He thumbs his nose at the Versailles Treaty which demanded the disarmament of Germany."

"That's right, Poppa. We can only hope that Roosevelt will be able to convince Congress to meet the threat by building up our armed forces. However, his hands are full with his New Deal."

"Who's that coming up the road, Poppa?" Dad asked.

"Can't see for the steam . . . the radiator's boiling over! Wait until he gets a little closer . . . now I know . . . it's Henry Lucas, a friend of Little George's. Guess he wants water for the hot engine."

The overheated Chevrolet sedan rolled to a coughing stop. Henry Lucas emerged and proceeded to fan the billowing steam with his straw hat. As he reached to remove the radiator cap, Grandpa called to him, "Henry! Better let it cool down a bit before you take the cap off! Let it be! Come meet everybody and have a cool drink with us."

"Thanks, Mr. Jefferies! Don't mind if I do!"

Trans World Airlines asked Douglas Aircraft to design an all-metal commercial aircraft to carry twelve passengers. The DC-1 was designed and in July, 1933, it was successfully flight-tested. The twin engine plane cruised at a speed of 150 mph. *Only one DC-1 was built.* A decision was made to stretch the fuselage by two feet, thus increasing the number of seats from twelve to fourteen. The new version was identified as the DC-2. Impressed with the plane, TWA ordered twenty-five. Other airlines quickly placed their orders for the passenger plane. American Airlines ordered twenty. The DC-2 became an obsolete airliner with the introduction of the DC-3 in December 1935.

Over a glass of lemonade, Henry Lucas explained that he had just left Little George at Sports Lake and that they had had a most serious discussion.

"About what, Henry?"

"Well, I should let Little George tell you first, but since you asked, I'll tell you of our decision."

"What decision, Henry? What are you and Little George up to now?"

"We're both signing up with the CCC!"

"That's good news, Henry! . . . Yes, indeed . . . I think that's just fine! I'll miss having Little George to help me with the farm, but he has to get out on his own sooner or later, and jobs are hard to find. The CCC will be good for both of you! It's one of the best programs Roosevelt has come up with. Here comes Little George now. He can tell you in his own words."

"Hi, folks! Mind if I join you?"

"Little George, Henry has told us that you're signing up with the CCC."

"Yes, Poppa. We will enlist in about ten days. I want to wire up this house before I leave. You can then put away those lamps, Momma."

"What a blessing that will be!" Grandma exclaimed.

"Well, folks, thanks for the lemonade!" Henry said. "Better fill the radiator and get going . . . have to be in Columbia . . . I have a date with a pretty girl."

"I'll go to the well and fill a couple of gallon jugs, Henry."

"Thanks, Mr. Jefferies!" After Henry Lucas sped away in his cooled-down Chevrolet, Uncle George sat with us and talked of current events. "Have you heard that men's underwear sales have suffered a serious decline?" he asked.

"No, Little George, pray tell us why," Grandma asked.

"Well, it's true! After moviegoers saw Clark Gable in the new movie, *It Happened One Night*, and learned that he wore nothing under his shirt, men have stopped buying undershirts."

"Little George, you do come up with the most ridiculous things!"

"What other earthshaking news do you have for us, Little George?"

"More strange news out of Germany, Poppa. Heinrich Himmler, head of the Nazi SS, has started a state breeding program . . . asking young, 'pureblood' women to mate with their SS officers to produce a pure race."

"They are an evil bunch! We would have to be blind not to see that Hitler is bent on paying the Allies back for Germany's defeat in 1918."

"That's right, Poppa. Looks like things are shaping up for another war."

The autumn of 1933 arrived in a blaze of color. An early frost transformed the leaves into a canopy of russet and gold. I was awakened one morning by the honking of geese flying overhead. I quickly dressed and stepped outside. The early morning air was exhilarating. I reflected over the events of the past few months. In contrast to the

It Happened One Night—Columbia Pictures 1934 film. A romantic comedy, the award-winning film tells of a runaway heiress (Claudette Colbert) who falls in love with the reporter (Clark Gable) who is following her.

❋

News from Germany reported that a radical wing of the Nazi Party had plotted against Adolf Hitler. Upon learning of the plot, Hitler's storm troopers killed all seventy-seven dissidents.

urban life in Niagara Falls, the small town of Bremo Bluff offered us freedom to explore the open fields, the pine forests, and the banks of the James. Matt and I spent the summer eagerly seeking new experiences. We climbed trees, walked fences, skinny-dipped in bottomless quarries, fished in the creeks, went boating on Sports Lake, crossed over the river on the railroad trestle, visited neighboring farms, and became acquainted with many residents of Fluvanna County. We attended elementary school and were members of Grace Episcopal Church. Matt and I sang in the church choir. Our visits to the Cumberland County farm were frequent. It was indeed a blessing to live so close to our grandparents. Surely, I concluded, we had all one could ever desire, a loving family, food on the table, a comfortable home, and our faith in God. Overhead, the honking geese gracefully flew to warmer climates.

Two momentous events occurred in December: the prohibition against the sale of alcoholic beverages in America ended on December 5 with the repeal of the Eighteenth Amendment, and, more importantly to us, Matt and I received bicycles for Christmas! The bikes were identical except that Matt's was blue and mine was red. Both were equipped with a rack and a headlight. The bikes allowed us to travel far and wide in three counties.

Although he had only hand tools to work with, Dad accomplished wonders in making furniture; tables and chairs were his specialty. Each piece was painstakingly worked to perfection. We derived great pleasure in observing his skill at sawing, planing, shaping, sanding, gluing, clamping, and finishing the wood. He preferred working with the hardwoods native to the area: walnut, oak, and cherry. The three of us pitched in and helped with the sawing and the sanding.

One summer evening, we assembled indoors, oblivious of a rain storm raging outside. Mom was sewing. Matt and I were building model airplanes. Phil was drawing. Dad was reading the Richmond paper.

"Anything newsworthy in the paper, Walter?"

"Well, yes, there is! Two new comic strips are now in the *Richmond Times Dispatch*. 'Flash Gordon' is another 'world of tomorrow' space adventure. The other strip is called 'Li'l Abner.' Abner is a handsome young boy who lives in the fictitious hamlet of Dogpatch, Kentucky."

We gathered around Dad and he read "Flash Gordon" and "Li'l Abner" aloud. Mom laughed when Dad showed her a picture of Daisy Mae, Li'l Abner's pretty girlfriend. After viewing "Flash Gordon," Matt made several sketches of the space ships and compared them to those that Buck Rogers and Wilma flew in their explorations of the planets.

VEPCO allowed their employees to grow crops in the bottom land adjacent to the power plant. In the early spring, Matt and I helped Dad cultivate an acre of ground for planting corn. The rich loam was comparatively easy to turn and shape into rows. Soft spring showers and an abundance of sunshine encouraged the corn to grow rapidly. However, upon returning to the field in June, we were astonished to see a prolific growth of Johnson grass robbing the stalks of ground moisture and threatening to overwhelm the corn. "What do we do now, Dad?"

"We've got to chop out the Johnson grass . . . or there won't be any corn!"

In 1934 "Flash Gordon" appeared in the comics to challenge the popularity of "Buck Rogers." Flash emulated the exploits of Buck by landing on Planet Mongo and doing battle with the evil inhabitants. Episodes had beckoning titles:

"Flash Gordon on the Planet Mongo."

"Flash Gordon and the Power Men of Mongo."

"Flash Gordon and the Monsters of Mongo."

Flash Gordon's rocket ships were more streamlined and the structures on the planets were ultra twenty-fifth century.

©1939 King Features Syndicate

❈

The bottom land acre of corn was not our only agricultural effort. Behind our house we planted a garden: rows of peas, tomatoes, snap beans, beets, cabbage, yams, lettuce, and turnips. Patches of the garden were set aside for cantaloupe and watermelon. Throughout the long, hot summer, our table was well-supplied with a cornucopia of fresh, garden vegetables. Mom's pantry was soon filled with rows of colorful Mason jars.

Flash Gordon

Alice S. Harvey, 1853–1936. When she was a young girl of ten on her parents' farm in Westmoreland County, a Union Cavalry Officer raided the premises and stole whatever he took a fancy to, including a set of bone-handled knives and forks given to her as a birthday present by her father. Alice pleaded for him to give them back. Apparently softened by her tears, the officer retrieved a fistful of the utensils from his saddle bag and threw them to the ground at her feet.

Alice S. Harvey Sanford's Eightieth Birthday

We soon learned how challenging the elimination of Johnson grass can be. Deeply rooted, the wild, creeping grass stubbornly resisted our attack. At times, I would pause and look back over my shoulder to see if the Johnson grass was growing faster than we could destroy it. We returned to the field many times throughout the summer to combat the menace. Our labors were not in vain, as we were rewarded with many bushels of fine, sweet corn. "You boys have been a great help to your mother and me this summer, so we've decided to take a few days off and drive to Ottoman. It may be the last chance you'll have to visit the farm because your grandparents are planning to soon leave Ottoman and live with your Uncle Harvey in Richmond. They are both getting along in years. Your grandmother just turned eighty, and the farm is too much work for them."

Grandma and Grandpa Sanford were overjoyed to see us. We had to stand up straight with our backs to the wall while our heights were compared to previous marks.

As in previous visits, we lost no time in dashing outdoors to explore the farm. In the orchard, we found a plentiful supply of apples and peaches clinging to the branches. From the watermelon patch, we selected a beauty and carried it back to the house. Grandpa said that it was the very one he had planned to save for us pending our arrival.

"Boys," he said, "I promised that you could ride Hampton, so finish your watermelon and come with me to the barn."

George M. Sanford, Phil, Matt, and Dick

We led Hampton out of his stall. None of us had ever been on a horse before, so Grandpa showed us how to mount, hold the reins, and to tell Hampton what we wanted him to do. To demonstrate, Grandpa mounted and galloped several times around the barnyard, stirring up a cloud of dust. Each of us was given the chance to ride until we became quite at ease in the saddle. Hampton obliged us with an afternoon of riding.

"Now boys, Hampton is tired, so lead him to the trough for water and then take him to his stall. Give him some hay and corn. Be sure to shut the barn door when you leave. Do as you wish for the next couple of hours before supper. You may want to go up the hill behind the house and see the beacon that guides airplanes at night. Now, I want you to promise not to attempt to climb the ladder on the side of the tower. You may fall, so do as I say! Better to be safe than sorry!"

After tending to Hampton, Matt and I took off running. Phil, saying that he was tired, returned to the house. We clambered up a steep, brush-covered path to the top of the hill. There, reaching skyward, was a tall, steel tower.

The view of the surrounding countryside was spectacular. From our vantage point, the little town of Ottoman looked like a miniature village. We paced off the concrete directional arrow and estimated its length to be seventy feet. From ground level, the steel tower appeared to be about fifty feet high. Atop the tower was a wide, grated platform on which a beacon and two smaller, stationary lights were mounted.

"If we climbed up the ladder part way, we could see much more."

"But Matt, Grandpa told us not to climb up the ladder!"

"No, he just said that we should just be careful! I'll climb up high enough to read the number on the roof of the shed."

Matt proceeded to slowly scale the ladder, a rung at a time, until he reached the half-way point, at which time, he paused to look around and to call down to me the distant sights.

"You'd better come on down, Matt!"

Ignoring my suggestion, Matt continued to climb until he reached the underside of the grated platform. A padlocked trapdoor prevented him from gaining access. He hesitated for a moment and then proceeded to try and climb around the iron cage surrounding the platform. Using only his hands for support, he struggled to inch his way upward but something prevented him from moving any further.

"I'm hung up on something, Dick!" he shouted. "I can't go any further and I can't go back to the ladder . . . can't hold on much longer . . . you'd better come up and help me!"

I have no clear recollection of climbing the ladder except that I quickly found myself at the top. Matt's belt was snagged on a protruding bolt which prevented him from moving in any direction. Fortunately I was able to reach out and release him. He barely had enough strength to work his way back to the ladder. We descended without saying a word. Reaching the base of the tower, Matt laughed and said: "Thanks, brother Dick! That was a close call . . . but it was worth it! You won't tell anyone about what happened, will you?"

"Of course not, Matt! It never happened!"

We had experienced a great day. Sadly, however, we realized that it would be our last opportunity to enjoy Grandma and Grandpa's Ottoman farm.

Airway beacons—Rotating beacons for guiding pilots towards their destinations were spaced at intervals of ten miles. Mounted on a seventy-foot long concrete *arrow*, a fifty-one-foot high, steel tower provided an elevated platform for a twenty-four-inch beacon. The million candle-power beacon was visible to pilots at ten second intervals. Two stationary course lights flashed coded numbers which provided the night flying pilots with the location of the tower. Power for the lights was provided by a gasoline powered generator in a shed standing on the *feather* end of the concrete *arrow*. Painted on the roof of the shed was a number which corresponded to the number on the pilot's map.

Note: In the picture of the three of us eating ice cream, note the toys underfoot … Matt's airplane and my Mack truck. Phil's sketchbook is on the bench. Hampton posed with us and looked straight into the eye of the camera.

Phil, Dick, Matt, and Hampton

After supper, we were treated to generous helpings of homemade ice cream. Hampton seemed pleased to join the party. Dad captured the occasion on film with his Graflex.

Late the following day, we told our grandparents "good-bye" and left for Bremo. We tearfully looked back at the home we loved so much and wondered if we would ever see it again. We had spent many happy days on the Ottoman farm. The thought of never returning was very sad indeed.

Dad had always cut our hair; scissors and hand clippers skillfully wielded to trim our unruly manes. With school only a week away, Dad announced that it was again time for our haircuts: "Who's first?"

"I am, Dad!" Phil responded.

While snipping away at Phil's summer growth, Dad informed us that he had decided to mix up a large batch of root beer. "Your mother has mixed the ingredients in boiling water and allowed it to stand for the past twelve hours. The root beer is now ready for bottling. That's where you can help!"

"What ingredients, Dad?"

"Molasses, sassafras root, sarsaparilla root, and yeast. A fellow at the plant gave me his recipe. He says we'll never taste better root beer!"

"Where did you get the sassafras and sarsaparilla roots?"

Sarsaparilla was introduced in Spain as early as 1545. Its name was derived from the Spanish words "zarza" and "parilla," referring to the thorny vines of the plant. Tea made from the roots was used medicinally for chronic rheumatism and skin disorders.

✳

The problem of the bottles blowing up was not uncommon. Fermentation resulting from the yeast acting on the sugar in the molasses produced a gas that expands as the mixture stands and cools. It was concluded that the cause of the exploding bottles was that they were filled too high. Dad's friend who gave him the recipe failed to say that the bottles should be filled to *within one inch of the top*.

"From your grandpa's farm, Dick. Both grow wild in Virginia. It's the roots that flavor the root beer."

Our haircuts completed, we entered the kitchen to find Mom stirring the root beer in a large vat. The sweet aroma of sarsaparilla greeted our nostrils as we leaned over the vat to inspect the contents. Two dozen green-colored bottles were lined up on the counter. Dad brought in a hand—operated capper for crimping the caps to the bottles. We were soon filling and capping the bottles with assembly line efficiency. Dad ladled the liquid from the vat and Phil held a funnel over each bottle as Dad poured. Matt and I took turns capping the bottles. "Good work, boys! We'll store the bottles in the basement where it's cool."

Sometime in the wee hours of the night, we were abruptly awakened by a loud blast, followed moments later by another. We heard Mom cry out: "Walter, wake up! Someone next to the house is firing a shotgun! I'm frightened to death! Who can it be?"

Before Dad could reply several more blasts resounded throughout the house.

"Calm down, Grace! That's not a shotgun! It's coming from the basement! I think the root beer is blowing up! Must have done something wrong! I know we followed the recipe and used the proper ingredients. I don't understand it. I'll go down and take a look. You go upstairs to tell the boys. They're probably scared out of their wits!"

Now wide awake, we were still counting the mysterious blasts when Mom switched on the light.

One winter evening, after the dishes were washed and put away, Dad asked us to sit with him while he read our report cards from school. We waited while he quietly examined each of the reports before looking up and saying:

"Matt, it looks like you need to work harder on your arithmetic . . . B- is OK, but you can do better. Everything else looks good . . . A+ in reading . . . an A in geography . . . good . . . good . . . good . . . but what is this all about?"

"What, Dad?"

"You teacher has made a notation opposite your deportment saying that you are sometimes inattentive in class. What's your explanation?"

"When I'm bored, Dad, I guess my mind wanders."

"I'm not surprised, son. We are aware of your daydreaming. However, it is important that you pay attention in class even if the subject *is* boring."

"Now, Dick, you're next. You too have an A+ in reading. Geography is a B-; arithmetic a B; and spelling a C. Better get to work on your spelling and bring that C up to a B. Your mother is a good speller and she will work with you. Practice makes perfect, you know."

"Yes, sir."

"And now, Philip, let's see how you are coming along. Very good . . . good . . . very good . . . but you need to improve your arithmetic. You can do better than a B-. I'll help you go over your problems."

"Thanks, Dad."

Dad signed our report cards and we spent the rest of the evening with our hobbies. Matt and I had assembled several model airplanes from balsa wood kits. Our rubber band powered aircraft had made many successful flights and were in constant need of repair to keep them air-worthy. Phil moved from water colors to charcoal and pastels. He had a natural flair for painting and was content to spend hours perfecting his work.

On January 4, 1935, Roosevelt met with Congress and reported that retail sales were up dramatically, savings bank deposits were increasing, farm prices were higher, and automobile production was at an all-time high.

Courtesy of Patty Dickenson

Artist—Matt Jefferies

BOY AND A HAWK
Matt's fascination with flying was not limited to airplanes and gliders. The sight of a hawk or eagle circling overhead captured his attention. He would pause in whatever he was doing to study the raptor's effortless soaring.

"Sounds like Roosevelt's New Deal is getting results."

"Sure does, Grace! However, millions are still unemployed. Five years of depression has severely crippled our country. Recovery will take time."

"Now, boys, I have news for you! Your Aunt Mattie has written that she has taken a nursing job at the Old Soldiers Home in Richmond. Pluto, her German police dog, will live with your grandparents in Cumberland."

We were overjoyed with the thought of seeing Aunt Mattie often and looked forward to getting acquainted with Pluto.

One day Dad said that he wanted to have a private conversation with us. Mom retreated to the kitchen and Dad accompanied us upstairs to our bedroom. He quietly closed the door behind him.

As Dad said, we were aware of Matt's tendency to daydream. Airplanes and thoughts of flying captured his imagination. At the sound of an airplane, Matt would dash outside to catch a glimpse of the plane and wave at the pilot. He would return with a full description of the plane. Advertisements and Sunday school programs were meticulously converted into gliders capable of sailing great distances. One day in school, Matt launched a paper glider across the room, aimed at an open window. However, it veered off course and landed on the teacher's desk. Startled, she looked up from her book and demanded that the guilty party raise his hand. Matt sheepishly complied, said he was sorry, and explained that it was meant to go outside. "Very well, Matt Jefferies, but this is a reading class, not a hobby shop!"
She carefully studied the glider and said: "Now, let's see how well it soars!" She stood up, stepped to the window and sent the glider sailing. "Wonderful!" she exclaimed as the entire class applauded. Matt just grinned.

April 18, 1935

My Dears,
I have accepted a nursing position at the Confederate Old Soldiers Home in Richmond. I am to report on July 5th. I have truly enjoyed my work at the hospital here in Pennsylvania. Everyone has been wonderful to work with . . . doctors, nurses, orderlies . . . all dedicated people. I shall miss them all! However, I want desperately to be close to Momma and Poppa and you folks . . . and I have always loved Richmond. I've told you about Pluto, my beautiful German police dog. I can't have him with me at the Old Soldiers Home so Momma and Poppa are more than pleased to take him. He'll be free to run on the farm. You boys will find a new friend in Pluto. He's gentle and will accompany you on your walks to Sports Lake. I am looking forward to seeing you again soon.

I love you all,
Mattie

"Sit down, boys. I must have your undivided attention."

"What, Dad?" Phil asked.

"Your mother is going to have a baby!"

"A baby, Dad? Did you say a baby?"

"That's right, son."

"When, Dad?" Matt asked.

"In late January or early February."

"A boy or a girl baby?"

"We won't know until it arrives, Phil."

"Wow! A baby! Imagine that!" I exclaimed.

"Now boys, think for a moment . . . Is there anything you want to know about this blessed event? Now is the time to clear up any misconceptions you may have about how babies are made . . . any questions? Matt?"

"No, sir."

"Dick, what about you? Any questions?"

"No, sir."

"Phil?"

"Will a stork bring the baby, Dad?"

"Well, son, not exactly . . . but I suppose that's one way of explaining it. No more questions? Well, now you know! I want each of you to make a special effort to help your mother in every way you can. She will need all the rest she can get! OK?"

"Yes, sir!" we replied in unison.

After Dad left the room with Phil trailing along after him, I turned to Matt and said: "Why didn't you ask Dad for details?"

"Didn't need to! What about you?"

"Same here."

One afternoon in late summer as we dug up the last of the carrots and potatoes, Dad informed us that he would drive to Ottoman to pick fruit from the orchard. A friend had loaned him a two-wheel trailer to transport the baskets of fruit back to Bremo. Matt and I were to accompany him.

"When will we leave, Dad?"

"Friday . . . about midnight . . . after I get off from work. We'll get some sleep when we get there. Then we'll pick all the fruit we can load on the trailer. If we finish soon enough we'll rent a boat and do some deep water fishing."

A full moon illuminated the countryside. As we approached the Ottoman farm, we were saddened at the thought of our grandparents no longer living there. Hampton, the hogs and chickens—all no longer there—the place would not be the same without them. It wasn't! The tall hedgerow surrounding the front yard was overgrown and unsightly. Broken tree limbs cluttered the unmowed lawn. Upon entering the vacant house we were startled by several large bats that swooped down from the ceiling over the stairway to challenge our presence.

"How did they get inside, Dad?"

"My guess is that they entered through a crack somewhere beneath the eaves. Tomorrow we'll have to try to find the opening and plug it up."

"How can we get them out?"

"Come with me upstairs. I'll open a window on the second floor and we'll try and scare them into flying out. Here, Matt, you hold the flashlight!"

Disturbed by our loud shouts and hand clapping, the screeching bats flailed around in a wild frenzy until—finally—they soared through the open window. Dad quickly closed the window.

"Well, that's that!" Dad said. "Let's get some sleep!"

Dad awakened us at sunrise saying that the sooner we got started the better our chances of going fishing in the afternoon. "I've lit a fire in the kitchen stove. Breakfast will be ready in a jiffy."

Although it was evident that others had helped themselves to much of the fruit, there was still a plentiful supply, enough to satisfy our needs. As the bushel baskets were filled, Matt and I paired up to carry them to the trailer. By noon, the trailer was loaded and the contents covered over with a tarp.

"Good job, boys! Now, we'll do some fishing!"

We drove to a nearby dock in Ottoman. Dad rented a flat-bottomed boat for three dollars. Fishing lines, hooks, sinker weights, and a pail of soft-shell crabs for bait were purchased for a dollar. We shoved off from the dock and Dad rowed for a short distance to deeper water.

"Now, boys, I want you to move to the bow."

Dad removed the oars from the oarlocks and placed one in the bottom of the boat. Grasping the other oar, he stood, turned, and stepped to the stern.

"OK, boys, hold on to the gunwales! Sculling will get us out there faster than rowing."

He positioned himself in the stern, his legs spread wide apart for balance. With the stern-post as a fulcrum, the long oar was rotated in a figure eight pattern. The boat was speedily propelled forward. As we sliced into the waves, the bow of the boat lifted. When we were clearly a mile from shore, Dad ceased sculling and dropped anchor. We chopped up the crabs and baited the hooks. Three hooks, spaced at six-inch intervals and weighted down with a lead sinker, were tied firmly to the line. With the crab bait securely hooked, the line was dropped over the side and allowed to fall freely into the depths.

"How much line should I pay out, Dad?" Matt asked.

"We're in deep water, son. A hundred feet of line should do."

We watched Dad as he moved his line up and down to attract fish to the baited hooks. I had barely started to do the same when I felt a strong tug on the line.

"I think I've hooked one, Dad!"

"Take your time, son, and slowly pull in your line . . . that's right . . . not too fast . . . just a steady pull."

"It must be a big one, Dad! It almost pulled the line out of my hand!"

Before I caught sight of my catch, I heard a croaking sound emanating from the depths.

"You've caught a croaker, Dick! Pull him in and toss him into the boat."

"Wow . . . ! Look at that . . . I've caught fish on two of the hooks!"

"I've got one, too!" Matt yelled.

"So have I!" Dad said.

We must have anchored over a school of fish, for within an hour, we had pulled in twenty croakers, nine trout, two ugly toadfish, and a small swordfish.

"Boys, I think we had better quit and head back! We have enough fish for one day and it looks like a storm is coming up. Pull in your lines and toss out the remaining bait. We'll probably get a soaking before we reach the dock."

Dad raised the anchor and we were quickly underway. Suddenly the weather took a turn for the worse. The sky darkened. Powerful wind gusts whipped the waves into a frenzy. A slashing downpour soaked us to the skin. At times our little boat was tossed around like a cork, but Dad's powerful sculling brought us back on course. When the bow sliced into a large wave, water cascaded into the boat.

"Matt, you and Dick take turns bailing water out of the boat! Use the bait can and bail as fast as you can! We're making progress, but . . . ."

Dad's voice was drowned out by a loud thunderclap. Flashes of lightning illuminated the darkened sky. The fury of the storm was relentless and frightening. Just as suddenly as the storm arose, it abruptly tapered off. The sky brightened and a beautiful rainbow arched over the horizon.

"You can relax now, boys! We'll be back at the dock in a few minutes."

We looked to Dad, who was tenaciously applying all his strength to the sculling oar, his wet shirt clinging to his arms and shoulders. "Well, that one snuck up on us!" he said, as he tied the boat to the dock. "Leave it to the Rappahannock River to give us something to remember!"

At Fickland's store, Dad bought a large block of ice and a bag of rock salt. Mr. Fickland was surprised to see Dad and asked if we had come to Ottoman to fish. Dad said that our main purpose in making the trip was to gather fruit from the orchard.

"Will we have fish for supper tonight, Dad?"

"Sure will, son! Then, after we've eaten, we'll clean the rest of the fish and pack them in chipped ice. We'll take some to your Aunt Mattie at the Old Soldiers Home; the rest, we'll take home."

It was dark when we arrived back at the house. By lamplight, we changed into dry clothes as Dad lit a fire in the kitchen stove. Our clothes were hung up to dry. Dad cleaned three fish and soon had them sizzling in a skillet. Boiled potatoes, hot chocolate, and fresh fruit rounded out our meal.

"Now, boys, we have work to do! Bring the lamp outside and we'll clean and pack the fish."

We quickly teamed up to get the job done. Dad cleaned, Matt wielded an ice pick, and I packed the fish in a crate and covered them with layers of chipped ice and a sprinkling of rock salt.

"OK, boys, job's done. A kettle of hot water is on the stove. We'll wash up now and get to bed." Matt and I did not have to be persuaded as we were exhausted.

"Take this flashlight with you. You know where the outhouse is."

Following breakfast the next morning, Dad went in search of the opening where the bats had gained entrance to the house. Matt and I hastened to the parlor to play a few records on the Edison phonograph. We searched through the tall stack to find "In a Little Spanish Town." As Matt was winding up the phonograph, Dad appeared in the doorway and informed us that he had plugged up several openings beneath the eaves.

"Boys," he said, "we've got to go. Come along now. We must get back to Bremo in time for me to be at work by three o'clock."

"OK, Dad, but before we leave, we want to play your favorite record."

"Thanks, boys! Someday we'll take the Edison with us to Bremo. Wish we could do it now, but the trailer is loaded. The crate of fish will have to ride on the running board."

As we drove away from the farm we looked back at the deserted house and recalled the wonderful times we had when our grandparents lived there. Set well back from the country road, the whitewashed, clapboard house with its gingerbread roof trimmings and wide front porch was picturesquely framed by two stately trees: a towering oak and a blue spruce. The windows were shuttered. I remembered how, many times as we were leaving the house, Grandma would say: "George, did you check the stove and the blinds?" The safety and comfort of the house was an obsession with her. Closed blinds contributed to the interior being cooler in the summer and warmer in the winter. The danger of fire was a constant worry, so she was very careful to make certain that the stove fires were extinguished before departure. Viewed from our moving car, the shuttered windows suggested a once lively dwelling, now orphaned and lonely.

As the farm disappeared from view, we sat back and observed the passing countryside. Farmland, charming little towns, and Colonial churches flashed by as we progressed through Lancaster and Westmoreland Counties. Leaving the Northern Neck was always a sad occasion for us, but we knew that in the future, there would be other opportunities to return to Ottoman, to pick the fruit, to fish, and to romp around the old farm. However, it was dispiriting to know that we would never again hear Grandma admonish Grandpa about checking the fire in the stove and fireplace or closing the blinds.

Approximately fifteen miles from Richmond, we crossed the Chickahominy River near the town of Mechanicsville. Matt and I remembered Mr. Wakley, our YMCA director, telling us that a major Civil War battle had been fought here. We had informed Mr. Wakley that Southerners refer to the conflict as the "War Between the States."

Our route into the city placed us on Richmond's beautiful Monument Avenue. Gracing the wide, landscaped boulevard are the equestrian statues of Generals Lee, Jackson, and Stuart surmounting massive granite pedestals. The name of each general is chiseled in stone.

"Dad," I asked, "Mr. Wakley said that Robert E. Lee was the greatest general in the War Between the States. Would you agree?"

"No doubt about it! Lee was a clever tactician, highly respected by both sides. Even today, Lee is considered the War's most famous general."

"Was Ulysses S. Grant also a great general?"

Lee Monument, Richmond, Virginia

"Well, Grant was victorious, so the Union paid him the appropriate respect."

"It was a terrible war, wasn't it, Dad?"

"Indeed it was, son! The nation was divided. Many families were also split . . . brother pitted against brother and father against son. Each side felt theirs was the right cause. For the South, however, it was a *lost* cause. It's best that the South lost the war."

"Why, Dad?"

"Because America was founded as one nation and should remain as one."

The Confederate Old Soldiers Home was nestled in a grove of towering trees. Manicured lawns, shrubbery, and flower beds bordered the antebellum structure. We were met at the entrance by a white-jacketed orderly. Dad informed him that he wished to see his sister, Mattie Jefferies. We were asked to wait in the vestibule where a lifelike, mounted horse was prominently displayed. We reached out to pat the horse's nose and stroke his mane as we so often did to Hampton. Moments later the orderly returned. Seeing us admiring the horse, he said: "Boys, have you any idea who owned this horse?"

"No, sir."

"This is 'Traveller,' General Robert E. Lee's favorite horse."

"We saw Lee's statue on Monument Avenue. Is he on Traveller?"

"Yes, his mount is Traveller all right! No doubt about it!"

"Mr. Jefferies, Nurse Mattie is so happy you have come to see her! She's out on the veranda with some of her charges. I will take you to her." Aunt Mattie was standing among several, very old, white-haired veterans. All were attired in their gray Confederate uniforms, their campaign medals proudly displayed on their chests. Some were in wheelchairs, and others, bent with age and leaning on their canes, were strolling around the grounds. A number were grouped around a massive cannon cradled atop a concrete pedestal. As we approached, Aunt Mattie smiled warmly and opened her arms to us.

"Pray tell, Walter, what brings you and the boys to Richmond?"

In May 1862, General George McClellan commanded the army of the Potomac. President Lincoln was not pleased with McClellan's failure to attack a smaller Confederate army in northern Virginia which could have enabled his army to quickly move on to RIchmond, the capital of the Confederacy. However, in spite of his concern, Lincoln agreed to McClellan's alternate plan to land on Virginia's York Peninsula and move against Richmond. However, his 25,000-man V Corps, under the command of General Porter, was stopped when they reached Mechanicsville. Lee ordered General Jeb Stuart, his "eyes of the army," on a scouting mission. Stuart's 1200 cavalry troopers rode completely around the union's V Corps without being detected. With the information provided by Jeb Stuart, General Jackson was successful in forcing General Porter to retreat. However, the battle casualties were heavy. Porter's loss in men killed, wounded and captured numbered 7,000. Lee's casualties were over 8,000. It was the beginning of McClellan's failed peninsula campaign to capture Richmond.

Robert E. Lee's monument is engraved **LEE**. The names of his subordinate generals are engraved:

STONEWALL JACKSON
J. E. B. STUART
The engravings are a clear indication of how Virginians rated Robert E. Lee.

The Confederate Old Soldiers home, Richmond, Virginia.

After viewing Traveller, Matt, always a stickler for details, questioned the identity of the horse. He saw no resemblance to the horse at the Old Soldiers Home and the one on Lee's monument. There was no doubt in his mind that the horse Lee was astride on the monument was Traveller. He suggested, that perhaps the horse we saw at the Old Soldiers' Home was Stonewall Jackson's charger, "Little Sorrel."

After Jackson was killed, Little Sorrel lived for twenty years and died in 1886 at **Richmond's Old Soldiers' Home.** Little Sorrel's hide was mounted. Today, Little Sorrel is in the Virginia Military Institute Museum in Lexington, Virginia. The famed horse is standing near the raincoat that Jackson was wearing when he was mortally wounded. Stonewall Jackson had been a professor at VMI from 1851 to 1861.

"We've been down to Ottoman to pick fruit for canning. Thought we'd leave a couple bushels with you, along with some croakers and trout we caught in the Rappahannock."

"That's very thoughtful of you, Walter. These men will enjoy the fruit! Tonight, after they are all tucked into bed, the staff will enjoy a fish fry. Now, I want you to meet some of my friends." She introduced us to several veterans who were delighted to meet us. One, Captain Cover, told us that he had served in the Fifth Virginia Cavalry and was wounded in a battle near Dumfries, Virginia. "Boys," he said, "when you grow up, I hope you won't have to go to war. We did what we felt was right at the time, but at a terrible cost . . . so many lives wasted."

"I'm sure glad you came through the war OK, Captain Cover!"

"Thank you, son. Now I want you to accompany me to see that big cannon over there under the trees. Brought here from Charleston, South Carolina, it is one of the surviving cannons from Fort Sumter. In its time, it was a powerful and effective long-range weapon."

Later, I asked Aunt Mattie to tell us more about Captain Cover. "He's ninety-five and very sweet . . . never complains. Tragically, he lost two brothers at Gettysburg. He's very patriotic, urging everyone to vote for Roosevelt and Garner for a second term." Aunt Mattie stood in the driveway and waved as we drove away. We were reminded of the night she waved to us from the illuminated porch of a hospital in the mountains of Pennsylvania.

When we arrived home, Mom and Phil rushed out to meet us. Mom's sad countenance suggested that she was deeply distressed.

"What's wrong, Grace?" Dad asked.

"The house in Ottoman has been destroyed by fire! I received this Western Union telegram two hours ago."

Dad read the telegram in silence and embraced Mom to comfort her. We were too distraught to speak. The thought of the house in ashes was more than we could bear.

"I can't understand how it could have happened. We had a fire in the kitchen stove but it was completely out before we left. I made certain that it was extinguished! Only thing I can think of is the possibility that there were sparks in the chimney that somehow caused the fire."

"Don't grieve over it, Walter . . . the house is now just something for us to fondly remember . . . you and the

The Western Union telegram:
YOUR OTTOMAN HOUSE BURNT TO THE GROUND STOP NOTHING SAVED STOP YOU WERE SEEN LEAVING OTTOMAN WITH A TRAILER LOAD OF FURNITURE STOP SUGGEST YOU RETURN TO OTTOMAN AT ONCE STOP

The telegram was sent by Mr. Fickland of Fickland's Store.

boys are safe . . . that's all that matters! All of you must be famished, so I'll make some sandwiches. Now go and wash up. You have to be at the plant in forty-five minutes."

Dad remained silent but the painful thought of the tragedy was etched on his face. He held Mom in his arms as she bravely fought back tears.

We ate in silence as Mom and Dad discussed the loss of the Ottoman home. It was only recently, we learned, that the deed to the house and farm had been transferred to them. There was some question about the insurance coverage, a possibility that there was no coverage for a house that was unoccupied.

"What will you do now, Walter?"

"Tonight, when I get off from work, I'll return to Ottoman. On my way back home, I'll stop by Harvey's and tell your mother and father about the fire."

"I know that will not be an easy task Walter, but they have to be told. I am worried how Mama will take the distressing news."

"May Dick and I come with you, Dad?"

"Yes indeed, Matt, but I want you both to get some sleep before we leave. I should be home by midnight and we will want to leave right away."

"Walter, can't you put it off until you have had some rest? Must you leave tonight?"

"Yes. I'm concerned about what was implied in the wire."

"Mom, who could possibly report that we had furniture in the trailer? It suggests that we took the furniture we wanted and set fire to the house in order to collect insurance."

"It certainly does, Dick, and it is indeed very troubling."

"Could someone have deliberately started the fire?"

"It's possible, Matt, but highly unlikely. All the folks we know in the Northern Neck are honest, hardworking, law-abiding Christians . . . all are genuinely fine people. I don't believe anyone would do something as wicked as setting fire to a house."

Through the night and early morning hours on our return trip to Ottoman we had the opportunity to discuss the tragedy with Dad. He reminded us of the thousands of Americans who lost their homes to bank foreclosures. Their losses, he said, were just as painful, though ours was due to a fire and theirs were results of the Depression.

The Virginia countryside was bathed in soft moonlight. We had fleeting glimpses of farm houses, barns and fenced fields, all dear to those who owned them. To us, however, Ottoman was more than a farm, a house and a barn. Rather, it was our memories of times past, of Grandma baking bread or feeding the chickens, of Grandpa hitching up Hampton to the plow or closing the blinds before departing for church services, of Mom cleaning and filling the kerosene lamps, of the many times we played records on the Edison phonograph, or lay in bed at night and listened to the rain beating on the tin roof. These were my fleeting thoughts as we traversed the miles to Ottoman, remembrances forever etched in memory to be happily recalled for a lifetime.

Dad must have sensed my feelings. Without speaking, he reached over and patted my hand. "Thanks, Dad," I whispered just before I dozed off.

Although I had visualized the ruins in my mind's eye, I was not fully prepared for the totality of the loss. Only a heap of smoldering ashes remained of the lovely old home that we loved so dearly. The tall spruce and oak trees which had shaded the house were reduced to unsightly, skeletal timbers. A front porch railing—which someone had pulled away from the burning house—lay across Grandma's rose garden. Circling the site, we could easily determine the location of each room on the ground floor. The brick chimney collapsed onto the cast-iron kitchen stove. Grandpa's old safe from his Hopewell store was topped with a pyramid of ashes. Twisted metal rails and springs were all that remained of the beds. I was surprised to see a ceramic pitcher lying intact among the ashes. I reached out with a long stick to snag the handle, but upon contact, the pitcher fragmented into a thousand pieces. The tin roof had fallen to one side of the house and lay crumpled on the ground. Window panes had melted and solidified into crystal-like balls of glass. Window sash weights lay scattered alongside the glass balls. Pausing to examine the area which had been the parlor, I was astounded to see the stack of Edison records still intact. However, there was no sign of the phonograph. I leaned over the hot ashes for a closer look and was amazed to find that the label on the top record was still legible. The record lay where we had placed it. It was "In a Little Spanish Town." A touch of the stick and the stack of records collapsed into a pile of ashes.

"To every thing there is a season. A time to every purpose under the heaven. A time to be born, and a time to die. A time to weep, and a time to laugh. A time to mourn, and a time to dance. There is nothing new under the sun."

—Ecclesiastes

※

THE HISTORY OF WHITE POINT HOUSE AND FARM. NOW THE "OLD HOTEL" AT COLONIAL BEACH, VA.

In days gone by this house was a resting place for a bunch of 'lively sports' who went out for fishing and bathing and large oyster roasts on the beach. These sports were Livingstons, Lees, Stuarts, Cox and others. For a short time Henry Lee owned the property. He sold it to James Stuart who, in turn, sold the property to James Cox, my grandfather, who married Lucy Brockenbrough of Tappahannock. Cox remodeled the house and made it into a beautiful, picturesque home and farm. He had four daughters and one son, John Livingston Cox, by his first wife, Lucy Brockenbrough. His second wife was Catherine Bowie. My mother, Mary Cox, was married in the house to George Carmichael Harvey in 1835. They sailed away to Alexandria to live in a new home, a bridal gift from her father. He gave homes to all of his daughters.

Some of the old paper mulberry trees planted by Cox are still living in the hotel yard. White Point, now Colonial Beach, is an incorporated town, now a great summer resort.

—AHS

I had seen more than enough to satisfy my curiosity. I retreated to the car and waited for Dad and Matt. Left alone with my thoughts, I somehow found comfort in the biblical passage: "To every thing there is a season." We had loved the old home and had many precious memories of the good times we had there. In our hearts it would always be Grandma and Grandpa's home but there came a time when they had to leave the farm. Without them, without Hampton, and the hogs, and the chickens, the home had become just a house. Now it too was gone.

"Lord have mercy, Walter! What a surprise! Matt, Dick, come give your grandma a big hug! My, how you have grown! Is Grace with you, Walter? Is she all right?"

"Yes, Mrs. Sanford—she's in Bremo. The boys and I have been in Ottoman. We have some sad news . . . I'm so sorry to have to inform you . . . the house in Ottoman has been destroyed by a fire."

"Was anyone hurt?"

"No, Mrs. Sanford . . . no one was there when it happened. You see, we went there yesterday . . ."

"Never mind, Walter. It's not important. George is asleep . . . I will tell him in the morning."

Grandma had been reading her Bible. She clutched it tightly as she looked to each of us and smiled. "Thank the Good Lord for watching over you. We must count our blessings. Now, it's past my bedtime, so I will say goodnight. I love you all." She took a deep breath, kissed each of us and retired to her room.

Grandma's unemotional reaction to the loss of her home left us dazed. Her home had been her refuge—lovingly tended to and fretted over for so many years. Always cognizant of the threat of fire, she regularly cautioned everyone about carelessness in the handling of matches. The kerosene lamps posed an even greater threat. Grandma's admonition was vividly recalled: "Do be careful, boys! Fire is not to be played with. It is our best friend . . . providing heat and light . . . but, also, our worst enemy!"

"Walter," Uncle Harvey said, "I can't believe what we just witnessed! I expected Mama to cry out and agonize over the tragic news, but . . . well, what can I say?"

"She's a pillar of strength, Harvey. The house is insignificant compared to the safety of those she loves. She is a most extraordinary lady!"

Following an early frost, autumn arrived in a blaze of color. Matt and I enrolled in a new high school at Carysbrook, eight miles from Bremo. Rather than commute by bus, we preferred to ride our bicycles, irrespective of weather conditions. Although the air was crisp, we occasionally stopped by an abandoned quarry located deep in the woods. We had great fun diving and swimming in the frigid water. We found the great outdoors to be exhilarating and challenging. Nothing escaped our curiosity.

On Halloween, we were invited to a costume party at the home of a classmate. Matt wore patched bib overalls, a bandana, and a straw hat. He said that he was a scarecrow. I went as a masked gunman armed with two six-shooters. Phil, draped in a blanket, and wearing a feather in his hair, was a young Indian buck, appropriately armed with a bow and arrow. We played "Pin the Tail on the Donkey," bobbed for apples, and kissed the girls.

When we returned home around midnight, we were shocked to see that an outhouse had been deposited on our neighbor's front lawn.

Matt and I sang at the Sunday services at Grace Episcopal Church. Bible studies were held in a parish house adjacent to the church. The vicar was a dedicated minister who encouraged us to emulate Christ in our lives.

During the holidays, a winter storm blanketed central Virginia with snow.

A particularly heavy snowfall closed the hillside road to Lower Bremo. Only the tops of parallel fence rows outlined the snow-covered road. Swirling wind gusts sculpted deep drifts into soft,

Grace Episcopal Church, Bremo Bluff, Virginia

undulated patterns. The evergreens suffered the fury of the vicious storm, their boughs bent earthward under the sheer weight of the glistening snow. Limbs snapped with a sharp report, like the crack of a rifle shot. During the long night hours, the eerie sounds were unnerving. At long last, the storm subsided. The break of dawn on the third day revealed the countryside snugly blanketed in silent whiteness. I arose and stepped outside to marvel at the beauty of the morning. The rising sun cast sparkling reflections off a crystalline landscape. The frigid morning air was pure and crisp. Only distant columns of smoke from scattered chimneys suggested any sign of human habitation. Birds miraculously appeared from their sheltered retreats to hungrily seek food. I was amused to observe a field mouse, having nosed his way to the surface, shake the snowflakes from his furry head, survey his surroundings, and quickly return to his snow-covered burrow. As the early morning progressed, the stillness was broken by the faraway barking of dogs, the percussive sounds of wood chopping, and the scraping of snow shovels on porches, roofs, and walkways.

Voices, audible and excited, carried over great distances, imploring all within earshot to bring shovels and work their way along the snowbound road to the brink of Bremo Hill. The steep curving road to Lower Bremo was the focus of the early morning migration.

A downhill course was being methodically contoured and compacted for sledding.

Dad's return home was delayed by the deep snow. He had to hike the distance, so his trek included having to climb Bremo Hill. Matt and I ran to meet him and peppered him with questions about the activity on the hill. He responded by stating that dozens of people were engaged in the effort. In addition to the sledding course, an adjacent path had been prepared for the return hill climb. "OK, boys, I know you want to go sledding on the hill, but you must be back before dark! There will be some daredevils out there and we don't want you to get hurt!"

We retrieved our one-man *Flyer* from the garage rafters and worked to prepare it for action. The rusted runners where filed and polished to a mirror finish. The frayed rope was replaced with a stronger one and tightly knotted in place.

After eating lunch, we quickly dressed, each donning two pairs of trousers, two shirts, a heavy jacket, woolen cap, earmuffs, gloves, and boots.

We arrived at the brink of the hill to find sledding already underway. A large crowd was gathered around a blazing bonfire. Some, we learned, had come from as far away as Richmond to participate in the frolic. A line had formed at the approach to the downhill course. I recognized the authoritative voice of the self-appointed leader whom I had heard in the early morning hours. He was Harold Jones, the undertaker. Matt wryly commented that he was probably present to drum up business! Mr. Jones had stationed

The *Flexible Flyer* sled was patented in 1889 by Samuel Leeds Allen of Philadelphia. During the early 1900s the popular sled was marketed by Wanamaker's in Philadelphia and R.H. Macy Co. in New York.

himself at the starting point. With a stopwatch, he timed each departure in precise intervals of thirty seconds. As we awaited our turn, it was decided that Matt would make the first run. The delay enabled us to observe the various methods employed to initiate a rapid start. Some ran and flopped on the sled in a prone position. Others positioned themselves in a sitting position with their feet on the steering bar and the rope tightly grasped.

"OK, son, your turn!" announced Mr. Jones. "And, son, if you spill, hold onto your sled and quickly move off the course—or you'll get run over!" Matt made a running start and threw himself on the sled in the favored prone position. As he descended, all I could see was the rapidly disappearing soles of his boots.

Returning to the bonfire I paced nervously, wondering if Matt had made it safely or was lying in a bloody heap in a snow bank. As this dreadful thought crossed my mind, I was approached by a pretty girl carrying a thermos bottle. "Hi!" she said with an inviting smile. "You look cold! I've saved some hot chocolate for you. Have you made a run yet?" As she filled a cup with steaming hot drink, I thanked her and explained that I was waiting for my brother to return. I added that it was our first run and that naturally, I was worried about him.

"Oh, I'm sure he's all right! It can take up to forty-five minutes for them to get back." She smiled, said good-bye, and drifted off into the crowd. About the time that I resorted to prayer, Matt emerged, huffing and puffing from the climb, but excited about his fantastic ride. Handing the sled over, he cautioned me about the junction with the cross street at the bottom of the hill: "There's a jog in the course as it levels off . . . keep going straight and I guarantee you'll end up in a bonfire! You'll have to steer way over to the right or you'll burn for sure!" Leaving Matt to warm by the fire, I took my place in line and concentrated on how I could emulate his flawless starting performance. Within moments it was my turn. Mr. Jones repeated his warning. Holding the sled to my side and taking several swift, running steps, I slammed my torso atop the sled as it hit the slope. The sensation of rapid acceleration was spontaneous. An icy blast of air brought a flood of tears to my eyes. I had little control over the wild descent. The sled and I had become one and we were free-falling! The speed, the blast of cold air, and the soft, swishing sound of the runners on the packed snow was exhilarating! Within an instant the first banked curve loomed into view. Slicing into the curve, I tightened my grip on the steering bar and guided high up on the elevated bank. I felt my weight press against the sled as the curvature reached its apex, and then lessen as it proceeded in a gradual but swift descent to the next straightaway.

The downward travel from the banked curve had the effect of further increasing my speed. In traversing the straightaway, instinct commanded my every action. I took another curve in the opposite direction and then another straightaway, all in rapid succession. Along the way I was vaguely aware of the voices and cheering of those on the path alongside the course. Visually they were but a fleeting blur of color. Having attained what was surely maximum speed, I entered the final straightaway. Directly in line with my path of travel loomed the dreaded bonfire Matt had warned

about. As I neared the junction at the bottom of the hill, I leaned over to maneuver around the obstacle. Miraculously, I managed to avoid the blazing fire.

I quickly headed back up the hill. along a steep, slippery path. Matt, eagerly awaiting my arrival, reached for the sled and took his place in line. Soon he was off again, running, flopping and sledding like a professional. Before sunset each of us had made three runs. The fading light of day made it all too apparent that there was not enough time for each of us to make another run. Other enthusiasts had arrived on the scene and the line was lengthening. We then had a brainstorm: our final run would be made together! Two could not sit on the one-man sled, so we decided to ride piggyback. I would lie on the sled and steer. Matt would lie on my back and hold onto the runner struts. When we arrived at the starting point, I quickly mounted the sled. Matt pushed it along to the brink, flopping atop my back as we plunged downhill. Although we were top-heavy, and seemingly faster than our solo runs, the descent went smoothly. As it was then quite dark, the sense of speed heightened. The steel runners struck bits of gravel embedded in the snow, and bright, flashing sparks were emitted, adding a new dimension to the thrilling downhill plunge. As we rounded the final curve and headed into the straightaway, we faced our most imposing challenge—swerving clear of the raging bonfire. Our attempt to turn was futile as we rapidly approached the fire.

"Lean, Matt! Lean! . . . More! . . . I can't steer! Watch out!" With that shouted exclamation, we plowed into the inferno! Burning wood, red hot embers, and a tremendous shower of sparks scattered in every direction. The sled came to a halt in the center of the fire. An alert bystander picked up each of us by the seat of the pants and tossed us into a snow bank.

Unharmed, Matt shakily asked if I was injured. Feeling no pain and seeing that I was not on fire, I blurted out that I was apparently OK. "The sled!" Matt shouted. "It must still be in the fire!" After clawing our way out of the snow bank, we were relieved to learn that it had been retrieved and had suffered little damage—a few slats blackened and blistered. We were grateful to our rescuer and thanked him. The crowd around the bonfire obviously enjoyed the free entertainment. Someone remarked that when we hit the fire it was like the Fourth of July!

Returning home as quickly as our tired legs would carry us, we returned the singed sled to the garage rafters and approached our waiting parents as though nothing out of the ordinary had occurred. We excitedly told them of the fantastic time we had sledding the treacherous course.

Later, bedded down for the night, I thought back over the events of the day. I recalled the pristine morning when all was silent and the beauty of the landscape had so moved me. Then there was the awakening of the local gentry followed by the preparation of the course. I recalled my anxiety in awaiting Matt's return from that first run. A stranger had given me a cup of hot chocolate. The excitement of my first run was repeated on those that followed. Matt and I were indeed fortunate that no harm had come to us when we landed in the bonfire. We had had a great experience! Slipping into dreamland, I was again sledding on Bremo Hill.

On New Years Day we drove to Cumberland to visit Grandma and Grandpa. Much to our delight, Uncle George was the first to step out and greet us: "Happy New Year, folks! I'm so glad you made it over . . . sure didn't want to miss seeing you!"

"Happy New Year, George! So, the CCC gave you time off for the holidays."

"Only a few days, Walter. They've had us shoveling snow and getting food to the people who are snowbound. Quite a storm, wasn't it?"

"Indeed it was! However, it gave Matt and Dick the opportunity to sled down Bremo Hill. It was a real thrill for them!"

"You look wonderful, George!" Mom said. "The outdoor life has been good for you!"

As the year 1935 drew to a close, the mood of the country was one of guarded optimism. President Roosevelt had succeeded in convincing Congress to pass the Social Security Act. He had long recognized that among the most pitiable victims of the Great Depression were the millions of aged Americans who saw their savings wiped out by the economic catastrophe. To provide monthly benefits to retired workers, the act would be funded by a payroll tax shared equally by employee and employer. On signing the bill, President Roosevelt declared it to be the *supreme achievement* of his administration.

※

Sir Malcolm Campbell, the English racing driver, drove his Bluebird at 276 miles per hour over sand at Daytona Beach, Florida.

"Thanks! By the way, Grace, aren't you about ready to provide me with another nephew . . . or will it be a girl this time?"

"In about a month, George . . . sometime in early February . . . and we'll just have to wait and see."

"What about it, boys, are you wishing for another brother?"

"Makes no difference, Uncle George, but except for Mom, we've never had a girl in the house."

"Well, good gracious, look who's here!" Dad exclaimed as Aunt Virginia emerged from the house. "Virginia, you're a sight for sore eyes!"

"Well, Walter, you're mighty handsome yourself! Grace, you must be taking good care of my big brother! Boys, come here and give your Aunt Virginia a big hug . . . and all of you come on in! We were about ready to sit down for lunch."

Grandma's steaming hot rabbit stew, cornbread, lima beans and sweet potato pie were enjoyed by everyone. The family gathering was indeed a blessing for our grandparents. The banter around the table was lively and the range of knowledge remarkable.

"Dick, what book have you enjoyed reading lately?" Aunt Virginia asked.

"*David Copperfield.* I feel I've gotten to know the characters personally."

"Oh yes, one does indeed! And, Matt, what have you read?"

"Zane Gray's *Riders of the Purple Sage* . . . a great Western!"

"I want you boys to continue to read. Books will open up worlds of knowledge that will sustain you throughout you lives. I have endeavored to promote elementary student reading through the Cooperative Education Association, of which I am an active member. Are you participating in the Junior Community League Reading Course?"

"Yes, ma'am," Matt responded. "Dick and I will receive our reading certificates in May."

"Good! Now, if you are searching for additional reading material, remember that I have a substantial number of books here at your grandmother's house. You may borrow them, but they must be handled with care and returned after you have read them. Understand?"

"Yes, ma'am," we replied in unison.

"I know how much you like to read "Buck Rogers" and "Flash Gordon," but there is a great deal to be learned from the past, so I encourage you to read history, biographies, poetry, and the classics."

"Yes, ma'am."

We returned home to find a letter in our mailbox from Dad's friend, Charles Huneke, who had left Hopewell with Joe Roberts and their families to find work on the Boulder Dam project. Knowing that we would be interested, Dad read the letter aloud. He was delighted to learn that Mr. Huneke would soon return to Hopewell.

During the final week in January, the weather forecast called for more snow. Apprehensive about a blizzard possibly closing the highway, Dad drove Mom to Richmond to stay with Uncle Harvey until she was ready to enter Grace Hospital. Dad's job necessitated his return to Bremo until notified that the baby was due.

Birthday celebrations customarily included a home-baked, multi-layered cake. However, with Mom in Richmond and Dad at work, Matt took it upon himself to bake a cake for my thirteenth birthday. He donned one of Mom's flowered aprons, rolled up his sleeves, and prepared to go to work. Bowls, pans, spoons, measuring cups, a spatula, an eggbeater, and a large knife were arranged on the counter top in the order of their pending utilization. A cookbook, conveniently propped up against the toaster, was opened to a recipe for a chocolate layer cake. The ingredients: flour, sugar, baking powder, eggs, and butter were similarly arranged. Sifting, measuring, mixing, beating, and stirring occurred at a furious rate. Simultaneously performing these operations while meticulously following the directions in the recipe was no easy chore, but Matt rose to the challenge. Periodic tasting of the batter reassured Matt that the cake was progressing nicely. Fully satisfied that the mixture was proper in every respect, he wielded a wild spatula to transfer the batter to a Pyrex pan. Within short order, he declared that the cake was ready for baking. The pan was placed into the oven and a wind-up timer was set for the precise timing. As the minutes ticked away, a delightful aroma filled the entire house. At the sound of the timer bell, Matt stood poised with a broom straw to test the consistency of the golden brown cake. Pleased with the results, he removed the pan from the oven and turned it over to deposit the cake onto a wooden cutting board. Before proceeding further he sliced

December 28, 1935

Dear Walt,
I hope this letter reaches you. After we left Hopewell in 1931, we lost track of you. We were told that you had moved to New York. Recently I returned to Hopewell for my father's funeral. I went by the post office and they were able to determine your current address. Our trip to Nevada did not go well! The truck broke down in Pueblo, Colorado. We did not have enough money to repair it so we camped out for a month and I went to work in a steel mill. Then, Joe's mother-in-law came down with pneumonia and died. We buried her in Pueblo. When we finally reached Las Vegas, there was no place for us to live so we camped out on the banks of the Colorado River. Two months later I was hired by the Six Companies as a haul truck mechanic. Joe was hired as a jackhammer operator and was badly injured two months later. He and his family had to return to Virginia to live with his folks on a farm near Roanoke. It was six months before we were provided with a house in the newly constructed Boulder City. I guess you know that they renamed the dam "Hoover Dam." FDR was here on September 30th to dedicate the dam. However there is still a lot of work to be done before it will be operational. We've saved our money and will leave here in about six months and move back to Hopewell. Best regards,

—Charles Huneke

off a small sample for tasting. Noticeably pleased, he sampled another piece . . . and then another. However, remembering how I always liked a jelly roll, he decided to transform the intended layer cake into two strawberry jelly rolls. Sliced in half, the cake was allowed to cool. Rolling the halves proved to be more difficult than expected, so any imperfections resulting from the rolling were disguised by a healthy application of strawberry jelly. Matt stood back, surveyed his masterpieces, and said: "Dick, you and Phil sit at the dining room table. I have a surprise for you!" "HAPPY BIRTHDAY, DICK!" Matt sang out as he appeared carrying the strawberry-red rolls adorned with flaming candles.

"Thanks, Matt!" I responded as I reached for a knife. The cake was delicious!

"Dick, because I baked the cake, I think it's only fair that you clean up the kitchen. Phil, you can help. I need to take a little nap."

Upon my return to the kitchen, I was appalled at the sight before me. Everything that Matt had used in making the cake was scattered in complete disarray. Flour, baking powder, sugar, egg shells, butter, and strawberry jelly were generously deposited on the stove, counter tops and linoleum floor. The cleanup task was a major undertaking. However, with Phil's help, the chore was accomplished. I truly appreciated Matt's contribution and he had indeed earned his nap.

On February 6, Uncle Harvey called Dad to suggest that he return to Richmond as Mom's delivery was near at hand. At 5:25 p.m. on February 8, 1936, Dr. H. H. Ware delivered a son to Grace and Walter Jefferies. He was named John Daniel. Aunt Mattie Daniel Jefferies was particularly pleased with the name and stated that our great-great-grandfather, John McKendree Jefferies, would "most assuredly look down and smile."

"Will we call him John?" Phil asked.

"No, son, we'll call him Jack."

"Why, Mom?"

"Because Dr. Ware said that he is a real crackerjack." Upon his arrival at home, Jack did not hesitate to make his presence known; his cries overpowered the howling of the March winds. However, once acclimated to his new surroundings, the protests diminished and he became just another member of the family.

There is an interesting legend associated with the dogwood tree. It has been said that Christ was crucified on a cross made of dogwood. The blossoms of the dogwood tree are in the shape of a cross, having two long and two short petals. In the center of the outer edge of each petal are rust-colored dots which are reminders of the nail prints. Spots of red suggest the blood of Jesus. The center of the flower is akin to the crown of thorns. All who see the blossoms will remember the Passion of Christ.

The State Flower of Virginia is the flowering dogwood.

Spring showers transformed the rural landscape into brilliant splashes of color; the blossoming of trees and wildflowers accompanied the greening of the forests. Flowering dogwood brightened the roadside, and the sweet fragrances of honeysuckle and sumac permeated the air. The coming of spring enabled Matt and me to continue to explore the vast countryside on our bicycles. One of our favorite discoveries was the Bremo mansion, home of General John Hartwell Cocke. We became acquainted with the caretaker and his daughter, Beverly, a classmate. Beverly's father told us a great deal about General Cocke. He was Fluvanna County's most prominent citizen of the nineteenth century and one of the founders of the University of Virginia. He served in the War of 1812 and attained the rank of Brigadier General. Returning to Bremo following the war, he built his mansion. It is located on a site overlooking the James River. The architecture, described as Roman Classical, was Thomas Jefferson's. Completion of the mansion was in 1820. General Cocke was a leader in the Temperance movement and actively worked for the general improvement of education. He was involved in the construction of the James River/Kanawha canal. When completed, a leisurely canal boat trip from Richmond to Bremo took twenty-one hours. Matt and I often rode to the mansion for an afternoon visit. Beverly was like a breath of fresh air. Her smile was genuine and her laughter infectious. Although exuberant and fun-loving, yet she had a serene disposition towards nature and the arts. She painted

Tradition reveals how General Cocke selected "Bremo" as a name for his home. His favorite hunting dog was named Bremo. One day while General Cocke was deer hunting on horseback, Bremo ran ahead and flushed a deer out of a thicket. Bremo pursued the deer to the brink of the bluff. To escape, the deer plunged over the edge. Both fell to their deaths. In honor of his faithful hunting dog, General Cocke named his mansion Bremo.

"BREMO," Bremo Bluff, Virginia

lovely landscapes in watercolor. She wrote poetry and quoted her poems with feeling and tenderness. She taught us to play tennis and patiently helped improve our performance. The tomboy in her challenged us to compete with her in climbing trees and swinging so high that her toes touched the leaves of the towering oak tree from which the swing was suspended. Her father sat with us under the sprawling branches of a giant mulberry tree and told us stories about General Cocke, his family, and his home. He particularly enjoyed telling us about General Robert E. Lee's friendship with General Cocke. Lee and his wife, Mary, were frequent guests of the Cockes. Fearing for Mary's safety when the Union army approached Richmond, Lee insisted that Mary accept General Cocke's invitation to stay with them in Bremo. Our afternoons with Beverly and her father were always great fun. We never tired of roaming about the grounds and exploring the interior of the beautiful mansion. One afternoon Matt brought his sketch book and made a detailed rendering of the Bremo mansion. When Mom and Dad saw his work, they asked if he might perhaps be interested in becoming an architect. Matt appreciated the compliment but assured them that his interests were still in aviation.

Across the James River from Bremo Bluff is the little town of New Canton. The only crossing between Bremo Bluff and New Canton was a C&O Railroad trestle. The closest highway bridge was at Columbia, fifteen miles east of Bremo Bluff. On a number

John H. Cocke Memorial Bridge

of occasions, Matt and I crossed the trestle to visit Aunt Dantie. She was married to Will Adams, who owned a general store in New Canton. She taught music in their home. Aunt Dantie loved to tell us of the times when, as a boy, Dad came to her former home, Clover Lea, to take violin lessons. "When you feel you would like to learn to play an instrument, let me know," she said. "You have a choice of piano, guitar, banjo, violin, or zither." Matt and I expressed an interest but felt that crossing the James on the railroad trestle was too risky to attempt on a regular basis. Although we always pressed an ear to the rail to listen for an approaching train before crossing, on several occasions we had to madly run from mid-span to avoid a deadly encounter.

It was announced that the Highway Department had awarded a contract for the construction of a highway bridge across the James between Bremo and New Canton. Construction of the *John H. Cocke Memorial Bridge* was started immediately. Matt and I saw this project as a golden opportunity to earn a little money. We visited the

Willie Daniel Hanes Adams, (1873–1967), Aunt Dantie, was Grandma Jefferies's sister.

When only a child she was thrown out of a donkey cart and broke her back. During the many months of recuperation, she discovered that reading diverted her attention from the pains she suffered. The study at Vue Monte was well supplied with a wide variety of books. She read profusely and found comfort in the written word. It was then that she thought she might want to become a writer, so she regularly contributed articles to the newspaper. Music, however, was her overriding passion. She had taken piano lessons and was told by her teacher that she had an "ear for music" and a "God-given talent." These words of praise encouraged her to become a music teacher.

site and met the project manager to ask if he had something we could do to help. He agreed to pay us a quarter for every pail of water we carried to the workers. As the month of June was exceedingly hot, the job turned out to be more than we had bargained for. Our long trek from a water truck to the crews working on the bridge deck was exhausting. After several hours of toiling, our hands were blistered and our tortured bodies bathed in sweat. Our employment was short-lived, however, as the project manager, seeing us toting pails of water the length of the bridge, declared that we were too young to be working on the site. We were paid and dismissed. When the bridge was completed and opened to traffic, Matt and I visited Aunt Dantie more often. She was an extraordinary woman who took a great deal of interest in "Walter's boys." Matt informed Aunt Dantie that he would like learn to play the banjo. I selected the piano. Thus began our biweekly visits to New Canton to take Aunt Dantie's music lessons. She was a gifted teacher who patiently encouraged us: "Now, Dick, listen carefully when you play . . . the sharp notes are raised a half-step in pitch and the flat notes are lowered a half-step, understand?"

"Yes, ma'am."

One warm, summer evening after a day of chopping the detestable Johnson grass in our lowland cornfield, Dad brought out his violin and entertained us with a few tunes he had memorized. Placing the violin back in the case, he turned to Matt and said: "Now, Matt, it's your turn. We could use a little toe-tapping banjo music to liven things up." Matt picked up his banjo and plucked the strings to render his favorite tune: "Red Sails in the Sunset." We enthusiastically applauded his accomplishment. Mom and

"The Prisoner's Song"—Although we knew this popular song as "the Prisoner's Song," it was in fact entitled "Moonlight."

Meet me tonight, lover, meet me. O meet me in the moonlight alone. I have a sad story to tell you. Must be told in the moonlight alone.

I'm going to a new jail to-morrow, and leave my poor darlin' alone. With the cold prison bars all around me, and my head on a pillow of stone.

Your father and mother don't like me, or they never would have drove me from their door. If I had my life to live over, I would never go there any more.

I wish I had never been born, or had died when I was young. I would never have saw your sweet face, or heard your lyin' tongue.

If I had a-minded my mother, I had been with her today. But I was young and foolish, and you stole my heart away.

I have three ships on the ocean, all laden with silver and gold; and before my darlin' should suffer, I'd have them all anchored and sold.

If I had the wings of an angel, across the wide sea I would fly. I would fly to the arms of my darlin' and there I would stay till I die.

I sat at the piano and played "Easter Parade," the song I had been practicing for weeks. To conclude our evening of musical entertainment, Mom softly played some of her favorite hymns. We all joined in singing "Home on the Range" and "The Prisoner's Song." The evening was one of music, fun, and laughter.

It seemed that the summer months had passed all too quickly. With school only a few weeks away, Matt and I continued to seek new experiences. One day while riding our bicycles we observed a house under construction. Curious about the structure and intrigued by the smell of freshly cut lumber, we proceeded to explore the unfinished house. Seeing us climb up to the second floor, a carpenter cautioned: "Be careful, boys! Don't want you to get hurt!"

"Yes sir!" Matt said. "We just wondered what you are doing."

"We're shingling the roof."

"Is it OK if we bring some shingles up to you?"

"OK, son, but be careful. It's a long way to the ground!"

Returning to the second floor with an armload of shingles, Matt gingerly stepped out onto a scaffold and moved towards the corner of the roof. A plank which was not secured, tipped, and Matt dropped to the ground. I ran to where he lay and asked if he was hurt. His response was that, except for the wind being knocked out of him, he was fine! However, as he started to rise from the ground, it was painfully obvious that all was not well after all—his right leg was fractured, the thigh doubled over the break. As a result of the accident, Matt spent his fifteenth birthday in the same hospital where Jack was born. I was left to care for six-month-old Jack while Mom and Dad visited Matt at Grace Hospital in Richmond.

Aunt Mattie regularly visited Matt and brought him reading material and art supplies. Phil and I accompanied Dad to Richmond on several occasions to visit the hospital. Matt was lying in bed with his leg supported by a cable, pulley, and weight apparatus, providing the required tension to realign his fractured femur. His bed was cluttered with books and drawings. A serving tray, tilted at an angle, served as an easel. A model plane hung overhead.

One night, Mom and Dad returned from Richmond around midnight. I was tending to Jack who had awakened and refused to go back to sleep. I asked about their visit with Matt.

It was during Matt's extended stay in the hospital that his talent for drawing and painting became apparent to all who viewed his work. The attention given to detail in his drawings of airplanes and automobiles was remarkable. Lying in traction, unable to turn or to leave the bed, Matt must have been very uncomfortable. He never complained. Rather, he appeared to relish the time away from school to perfect his drawings and water colors.

✳

Alice Stephania (Harvey) Sanford (1853-1936) was born and raised in Westmoreland County. Her parents, George Carmichael Harvey and Mary Susan (Cox) Harvey were natives of the Northern Neck. In 1882, Alice married George Mottrom Sanford (1858-1943). The Harveys and the Sanfords worshipped at Old Yeocomico Episcopal Church.

"After leaving the hospital and dropping Mattie off at the Old Soldiers' Home, we drove across town to your Uncle Harvey's. We had a fine dinner with Harvey, Katy, the children, and your Grandma and Grandpa. All are well and send their love to you."

Before sunrise, I was awakened by a gentle touch. "Wake up, Dick, your mother and I have to return to Richmond right away. You'll have to stay home from school and tend to Jack until we return."

"What happened, Dad? Is Matt OK?"

"Yes, Dick, Matt's fine! It's your grandmother. She is very ill."

"But you said Grandma was well yesterday."

"I did, indeed, Dick. However, she became ill shortly after we left." An hour after Mom and Dad arrived at Uncle Harvey's, Grandma died. Her final words were of the love she had for us all.

The shock of Grandma's passing was almost too much for us to bear. We were devoted to her. As far back as we could remember, Grandma's heart and arms were always open to us. She truly loved her children and grandchildren. In her presence, the world was always a better place.

Grandma was laid to rest on the grounds of Old Yeocomico Episcopal Church in Westmoreland County. Many times in the past we had attended Sunday services at Old Yeocomico with Grandma and Grandpa Sanford. Following Grandma's funeral, the entire family gathered at Uncle George Sanford's home near Hague for refreshments and remembrances. The pain of our loss eased as we acknowledged that our beloved grandmother had peacefully joined the angels.

Old Yeocomico, a brick structure constructed in the form of a cross, was built in 1706. It replaced a frame church which had stood on the site since 1655. Among its various congregations were persons associated with the founding of the Maryland and Virginia Colonies. Mary Ball, George Washington's mother, had worshipped there as a child. After the Revolution and withdrawal of the English clergy, the church was deserted for a number of years. During the War of 1812, soldiers occupied the structure and used the communion table as a chopping block and the baptismal font as a wine bowl. In 1906, on the two-hundredth anniversary of the building of Old Yeocomico, the church was restored.

Old Yeocomico Church, Westmoreland Country, Virginia

After six weeks in the hospital, Matt returned home.

Although his leg was in a cast, he refused to use crutches. Rather, he hobbled around on one foot and went about his usual activities as best he could. His return to school was postponed until after the Christmas holidays. Unable to ride his bicycle, he devoted his time to building model airplanes. Although supplied with a number of model kits during his hospital stay, he also constructed planes of his own design. Sheets of balsa wood were sliced to his requirements. Completed models were sanded and painted. Fuselage, the wings, and the tail were decorated with colorful insignias. Particular attention was given to building strength into the components to withstand crash landings. His collection of vintage model planes multiplied to where there was not enough space in our bedroom to display them. His solution to the dilemma was to hang them from the ceiling. Ultimately, there was an air armada overhead.

I arrived home one afternoon from Fluvanna County High School. Matt was helping Dad install a new battery in the Pontiac.

"Dick, I'm glad you're here. There is something I want to discuss with you before I leave for the plant."

"I'm all ears, Dad! What is it?"

"Your mother and I are seriously considering a move to Richmond."

"Why, Dad?"

"I've been offered a better paying job . . . that's one reason. Another is that we feel that you boys can receive a better education in Richmond. As a matter of fact, you and Matt would attend Thomas Jefferson High School, a new, well-staffed high school, which has far better facilities than those at Fluvanna. We spoke to some parents who have their youngsters at Thomas Jefferson and they said that the school's curriculum is far superior to those of the country schools. It's very important that you receive the best education possible! So, Dick, how would you feel about a move to Richmond?"

"Well, Dad, I can think of one thing I won't miss!"

"What's that, son?"

"Johnson grass! But seriously, Dad, I loved living in Hopewell . . . and in Niagara Falls . . . and I've enjoyed the country living here. I'm game for a return to life in a city, especially Richmond, where there is so much to see and do . . . and we'll be close to Aunt Mattie!"

"Well, then it's decided. Matt and Phil feel as you do. I will have to give VEPCO sufficient time to bring in an operating engineer to take my place."

"Who will you be working for, Dad?

"The Richmond Dairy Company. They need a combustion engineer to oversee their power plant and refrigeration equipment." Ten days later, Dad informed us that he had accepted the job in Richmond. He was to report to work on November 20. We accompanied Dad to Richmond to sign

During our trip to Bremo, Mom told us of an experience she had as a young girl in Westmoreland County. Grandma and Grandpa were waiting at the dock for her to arrive on a steamboat. She lost her balance while crossing the gangplank and fell into the river. Several young men dove into the water to rescue her. After she was delivered safely on the dock, Grandma took one look at her dripping clothes and said: *"I'm glad that you wore one of your best dresses for your dramatic performance."*

November 1936—As election day approached, President Roosevelt and his Vice President, John "Cactus Jack" Garner, campaigned vigorously for a second term. "The only sure bulwark of continuing liberty," Roosevelt proclaimed, "is a government strong enough to protect the interests of the people." Roosevelt-Garner won every state except Maine and Vermont. It was a vote of confidence in FDR's New Deal policies.

Boeing Aircraft Company successfully flew the B-17 bomber, originally designated as the YIB-17. The four engine plane weighed 21,600 pounds. With four machine gun positions it was appropriately dubbed: *The Flying Fortress*.

RMS *Queen Mary*, Britain's new passenger liner, made its maiden voyage on May 27, 1936. The crossing of the Atlantic was made in four days. The ship was 1,019 feet long and weighed 81,227 tons. The liner carried 1,957 passengers and a crew of 1,174.

WAR SERVICE

March 1940–September 1946, the *Queen Mary* served as a troop ship, carrying up to 15,000 troops at one time.

up for school and to search for a house to rent. One was found at 2014 Park Avenue. Its location would allow us to walk to school and for Dad to ride a streetcar to work.

Moving away from Bremo meant leaving behind our many friends and classmates. Beverly and her father were very sorry that we would no longer be neighbors. At our last choir rehearsal, the vicar and members of the choir surprised us with a farewell party. The most difficult part of leaving was the knowledge that Grandma and Grandpa Jefferies, Uncle George, and Aunt Dantie would no longer be close by. We promised to not allow distance to prevent us from visiting those who meant so much to us.

CHAPGER SIX

One cannot walk the streets of Richmond without being aware of the city's place in American history. The gentle rustle of the past is all too evident. Our move to Richmond enabled us to follow in the footsteps of the Colonists, the Settlers, and the Founding Fathers. Dad accompanied us to a bridge spanning the James River. From our vantage point we observed the river flowing over a rugged accumulation of fractured rocks and boulders. Dad explained that many years ago a waterfall existed at this location.

"But, Dad," Matt asked, "what happened to the waterfalls?"

"Years ago, the rock ledge was dynamited in an effort to make the river navigable. As you can see, no boat could possibly move across those rocks."

"Was Richmond located here because of the waterfalls, as was the case with Niagara Falls?"

"Indeed it was, Dick."

"What about the canal alongside the river, Dad?"

"That was George Washington's idea. He proposed a canal to bypass the falls and to link the James River with the Kanawha River in western Virginia."

"Too bad they dynamited the falls! It would have been a lot prettier than those shattered rocks."

"No doubt about it, Dick! It was a foolish idea."

Dad drove us to see the historic sites in the city. We visited St. John's Episcopal Church, where a group of patriots had

Richmond—The presence of the James River falls brought about the location of the city. Fifty miles downstream is where the English established the first colony in America. They named it *Jamestown* in honor of King James I. A party of colonists pushed up the James River to find a water route to the Indies. However, the exploration ended when they reached the falls. Realizing that navigation of the river at this point was impossible, they turned back. Later, another group of colonists built a frontier post adjacent to the falls, followed by the erection of *Fort Charles* to protect the settlers from the Indians. From this beginning the settlement grew into a major river port and ultimately, the ***city of Richmond***.

"GIVE ME LIBERTY OR GIVE ME DEATH"
—Patrick Henry

Thomas Jefferson High School, Richmond, Virginia

Thomas Jefferson High School. Opened in 1930, it displayed the highly-praised art deco style of architecture. Precast marble chip facing of the concrete structure was highly decorative. Two large podiums frame the central block, which is capped with a pyramidal tower. A quotation from Thomas Jefferson incised on one podium reads: "TO ENABLE EVERY MAN TO JUDGE FOR HIMSELF WHAT WILL SECURE HIS FREEDOM."

gathered in 1775 to discuss methods of averting war with England. It was here that Patrick Henry rose and advocated the arming of the Virginia militia to fight the British and drive them out of the colonies. He concluded his oratory with the immortal words: "Give me liberty or give me death!"

Matt and I attended Thomas Jefferson High School, a short walking distance from our home. We were both in the class of 1940. Mr. Ernest Shawen, the principal, and his assistant, Louise Weisner, administered the school with dedication and authority. Misconduct was not tolerated. Boys and girls alike conducted themselves in a friendly and courteous manner.

Selected for their expertise in teaching, the faculty was extraordinary. We were soon immersed in our studies. Classes, special programs in the great auditorium, and extracurricular activities consumed our hours at school. Weekends and holidays allowed us to visit Richmond's historic sites. One of our favorite places was the Virginia State Capitol. Located atop a hill overlooking the James River, the capitol is an imposing structure. In 1785, Thomas Jefferson was asked to aid the director of public buildings in selecting the most appropriate design for the capitol building. Jefferson, who, at the time, was minister to France, chose to model the capitol after a Roman temple in Nimes, France. The cornerstone was laid in 1785. The

Virginia State Capitol

Beneath the Rotunda is a life-size statue of George Washington, which was executed from life by the famous sculptor, Jean A. Houdon. Another of Houdon's originals in the capitol is a marble bust of the Marquis de Lafayette. In the House Chamber is a bronze likeness of General Robert E. Lee standing where he stood when he accepted command of the Confederate Army in 1861.

Capitol is a magnificent monument to Virginia's past and present.

One morning I awoke before sunrise and listened to the sounds of the city as it gradually stirred to life. From afar, the chugging of steam locomotives and the clamor of shunting rail cars in the switching yards disturbed the early morning silence. Train and factory whistles contributed to the cacophony. I heard the approach of a horse-drawn milk wagon moving from house to house and the tinkling of glass bottles being carried and deposited on the doorsteps. I knew it was five o'clock when Mom and Dad's "Little Ben" alarm clock sounded, followed by their whispered voices as they rose to face another day. The aroma of percolating coffee and frying bacon and eggs wafted into the room. I hastily dressed and went downstairs to spend a few moments with Dad before he left for work.

"What are you doing up so early, Dick?" Dad asked as Mom refilled his coffee cup.

"I heard the milkman. It reminded me of something I've wanted to ask."

"What's on your mind?"

"Well, Dad, Matt and I would like to visit the dairy and see how milk is processed. We've heard you talk about the bottle washers and the refrigeration equipment, but we would like to see the entire process from receiving of the raw milk to the bottling."

"Good idea, son! We'll tour the facility on Saturday."

Located one block off Broad Street, Richmond's principal commercial street, the Richmond Dairy occupied an entire city block. The four-story brick structure, built in 1900, was architecturally unique. Flanking the main entrance were two fifty-foot replicas of a milk bottle, one on each corner. Painted milk white, the soaring masonry structures were an imposing sight. Upon entering a white-tiled lobby, Dad introduced us to the receptionist who was seated at a cream-colored desk, and a cashier who was positioned behind a brass-barred window. Both ladies were very cordial and promised a frozen treat for us after the tour.

We followed Dad to the receiving dock where cans of raw milk were unloaded from trucks and farm wagons. It was fascinating to observe the dock man's skill at manhandling the heavy cans across the dock and onto a conveyor for transport into the building. Dad methodically explained every step in the automated system: pasteurization, homogenization, filling and capping, and finally, conveyance of the filled bottles to the loading dock.

Another room contained two enormous, bottle washers. Rows of empty bottles mounted on a revolving drum were

Boulder Dam (Hoover Dam)
The Colorado River project was completed after twenty-one months of construction. When filled, Lake Mead would be 115 miles long and would provide irrigation for 25,000 acres of farmland.

Richmond Dairy introduced a new method of capping milk bottles. An automated machine placed a stopper into the mouth of the bottle. A paper cover was then crimped around the neck of the bottle. Finally, the paper cover was wired into place. The new capping was well received by consumers. *On very cold mornings, no longer will the paper stopper stand an inch higher than the bottle.* The cap on the 55-foot-tall replicas of a milk bottle is of the innovative design.

Richmond Dairy Company

sprayed with steaming, high-pressure water. Workers loaded the bottles on one side of the machine and unloaded them on the opposite side. The rattle of bottles and the sounds of the steam and water jets were deafening.

"Of all the machinery in the dairy, these are the most troublesome," Dad said. "Sometimes, bottles shatter and the broken glass drops into the chains and sprockets, interrupting the machine's rotation. Management has given some thought to throwaway packaging, but customers want to receive their milk in glass bottles."

Our tour concluded with a visit to the ice cream department. The manager explained the process from the initial mixing of the ingredients to the final freezing and packaging of the ice cream.

"From the looks of it," Matt said, "you make more vanilla than any other flavor."

"That's right. About half of our production is vanilla, or plain, as people like to call it. We have a saying in the industry that if you can make good quality vanilla ice cream, you can make any flavor taste good!"

"How do you know when the ice cream is considered good?"

"We employ tasters. We have three and all they do all day long is taste ice cream."

"Sounds like the kind of job I'd like," Matt commented. We returned to the lobby where we were again greeted by the two ladies. "Now," the receptionist said, "I promised you a frozen treat. Go to the freezer against the wall and choose whatever Popsicle you wish."

Richmond continued to offer unlimited opportunities for us to experience the pulse of a gracious southern city. Rich in historic landmarks, spacious parks, tree-lined streets, recreational facilities, and cultural centers, the city was vibrant and exciting. Everything was

On January 20, 1937, President Roosevelt was inaugurated for a second term. Although the focus of his administration was a continuation of his New Deal measures to return America to a strong economy, he had grave concerns about developments abroad. Germany was bombing Spain in support of General Franco. Japan was continuing its aggression against China. There was every indication that Germany and Japan were becoming militarily strong and a collective threat to world peace. Roosevelt urged Congress to support his recommendations for strengthening America's armed forces. However, Congress and Americans were more concerned about jobs and a return to prosperity. After all, many reasoned, Asia and Europe were oceans away and there was no threat to the United States of America.

readily accessible, with many attractions located within walking distance of our home. More distant places were reached by biking or riding the streetcars. Dad, of course, derived great pleasure in driving us to special events, to visit relatives, or to venture beyond the city limits.

On November 11, 1937, we attended a colorful Armistice Day celebration. The parade route terminated at Richmond's War Memorial, a carillon tower dedicated to those Virginians who died in the Great War. Bells atop the soaring structure attracted a crowd of thousands. Following patriotic speeches from a flag-draped platform, a volley of rifle shots and the sounding of taps signaled the conclusion of the solemn ceremonies. We departed the memorial in silence.

"Matt, you and Dick are unusually quiet. Is something troubling you?"

"We were just remembering what the general said at the War Memorial. He said that the soldiers who died in the Great War may have died in vain. Is there going to be another war, Dad?"

"We pray not, son. However, he warned that something must be done to stop Germany and Japan's aggression. He urged all Americans to write to their congressmen and insist that we rebuild our armed forces. He stressed that America must be better prepared . . . and he's right!"

Again we were reminded that we were growing up in troubling times. Still struggling from the Depression, Americans were in no mood for our nation to get involved in foreign aggressions.

Matt and I discussed what might lay ahead for us in the

Join the National Guard

−NOW−

and help prepare our Country
for adequate defense

Daddy Fought For Me
I'll Fight For Him!

On July 7, 1937, the Japanese forces continued their aggression against China. In a span of only four months, Peking, Tientsin, Shanghai, and Nanking were bombed and occupied. The death toll of innocent citizens was staggering. In Nanking alone, 200,000 civilians were executed. Although world opinion condemned the aggression, no country came to China's aid. America continued to sell scrap iron and war materials to Japan for fear that if we cut off trade, it would have been considered an "unfriendly act."

future and agreed that we would willingly serve our country should the need arise.

"Two years from now," Matt said, "I'll be eighteen and old enough to join the National Guard."

"That's right, Matt, but I thought you wanted to be a pilot."

"I do, but experience in the Guard may make it easier to qualify for the Air Corps later on."

Overhearing our conversation, Dad looked up from his paper and saw apprehension etched on Mom's countenance. Her hands trembled as she filled his coffee cup.

"Enough of that talk for now, boys. I have a surprise for you. Your mother and I have decided to trade in the Pontiac on a new '37 Dodge sedan! It will be ready for us tomorrow morning."

Early Saturday morning, we accompanied Dad to the Dodge agency. A salesman enthusiastically greeted Dad by name and led us to our new car. Dad exchanged the Pontiac keys for those of the Dodge and we eagerly climbed into the shiny, new vehicle. It was sad to part with the '31 Pontiac but the thrill of riding in the new Dodge overshadowed our nostalgia.

"Where are we going, Dad?"

"To Westover—William Byrd's home. I thought you'd like to see where the founder of Richmond lived. The old Colonial mansion, built in 1730, has been restored and is open to the public."

In a setting of towering trees and spacious green lawns, Westover fronts on the James River. The grounds are

William Byrd's coat of arms. The Latin motto means, "No guilt to make one pale."

William Byrd—Born in Virginia and educated in England, William Byrd served in Virginia's House of Burgesses in Williamsburg. In 1737, he laid out, on his own lands, the town of Richmond. He recorded in his personal diaries a vivid description of life in Colonial Virginia. William Byrd was highly respected and devoted his life to serving his beloved state of Virginia.

April 5, 1709, William Byrd recorded in his diary: "The brick maker came this evening." In another entry dated June 3, 1712, he wrote: "The stonecutter came from Williamsburg to put up my marble chimney piece."

entered through a pair of ornamental, wrought-iron gates. William Byrd's cipher is contained in the scrollwork on the gate head. As we toured the beautiful mansion, Dad pointed out many of the unique architectural features: the Flemish bond brickwork of the exterior walls, the masterly carvings of the doors and arched window frames, and the hipped roof with seven dormers. The roof slate was imported from Wales and the bricks were fired in a kiln on the site.

Matt methodically made a detailed drawing of the Byrd family coat of arms embodied on the ornamental gates.

While returning home, Dad spoke of the effect technology was having on the world we live in. A good example, he said, was William Byrd's home.

"Beautiful as it was when Byrd resided there, it lacked amenities that we now take for granted. It had no electricity or running water. Fireplaces were the only source of heat; water was supplied from a well, and there was no inside toilet. The horse provided transportation. Contrast all that, with what we now have to make our lives easier, and we will surely appreciate what technology has given us . . . cars, airplanes, trains, electricity, refrigeration, radio, and the telephone."

Douglas DC-3 at Richmond's Byrd Field

The Douglas DC–3, powered with two radial engines and having a wing span of 95 feet, cruised at 155 miles per hour and had a range of 1,300 miles. The plane revolutionized the commercial aircraft industry. During World War II, thousands of the C–47 military version of the DC–3 served the armed forces throughout the world. The GI's affectionately called the plane the "Gooney Bird."

The *Graf Zeppelin* retired after 144 Atlantic crossings. It flew more than a million miles making 590 trips to London, Cairo, Helsinki, Rome, Rio, Tokyo, and around the world.
The *Graf Zeppelin* carried a total of 16,000 passengers, all without accident or injury to crew or passengers.

Amelia Earhart—July 2, 1937—On a trans-world flight with her navigator, Fred Noonan, Amelia Earhart vanished near Howland Island in the Pacific Ocean. No trace of the plane has ever been found. She was an aviation pioneer, courageous, imaginative, talented, and daring.

"Or replacing the horse-drawn milk wagons with trucks," Phil said.

"And steam locomotives with diesel engines," I added.

"In some cities, busses are replacing streetcars," Dad said.

"And airplanes are being made larger and faster."

"Quite right, Matt. By the way, I read in today's paper that the new DC-3 airplane is now flying into Byrd Field. The plane carries twenty-one passengers and can fly close to 200 miles an hour!"

"And it has a maximum payload of 9,000 pounds!" Matt added.

"I see you've done your homework on the DC-3, Matt. Eventually there will be even larger planes capable of flying nonstop coast-to-coast."

"Douglas Aircraft, Dad, is now designing a four-engine plane to be called a DC-4. It is expected to carry forty-two passengers," Matt added.

Later that night Matt and I lay in bed and continued to speculate on what technology would make possible in the future. We wondered if the space travel depicted in the "Flash Gordon" and "Buck Rogers" cartoon strips would some day become a reality. We wondered if the cars of the future would have automatic transmissions, tubeless tires, power brakes and interior air conditioning. Our bedtime discussion concluded with a decision to bike to Byrd Field to see a DC-3 land and take off.

A few weeks later we had an unexpected guest. Uncle George had completed his tour of duty with the CCC and was seeking work in Richmond. He asked to stay with us until he could rent a room elsewhere. I shared a bed with Matt, and Uncle George slept in my bed. It was great fun to listen to his tales of life in the CCC. When we told him of our plans to ride out to Byrd Field to see a DC-3, he talked at length about the exciting future of aviation: "Wouldn't surprise me," he said, "if someday they build planes to carry hundreds of people and tons of cargo."

On a clear December morning, Matt and I cycled to Byrd Field. Shortly after our arrival, a DC-3 landed and taxied to the terminal. The roar of the engines and the sound of the props thrilled us beyond description. We stood at the boarding gate and watched the passengers emerge from the cabin. The pilot, copilot, and a beautiful stewardess were the last to leave. They stood in the doorway and waved to the crowd. We remained at the gate long enough to see passengers and the crew board the plane. Many waved from the windows as the engines were started and the plane moved across the tarmac towards the runway. Watching the DC-3 take off into the wide, blue sky was a sight we would always fondly remember.

"Well, boys, what do you think of the DC-3?" an airline agent asked.

"It's a great plane!" Matt replied. "Someday I will become a pilot."

"You sound like a determined young man! While you boys are here, would you like to see an unusual aircraft . . . something quite unlike the DC-3?"

"Yes sir!"

"On the other side of the hangar is an odd looking plane called an 'autogiro.' Some jokingly call it a 'flying windmill.' The autogiro was invented in Spain. However, this one is a Pitcairn and was built in America. It has no conventional wings. Rather, the plane is supported in the air by a rotating, three-bladed rotor mounted on a shaft above the fuselage. The rotor spins by itself as it passes through the air. Forward motion is accomplished by an engine-driven propeller. One amazing thing about the craft is that it can descend almost straight down and land in a small space."

Autogiro

Thomas Edison once stated that the airplane wouldn't amount to much until someone developed "a machine that could act like a hummingbird."

※

The autogiro perfected by Stephen Pitcairn could land and take off in very short distances. Pitcairn autogiros were flown by several famous aviators, including Amelia Earhart. The U.S. Postal service used the plane to deliver mail directly to the roofs of the main post offices.

※

"The bumble bee should not be able to fly but the bumble bee does not know it, so it flies anyway."
—Albert Einstein

"How fast can the autogiro fly?" Matt asked.

"It's been clocked at a maximum of 120 miles an hour."

We crossed to where the autogiro was parked on the tarmac. It was indeed a strange-looking aircraft. As we examined the plane, a man in soiled, white coveralls approached. He was carrying a machine part in one hand and a tool box in the other. Smiling broadly, he greeted us with a cheerful "hello!"

"Hi!" we responded. "Are you working on the autogiro?" Matt asked.

"Yep! The pilot was en route to Washington but had to land here because of a cracked manifold. Fortunately, I was able to obtain a replacement."

"When can we see it fly?"

"The pilot plans on taking off early tomorrow morning if the weather is good. Should be around eight o'clock. You coming back?"

"We'll be here . . . you can count on it!"

We were up at the crack of dawn to return to Byrd Field. The weather was cool and the sky was clear, ideal for the autogiro to take to the air, we concluded as we approached the airport.

"There she is!" Matt exclaimed. "The autogiro is still parked in the same place. Look, there's the pilot with the mechanic." We stood alongside the fence and watched the two men as they circled the autogiro and checked to see that it was ready to fly. Then the pilot climbed into the cockpit, waved to us, and called to the mechanic to spin the prop. After a few spins, the engine came to life, and the plane taxied across the tarmac. The pilot paused for a few minutes at the end of the runway and then opened the throttle. The aircraft quickly gained speed causing the three-bladed rotor to begin turning. Magically, the autogiro lifted off the runway and quickly gained altitude. As it turned to fly toward Washington, the rays of the rising sun reflected off the spinning rotor blades in a brilliant display of flashing light.

That evening at the supper table, we told Uncle George about our visit to the airport. He listened attentively and said: "It'll be interesting to see what the future holds for this type of aircraft. I imagine that it will evolve into an aircraft with vertical takeoff capabilities. I have no doubt that we will also see the development of larger and faster planes. Wouldn't surprise me if someday planes will exceed the speed of sound. Ultimately this could lead to travel into outer space."

"Like Buck Rogers and Flash Gordon, Uncle George?"

"Yes, and just as illustrated in the comic strips, propulsion will be by rocket power."

General Motors introduced an automatic transmission in their 1938 Oldsmobiles. Under the name *Hydramatic Drive*, the long-awaited feature was widely acclaimed by owners.

Kate Smith, popular radio singer, asked song writer Irving Berlin to compose a patriotic song to "sort of wake up America!" Berlin obliged with "God Bless America."

Aviator V.P. Chkalov of the Soviet Union flew nonstop over the North Pole. His route from Moscow to Vancouver covered 5,400 miles.

Helicopter—The first practical and fully successful helicopter was built by Igor I. Sikorsky, a Russian engineer who had come to America in 1919 after the Communist revolution. The single-rotor helicopter lifted off the ground in 1940.

1939-40 New York World's Fair held in Flushing Meadow Park in Queens, New York. Its theme, "World of Tomorrow," attracted millions of visitors. New inventions exhibited included television, air conditioning, and nylon

"Why rockets, Uncle George? Won't airplanes be able to fly into outer space?"

"No, Phil. You see, an airplane must have air flowing over the wings to allow it to fly. In outer space there is no air. Rockets do not need air to push against . . . they will fly where there is no air."

"We learned that in our science class," Matt said. "An Englishman named Sir Isaac Newton stated that for every action, there is an equal and opposite reaction. So, in the performance of a rocket, the flow of gasses from the nozzle is the action, and the reaction is the continuous thrust of the rocket pushing against the exhaust gases."

"That's right, Matt. Newton's law makes it clear that rockets can travel in outer space."

In August 1938, we moved to 3207 Hanover Avenue. Uncle George landed a good paying job at DuPont's new cellophane plant in Richmond. He found living quarters close to the DuPont plant. He also announced that he was planning marriage. We were sorry to see him leave but were pleased that he was finally getting settled. Needless to say, Matt and I were happy to once again sleep in our own separate beds! We attended St. Mark's Episcopal Church as a family. Matt and I became members of the Young People's Service League. Actively supported by the clergy, the Y. P. S. L. participated in many of the church's activities. On Christmas Eve, a candlelight service was conducted entirely by our Y. P. S. L. members. Unfortunately, the candles we purchased dripped. The pastor, Reverend Henry Lane, was not at all pleased with the mess we had made and insisted that we return the day after Christmas to remove the wax drippings from the tiles.

March 1938—Hitler moved to annex Austria whose people were ethnic Germans. The so-called annexation was a start of his plan to *"protect the millions of Germans who live outside of Germany."* Two weeks later, Hitler turned his attention to annexing Czechoslovakia. Britain's Prime Minister Neville Chamberlain made three trips to Munich to protest the annexation. Hitler agreed to cease further expansion on the condition that Germany be allowed to take over a third of Czechoslovakia. Chamberlain returned to London and in a speech declared: *"I believe it is peace for our time . . . peace with honor!"*

March 1938—Hitler moved to annex Austria whose people were ethnic Germans. The so-called annexation was a start of his plan to "protect the millions of Germans who live outside of Germany." Two weeks later, Hitler turned his attention to annexing Czechoslovakia. Britain's Prime Minister Neville Chamberlain made three trips to Munich to protest the annexation. Hitler agreed to cease further expansion on the condition that Germany be allowed to take over a third of Czechoslovakia. Chamberlain returned to London and in a speech declared: "I believe it is peace for our time . . . peace with honor!"

In September 1938, Matt and I started our junior year at Thomas Jefferson High School. The curriculum offered a wide variety of elective courses. Matt enrolled in an art class and soon showed great promise as an artist. In a class contest he won the first place ribbon for a watercolor of Richmond Dairy's first delivery truck. Having given some thought to a career in engineering, I favored the science and math courses. Phil was enrolled at Binford Junior High School and, like his brother, excelled in art. I took a part-time job delivering groceries for the Black & White Food Store on Cary Street. Matt was hired by our Richmond Dairy milkman to help in the delivery of milk from a horse-drawn wagon. The compensation for his labor was fifty cents an hour and a quart of milk. Phil sold *Liberty* magazines door-to-door. Matt and his friends,

Left to Right: John Martin, Eddie Galeski, Abe Hertzberg, Matt Jefferies, Neil November, and Neil's cousin.

Neil November graduated from Thomas Jefferson High School in 1938. He took flying lessons at Richmond's Hermitage Airport. He was a naval officer in World War II. Following graduation from Washington & Lee University, Neil joined his family's clothing business. He continued to pursue aviation as a hobby. Planes he flew were: Rearwin Skyranger, Bellanca Cruisair, Piper Tri-Pacer, Piper Twin Comanche, and the Stearman PT–17. In 1987, Neil co-founded the Virginia Aviation Museum.

※

Matt, Neil November, Eddie Galeski, and John Martin were members of the *Richmond Model Airplane Club*, sponsored by the Richmond News Leader. Club meetings were held in the offices of the newspaper.

※

John Martin earned his BS degree in mechanical engineering at Virginia Tech. During WW II he served as a maintenance officer in a B-17 heavy bomber squadron at Fogia, Italy.

※

Following the war, John was employed by the Glen L. Martin Co. as an aero performance engineer.

※

Eddi Galeski earned his degree in aero engineering at MIT.

Matt—Richmond Dairy Painting

Eddie Galeski and Neil November, went into business selling model airplane kits to neighborhood model builders. They set up their retail store in Galeski's garage. Eddie's father owned the Galeski Optical Company.

One evening I arrived home to find L. B. Cottingham, our cousin, having a serious conversation with Mom and Dad. He was deeply concerned about the threat of war in Europe and the real possibility that America would be drawn into the conflict. I listened attentively to all that he said. It was in Matt's and my best interest, he said, to enlist in the Virginia National Guard. He had been in the Guard for a year and had recently attained the rank of corporal in Headquarters Company, First Infantry Regiment of the Twenty-ninth Division. He had only to report for training at the Grays Armory in Richmond once a month and to go on field maneuvers for a couple of weeks in the summer. The commander of Headquarters Company was Colonel John F. Bright, who was also the mayor of Richmond.

L.B. said that he knew Colonel Bright personally and could arrange for us to enlist even though we were underage.

Twenty-ninth Division—Formed in 1917 from National Guard units of Virginia, Maryland, New Jersey and the District of Columbia, the Twenty-ninth Division was considered the best trained division in the country. Elements of one Virginia Brigade could trace its origin to the French and Indian Wars with George Washington as its commander. The 1st Infantry Regiment's Coat of Arms illustrates the history of the unit. *The shield is blue for Infantry. The gray saltire commemorates service in the Confederate States Army during the War Between the States. The fleur-de-lis symbolizes the service in France during the Great War. The red cross represents Revolutionary War service and the arrow the French and Indian service.*

"Matt will be eighteen in August," Mom said. "I agree that it is a good idea for him to join the Guard at that time. Dick is only sixteen, so he'll have to wait for a couple of years."

"I disagree with you, Aunt Grace! There is no time for waiting! Hitler is moving too fast! He is determined to occupy all of Europe and then fight for control of the entire world. America is at great risk! We must be prepared. That's the Guard's purpose . . . to be prepared!"

"L.B., we appreciate your concern, but I have to agree with Grace," Dad said. "It is not a good idea for these boys to lie about their ages. When they are eighteen, I certainly agree that service in the National Guard will prepare them for regular army duty should it eventually come to that."

"I'm sorry to say this, Uncle Walter, but I think you are wrong in postponing their enlistment! I suggest you rethink the matter and realize that their future survival may be at stake."

On June 14, 1939, Matt and I accompanied L.B. and his younger brother, George, to Grays Armory at 7th and Marshall Streets. We enlisted for a three-year tour of duty in Colonel Bright's Headquarters Company. We were briefly lectured on the training requirements, issued summer khaki uniforms, and instructed on the basics of close order drill. Our company commander, Lieutenant Charles Southward, informed us of the history of the 1st Infantry Regiment. "You will indeed be proud," he said, "to serve in such a distinguished infantry regiment."

"Well, boys, what do you think of the Guard?" L.B. asked.

"So far, so good," Matt responded, "but it's pretty obvious that the National Guard is poorly equipped!"

"How do you mean, Matt?"

"The uniforms are left over from the Great War and the rifles are the old, bolt-action, single-shot, 1917 Springfields."

"That's quite right, Matt, but hopefully we'll be issued the new Garand M-1 semiautomatic rifles next year. The Regular Army has to be supplied first."

The first time Mom saw us in uniform, her countenance mirrored the fear she harbored for her sons' future. However, she bravely endeavored to conceal her anxiety and told us that we were quite handsome and soldierly. Dad, on the other hand, was noncommittal, but inwardly proud and relieved that we were in the National Guard. Both realized that our military training would prove to be invaluable should we be called to active duty. No further mention was made of our being underage. In regularly scheduled drills, we were instructed in communications, map reading, execution of field orders, first aid, and close order drill. After preliminary instruction in the care and operation of the Springfield rifle and the Colt 45 sidearm, we were issued a limited supply of ammunition for target practice in the armory's firing range.

One evening, Lt. Southward read an order from Brigadier General Waller, Virginia's Adjutant General. It ordered an increase in the frequency of drills and announced that Third Corps field maneuvers would be held at Manassas, Virginia, from the 5th to the 19th of August. The Twenty-ninth Division and Pennsylvania's Twenty-eighth Division would stage a mock battle with a Regular Army division. Developments in Europe, General Waller stated, prompted those in command to evaluate America's fighting capability and to take whatever steps were necessary to strengthen the armed forces.

One evening after listening to President Roosevelt's Fireside Chat on the radio, Matt asked Dad why Lindbergh supported America's neutrality.

"Lindbergh is considered a top authority on aviation. He recently accepted Hitler's invitation to visit Germany and inspect their *Luftwaffe* air forces. He returned with the conviction

Ignoring the agreement he had signed with Britain and France, Adolf Hitler occupied all of Czechoslovakia. His ally, Benito Mussolini, fascist dictator of Italy, invaded Albania in the Balkans. Together they planned to continue the domination of all of Europe and the world. These disturbing developments in Europe prompted concerned Americans to reconsider the nation's isolationist position. Congress had not supported Roosevelt's determination to modernize the armed forces. The country was divided on the issue of neutrality. One side, supported by Charles Lindbergh, insisted that America remain neutral. The other side supported Roosevelt's urgent call for preparedness. Heated debates in Congress failed to change anything.

1862—In the Second Battle of Manassas General Longstreet's Confederate Army assailed General Pope's Army of the Potomac. The casualties in the two-day battle were horrendous with Pope losing 14,462 men and Lee's forces 9,474.

A number of countries sent high ranking officers to observe the maneuvers. Germany sent Gen. Friedrich von Boetticher. Major General Yamauti was sent by Japan. Having these potential enemy officers present to witness our inferior armament and fighting capability was to us foolish and unwarranted. We could well imagine what they reported to their superiors.

that Germany's military might is capable of defeating any forces allied against them. He insists that America remain neutral and allow the European nations to settle their own differences."

"Well, Dad, maybe something worthwhile will come out of the Manassas maneuvers our National Guard Division is participating in next week. Two weeks of field maneuvers against a Regular Army Division will quickly reveal our military strengths and weaknesses. The mock battles, we are told, will include tanks, field artillery pieces and strafing aircraft. News reporters and foreign observers have been invited to witness the action."

On Saturday at 5:00 a.m., the First Infantry Division assembled on the street in front of Grays Armory. Two convoys, each consisting of seventeen trucks, were lined up awaiting the boarding signal. At precisely 6:30 a.m., the first convoy departed, followed five minutes later by the second. In all, 170 motor vehicles in twenty-one different convoys from throughout Virginia were headed towards the staging area near Manassas.

We arrived and made camp in the vicinity of Gainesville, which is west of Manassas. Matt and I shared a pup tent. The weather was very hot and dry. An impressive 23,000 troops were involved in the field maneuvers. The next day we were engaged in a battle with a Regular Army Division. The opposing force was far better trained and equipped than our First Infantry Regiment. Our line was overrun by tanks and strafed by low-flying aircraft. However, our officers said that we performed quite well under the circumstances. Our Headquarters Company was cited for maintaining communications throughout the action. Two

Artist—Gerry Asher, Fort Worth, TX

gerald asher ©2006

weeks of extensive field exercises, marching, digging foxholes, dodging tanks, eating field rations, and sleeping under the stars, significantly altered our appearance. We were deeply tanned. Our khaki uniforms were soiled and tattered, our boots and leggings mud-caked, scarred, and worn. Daytime temperatures throughout the entire maneuvers were sizzling hot. Not a drop of rain had fallen. The grounds of our camp were pulverized. On the eve of our departure, dark storm clouds blanketed the countryside. A torrential rain, accompanied by violent winds, assailed our campsite. Few tents remained standing. The campground was transformed into a quagmire. We struggled through the night to break camp and load the trucks and trailers with mud-soaked gear and supplies. The trucks, deep in mud, had to be winched to solid ground. It was noon the next day before our convoy was formed and given the signal to get underway.

Except for the monotonous drone of the trucks, silence prevailed; absent was the usual banter and singing. The bone-weary troops of the Twenty-ninth Division, who had so valiantly battled the Regular Army and remained in high spirits, were soundly defeated by Mother Nature. It was well past midnight when we finally reached Gray's Armory in Richmond. We dismounted and formed ranks under the glare of the street lights. Those who were there to meet us hurried along the troop formations in search of friends or loved ones assembled under their company standards. Dad appeared out of the shadows and approached our position. He stopped short of our ranks and waited for our dismissal.

"Headquarters Company all present and accounted for, sir!" barked Sergeant Norman.

"Dismiss the company, Sergeant!"

"Yes sir! COMPANY DISMISSED!"

Dad's smiling face mirrored the pride he felt for his soldiering sons. "Good gracious! You two look like you have just emerged from the trenches!"

"That's about right, Dad! We wallowed in mud getting out of the campsite."

Dad chuckled and said: "Looks like you brought back most of Gainesville's soil. The farmers up there may not have enough left for spring planting!"

Home never looked so good! Mom embraced us and wept with joy. Wiping her eyes with her apron, she said: "Now, you two get out of those muddy uniforms and take a good hot bath. I've cooked up something special for you to eat before you retire. My goodness, you look like a couple of scarecrows!"

A week later, L. B. dropped by the house to accompany us to the armory. He and Dad briefly discussed the probability of Poland being invaded by Hitler. "Let's be realistic," L. B. said. "Hitler doesn't think for a minute that Britain or France will go to war to defend Poland. Militarily, both countries are pitifully weak."

"That's where Hitler is wrong," Dad said. "Britain will surely go to war to defend Poland . . . and France will do likewise. Any further expansion of Germany will ultimately threaten all of Europe."

Adolf Hitler's armies occupied Bohemia and Moravia. It was generally agreed that Hitler's next target would be Poland. Britain and France finally took a stand and promised to defend Poland against any attack. The two Allies asked Russia to join them but Joseph Stalin refused and signed a nonaggression pact with Germany on August 23, 1939.

"You're quite right, Uncle Walter. We'll know any day now what Hitler will do to trigger another war. Then, America will have no choice but to join the Allied nations."

"God forbid!" Mom exclaimed.

On September 1, 1939, the world learned that Germany had bombed and invaded Poland. Two days later, Britain and France declared war on Germany. Bold headlines around the world screamed the news: THE WORLD IS AT WAR! WORLD WAR II!

"Well, Grace, our worst fears have come to pass. The war in Europe will be a global one. The occupation of France and Great Britain will be next on Hitler's agenda."

"Walter, how can Hitler be stopped?"

"I'm not sure that he can! His army and air force are too well-equipped."

"Dad, isn't that what Lindbergh has been trying to say?"

"That's right, Matt. Lindbergh has been to Germany and seen Germany's military might firsthand. The occupation of Poland should serve as a wake-up call for those politicians who have resisted modernizing our armed forces. You and Dick have witnessed firsthand in the Manassas maneuvers how poorly equipped our armed forces are."

Mom and Dad impressed upon us the importance of our completing our education before giving serious thought to our roles in the military. It was good, they said, that we were in the Guard and getting valuable training which could greatly benefit us should we be called into active duty.

Aside from concern about employment, the cost of living, and retirement benefits, Americans were deeply worried about our country being drawn into the European conflict.

Poland—Utilizing their new concept in warfare called *blitzkrieg*, or "lightning war," Germany attacked Poland on land and from the air. Over 1,500 planes, including the Stuka dive bomber, rained terror over the defenseless country. To share in the occupation of Poland, Soviet troops invaded from the east. Polish forces made a gallant effort to resist but were quickly defeated. Warsaw surrendered to the Germans on September 27. On September 28, Poland was partitioned between Germany and the USSR.

A nonintervention movement was spearheaded by Lindbergh and former president Hoover. On September 17, Lindbergh made a radio speech urging America to remain neutral. He suggested that Stalin was as much a threat to the world as Hitler.

On November 30, 1939, the Soviet Union, seeking to expand its northern border, invaded Finland. The Finns fought gallantly but were finally compelled to cede strategic territories to the Russians.

On January 30, 1940, the first Social Security checks were mailed to pensioners. President Roosevelt in one of his Fireside Chats reiterated his pride in having Social Security finally become a reality. The first check, for $22.54, was presented to a Vermont widow.

Matt, Eddie, and Neil were expanding their model airplane business. Planes powered by rubber bands were made obsolete with the introduction of a miniature, single cylinder, two-cycle, gasoline engine. When brought to life, the little engine could be heard a block away from the Galeski garage. Neighbors complained, but to no avail. Matt and his friends were too busy selling the gas engines to be concerned about a little noise. A group of angry neighbors filed a lawsuit to stop the racket. After hearing their complaint, the presiding judge said: "These three boys are to be commended for their entrepreneurship. They are working—not stealing hub caps or breaking out windows. They are well within the law in the operation of their business. Case dismissed!"

We were saddened to hear that Uncle Travis had died. He was a good man. His carpentry work was appreciated by many in Cumberland County. When there was no work, he sold the boxwood shrubs which had graced the grounds of Vue Monte for decades. When there was no boxwood, he sold the furnishings from the antebellum house to buy his jugs of moonshine. We loved him for what he was . . . a good man! We would miss our Uncle Travis.

Following the declaration of war on Germany, Britain sent a large expeditionary force to France to bolster their defense against invasion.

However, Germany's superior forces crushed all who resisted their Blitzkrieg attacks. In rapid order, France, the Netherlands, Luxembourg, Denmark, Norway, and Romania fell to the Nazi onslaught. Only Britain and Russia stood in the path of Hitler's attempt at world domination. On May 7, Winston Churchill succeeded Neville Chamberlain as Britain's Prime Minister. In an electrifying speech to the House of Commons he declared: "I have nothing to offer but blood, toil, tears, and sweat! Victory at all costs . . . !"

America remained neutral, but a day of reckoning was imminent. To be prepared militarily, Roosevelt called for the production of fifty thousand warplanes a year and the appropriation of billions of dollars to modernize the armed forces. Congress supported his budget requests.

In France, the Allied armies of France and Britain were forced to retreat to the shores of the English Channel. Two-hundred thousand British and one-hundred and forty thousand French troops were evacuated from Dunkirk. Thirty-thousand were killed or taken prisoner. On June 10, Italy declared war on France and Britain. On June 22, France signed an armistice with Hitler and on June 24, with Italy's Mussolini. Hitler's *Luftwaffe* launched massive air attacks on Britain.

Following graduation from Thomas Jefferson High School, Matt and I discussed our future plans. He was determined to request a transfer from the National Guard to the Air Corps following summer maneuvers. I had decided to study engineering at Virginia Polytechnic Institute in Blacksburg which necessitated my resignation from the National Guard and enlistment in the college's Reserve Officers Training Corps.

Our National Guard drills were increased to twice a week. The antiquated Springfield was replaced with the new Garand M1, semiautomatic rifle. We were issued new uniforms which included the newly designed canvas leggings. We were informed that in August, the Twenty-ninth Division would travel by train to Ogdensburg, New York, to participate in two weeks of intensive maneuvers. President Roosevelt was scheduled to review the troops in the field following the conclusion of the military exercises. Matt and I were excited about the maneuvers and eager to go.

During the summer months Matt was employed by a clothing shop as an assistant to the advertising manager. His job entailed the design of graphic art for newspaper advertisements, window display designs, and freehand lettering of signs and price tags. I worked as a counter clerk for the Black & White Food Store. Phil continued in his sales of *Liberty* magazines.

Prior to our departure for the New York maneuvers, we were issued two pairs of woolen uniforms, a woolen overcoat, and two woolen blankets. As opposed to Richmond's summer heat, temperatures in upper New York could be "chilly to downright cold," we were told.

On August 5, the Twenty-ninth Division boarded trains for Ogdensburg. Ten hours later we arrived at our base camp near Lake Ontario's Thousand Islands. The vast area selected

GARAND M–1 RIFLE—First issued to the U.S. Army in 1936, the M-1 is a .30 caliber, clip loaded rifle weighing 9-1/2 pounds. The clip holds eight rounds. The rear sight is adjustable for windage.

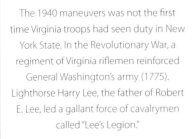

The 1940 maneuvers was not the first time Virginia troops had seen duty in New York State. In the Revolutionary War, a regiment of Virginia riflemen reinforced General Washington's army (1775). Lighthorse Harry Lee, the father of Robert E. Lee, led a gallant force of cavalrymen called "Lee's Legion."

for the maneuvers was fifty-five miles long and thirty-five miles wide. Our Twenty-ninth Division was part of America's First Army, numbering 90,000 men. Except for rifles and machine guns, arms were in short supply. Due to the shortage of tanks, trucks were draped with signs labeling them as tanks. Many of the field artillery pieces were merely sections of water pipe mounted on wooden frames. It was disheartening to see how ill-equipped American forces were in comparison to those of Germany, Japan and other countries. The first six days were devoted to small unit combat. Three days of brigade exercises, followed by three days of Division exercises prepared us for a week of mock battle between two opposing forces, the Blues and the Blacks. Our National Guard Blue Army took up defensive positions over a thirty-five mile battle line. An invading army, the Blacks, comprised a regular army division. On the eve of battle, dawn and a heavy rain broke simultaneously. Defending strategic territory against the invading Blacks in the heavy downpour was a real challenge. Digging and sleeping in water-soaked foxholes, surviving on field rations, and trudging through muddy fields left us miserable and exhausted. On the afternoon of the fifth day of battle, the temperature plummeted from ninety to forty degrees. Matt and I combined shelter halves and shared a pup tent. Where we had suffered from the heat in our winter uniforms and heavy packs, the woolen uniform, overcoat, and blankets were finally appreciated. Sometime during the long night, I was awakened by a chattering sound. Thinking that it was perhaps a snake, I roused Matt and whispered for him to listen for the startling noise. Grudgingly he said: "That's my teeth chattering, you dope! Go back to sleep!"

Aug. 23, 1940—Climaxing three weeks of maneuvers that ended in the defeat of an invader by outnumbered defending forces, Lieutenant General Hugh A. Drum, commander of the First Army, appealed to Congress and the nation to modernize America's armed forces.

"We are too few to meet the problems ahead and must demand that all able citizens be called to serve with us in preparing for the threatening crisis. We are wasting time and ignoring basic lessons of history by months of discussing the volunteer as opposed to the conscriptive system. Our troops in these maneuvers, national guardsmen, reserve officers and regular army, are all volunteers. The manpower requirements with which to create adequate armed forces to meet pending emergencies can only be secured by placing the burden on the population."

At the conclusion of the battle exercises, we made camp in an open field. Eighteen days of battle had taken a toll on our uniforms, so we did what we could to improve our appearances. Trousers, for example, carefully placed between cot and torso, emerged with some semblance of a crease.

On the morning of President Roosevelt's scheduled arrival, reveille sounded at five o'clock. Following a hurried breakfast, our Headquarters Company was assembled and meticulously inspected by Lt. Southward. We had been told what was expected of us—faces washed, boots shined, trousers creased, belt buckle shined, campaign hat brushed, rifle cleaned, etc. As we marched towards our destination, the usual banter was heard, some light-hearted and comical, others protesting the occasion.

"Lotta good it did to shine our boots," one griped. "We gotta walk five miles in the dirt and dust!"

"I suppose the president will personally want to peer down the bore of my rifle!" added another.

"Fat chance! He's crippled, you know . . . won't get out of his limo . . . doubt if we even see him!"

"Don't care if I do! Didn't vote for him anyway!"

"Knock it off, you two!" Sgt. Ballard shouted. "Whether you like him or not, he's our commander-in-chief and he's entitled to your respect!"

It was ten o'clock before we arrived at our appointed position in an immense, freshly-mowed wheat field. A cloud of powdered dust arose as the dry, stubbled field yielded to the tramping of marching men. As the sun neared its zenith in a cloudless sky, a hush fell over the massed

August 28, 1940—President Roosevelt and Secretary of War Henry L. Stimson, who inspected the troops in the New York maneuvers, expressed "complete satisfaction," but admonished that weakness demonstrated in the maneuvers required "immediate solution before our preparedness plans will be really effective."

October 29, 1940—The first peacetime
military draft is put into effect immediately. A National Guard mobilization bill
carried an amendment authorizing the
honorable discharge of all guardsmen
under age eighteen as soon as they are
called to active duty. "It is not right and
it is not the desire of Congress and the
people of the United States to force
children into the regular Army," Rep.
Massingale of Oklahoma asserted. "There
are hundreds of boys in the National
Guard of Oklahoma today who are not
eighteen years old," he stated. Matt was
nineteen on August 12, 1940. I was
seventeen and would not be of legal age
until February 3, 1941.

troops. Only the complaining crows, deprived of their feeding grounds, broke the silence. A gentle breeze from the direction of Lake Ontario softly snapped the flags and standards. Then, from afar, the booming of a twenty-one gun salute alerted us of the president's arrival. The resounding tribute was followed by an aerial display of over one-hundred aircraft comprising a variety of fighters, bombers, and observation planes. As the roar of the low-flying armada faded and disappeared from view, we patiently waited.

Presently, the strains of "Hail to the Chief" emanated from the far end of the field, our Twenty-ninth Division's tribute to the president. His progress down the long line of troops was easily gauged by the shouted commands of the unit commanders: "COM-PA-NEE-A-TEN-SHUN! PRE-SENT . . . ARMS!" The New York State police and secret service-men escorted the president. American flags mounted on the front bumper of his limousine flapped patriotically in the breeze. From the rear seat of the open convertible, President Roosevelt flashed his famous smile and waved. Later, in discussing our viewing of the president, many shared the impression that he had made eye contact and directed his smile to each of us personally.

As we returned to Richmond, I thought about General Drum's words and the threat facing our nation. France had conceded defeat. Hitler's mighty *Luftwaffe* continued to conduct massive bombing raids on Britain. The Royal Air Force responded by sending squadrons of Spitfire pursuit planes to intercept the Nazi bombers. In one week alone, one-hundred and eighty German planes were shot down over Britain. "Never in the field of human conflict was

Germany started all-night bombing raids on London, killing and injuring thousands. Hitler further tightened the noose by proclaiming a blockade of British waters. Churchill asked Roosevelt for help but there was little the president could do without America entering the war. To provide some aid to the British Royal Navy in their attempts to penetrate the blockade, Washington handed over fifty aging destroyers to London in exchange for the rights to build U.S. Air and naval bases on British territory in Newfoundland and in the Caribbean. The severity of the threat of war coming to America was finally being recognized by the government and the people.

so much owed by so many to so few!" proclaimed Winston Churchill in tribute to the Royal Air Force pilots.

It was indeed wonderful to be back home. Somehow, we felt that we were "boys" when we departed Richmond and "men" when we returned. We had marched and crawled and fought with the best of fighting men and our Twenty-ninth Division had performed admirably. I regretted having to leave the Guard in order to enter Virginia Tech's ROTC program.

Particularly difficult was the thought of being separated from Matt. We had seventeen years together and our brotherly bond was indelible. On the morning of my departure for Blacksburg, I awoke to the aroma of percolating coffee. John Martin, a friend of Matt's—also an aviation enthusiast, and a junior at Virginia Tech—had said that I could ride with him and his mother to Blacksburg. They arrived shortly after we finished breakfast. Jack, now four, was seated on the porch step, cuddling a small puppy. Tears streamed down his face. As we pulled away from the curb he waved good-bye. Mom, wiping her eyes with the tip of her apron, smiled bravely. Dad reminded me to keep my slide rule well-oiled. Phil promised to keep me informed about his school and art work. Matt grasped me firmly by the hand and said, "Go get 'em, tiger!"

John Daniel Jefferies

CHAPTER SEVEN

o capitalize on the lessons learned from the New York maneuvers, the commander of the Twenty-ninth Division ordered specialized training exercises for all higher staff and communications units. Col. Bright, commander of the First Infantry, issued this statement: "Every officer and man realizes that President Roosevelt's proclamation of a limited emergency is a severe step. Adequate preparedness will save us from the world-wide madness of war." Matt left Richmond with his unit on November 19 for two weeks' encampment at a Virginia Beach military reservation.

On November 10, Hitler's *Luftwaffe* pulverized Coventry, England. Thousands of Britons were being killed in the air raids. Germany's invasion of Britain was only a matter of time. After Britain's defeat, it was widely believed that Hitler would set his sights on America!

In the November elections Roosevelt was elected to a third term in office. The vote of confidence enabled him to win passage of the Lend-Lease Act enabling America to provide war materiel to besieged Britain.

Matt announced that he had resigned from the National Guard and applied for active duty in the Regular Army. He had orders to report for induction at Fort Meade, Maryland, on February 3, 1941. He explained that it was much more likely for him to transfer to the Air Corps from a Regular Army unit than from the National Guard.

Following the New York maneuvers, officers of the Virginia National Guard attended a National Guard Association convention in Baltimore. They returned convinced that the army's expansive preparations meant peace rather than war for the United States. Speaking at the convention banquet, the Secretary of War declared: *"Let me tell you there is no man in public life today who is more determined than your Secretary of War that your sons and my sons shall not march forth to war!"*

Matt—Upon his return from the Virginia Beach exercises, Matt was promoted to corporal.

September 1940—Richard registered at Virginia Tech for a four-year curriculum in mechanical engineering. He enlisted in the ROTC and was assigned to Engineer Company "E" of the Second Battalion. His roommate, Russell Starke, was also from Richmond. The Corps of Cadets was issued the 1903 Springfields. In a letter home, he explained that it was in his best interest not to reveal that he had served eighteen months in the National Guard. "Better," he said, "just to become a fast learner!"

June, 1941—The U.S. Air Corps is renamed: "U.S. Army Air Forces."

PVT. Matt Jefferies, U.S. Army Air Forces

❋

Summer, 1941—Richard was employed by Richmond Engineering Company as a blacksmith's helper forging chain links for anti-submarine nets. A government contract for 160 steel floats to support the nets was considered high priority. Sixty floats would support a net across San Francisco Bay and 100 across the New York Harbor.

❋

Harvey Booker Sanford—News of "Uncle" Harvey's sudden death at age fifty-eight distressed all who knew and loved him. He was laid to rest in the family plot at Old Yeocomico Church.

❋

Leaving Uncle Harvey's funeral at Old Yeocomico, Richard was notified that his college roommate, Russell Starke, had been killed in an automobile accident. Russell's father owned Richmond Engineering.

On April 6, Yugoslavia and Greece were invaded by German troops. On May 20, German paratroopers invaded Crete, driving out the British. The Germans captured 200,000 Greek and 300,000 Yugoslav prisoners.

Encouraged by his victories, on June 22, Hitler invaded Russia with over 250 divisions along the entire Russian frontier between the Black Sea and the Arctic Ocean. The invasion was dubbed "Operation Barbarossa." Europe and Asia were rapidly being gobbled up by the Axis armies.

Matt wrote from Fort Meade to say that he was assigned to the Twenty-ninth Division's 176 Infantry. Having experienced two maneuvers in the Virginia National Guard, he confessed that basic training was a snap! While awaiting transfer to the Army Air Forces, he was promoted to sergeant and assigned to Army Intelligence School. On September 4, he was notified that his transfer had been approved. Army policy required his discharge from the infantry and reenlistment in the Air Force as a private. He was allowed a week's furlough and returned to Richmond. Orders were received directing him to travel to Keesler Field in Biloxi, Mississippi, for Aircraft Mechanics school. In an exchange of letters, arrangements were made for Mom to visit with him for a weekend. He knew that she would enjoy the crawfish festival for which the antebellum city was famous. Another attraction that would interest his mother was the home of the former president of the Confederacy, Jeff Davis. She rode a bus to Biloxi. Unfortunately, she fell while emerging from the bus (en route, a metal step had dropped off). She was hospitalized for three days for a spinal injury. Matt was a frequent visitor to her bedside and his presence provided her much comfort.

Blacksburg, Virginia Sunday
December 7, 1941
I arose early and glanced out the window.
It was a clear day with no hint in the sky
that we could expect anything other than
sunshine and scattered clouds. It was a
great morning for walking into town; the
air was crisp and invigorating. I looked
forward to attending the ten o'clock
service at the Episcopal Church. It was
two o'clock when I returned to the barracks. The recreation room was crowded
with cadets gathered around a radio.
"What's going on?" I asked.
The Japanese have bombed Pearl Harbor,
America's largest naval base in the Pacific."

—Dick Jefferies

❋

December 8, 1941—In an address to
Congress, President Roosevelt angrily
declared, "December 7, 1941, is a date that
will live in infamy!"

❋

December 15, 1941—
Directive to all ROTC *cadets:*
"You have a duty to yourself and your
country to continue in your studies and
military training. In time your services
will be required by our armed forces. You
should direct your energies to acquiring the
knowledge and skills which will qualify you
to assume positions of leadership."

—Commandant

❋

**Ultimately, 110 Tech men would die
in World War II.**

The probability of America entering the war became increasingly real. The press hinted that measures were being taken to protect American harbors. Cargo ships were being armed. German U-boats had been sighted scouting the Eastern Seaboard. On September 11, President Roosevelt issued an order that German and Italian vessels sighted in U.S. territorial waters would be attacked. In response to this announcement, U-boats sank two U.S. destroyers with the loss of over a hundred lives. Meanwhile, in the Pacific, Japan's aggression continued with the seizing of Indochina. Japan signed a pact with Germany and Italy to support each other should the U.S. enter the war. The time had arrived for America to take action to weaken Japan's ability to wage war. Shipment of strategic materials including petroleum, petroleum products, and scrap iron was banned.

Sunday, December 7, 1941, The Japanese bombed Pearl Harbor, America's largest naval base in the Pacific. At 7:50 a.m. Honolulu time, hundreds of carrier-based Japanese planes bombed and strafed the American fleet anchored at Pearl Harbor. Two battleships were sunk, and six seriously damaged. Three destroyers and three cruisers were damaged. Four support ships were sunk. Hundreds of American aircraft were destroyed on the ground. The loss of life numbered in the thousands. There was no warning of the attack and our forces were unable to stage a meaningful resistance. The attack had crippled our Pacific fleet. That such a thing had occurred was beyond belief! "Japan, a small island nation—having the audacity to attack America!" exclaimed a newscaster. Japan was obviously well aware that America was militarily weak and unable to defend herself from swift attacks by superior sea and

I WANT YOU
FOR U.S. ARMY

Recruiting posters appeared in front of banks, post offices, and government buildings. The classic poster of World War I by James Montgomery Flagg again served to urge young men to enlist in the U.S. Army.

air power. It was feared that the Pearl Harbor attack would be followed by other aggressive strikes in the Pacific. The initial shock quickly turned to outrage. Reports from the Pacific continued to spell disaster. On the eighth of December, Japan declared war on Britain and proceeded to invade Malaya and Siam. On the ninth, two British warships, the HMS *Prince of Wales* and the HMS *Repulse*, were sunk off the Malayan coast. Japanese forces landed on the island of Luzon in the Philippines on the tenth and on Guam in the Marianas on the eleventh. Germany's pact to support Japan should America enter the war resulted in a formal declaration of war on the United States. Italy echoed the German declaration. On the same day, the United States declared war on Germany and Italy. The prospect of having to fight the Axis nations on two fronts was awesome. However, the nation responded with an outpouring of patriotism. Young men lined up at recruiting stations across the country to enlist for the duration of the war. American flags were displayed in store fronts, bank lobbies, the windows of homes, and in offices and factories. America had a new battle cry: "REMEMBER PEARL HARBOR!"

In January, Matt was transferred to Chanute Field, Illinois, for three months of training in the Aircraft Electrical Specialist School. Although only fifty miles south of Chicago, Chanute Field could just as well have been an ocean away as wartime restrictions required Air Force personnel to remain on base. A postcard expressed his view of the Windy City on a rare occasion when he was granted permission to be absent. "This metropolis has recovered well following the Great Fire of 1871. No sign of Mrs. O'Leary's cow, however."

During the first three months of 1942, the situation in the Pacific continued to deteriorate. The Japanese occupied Manila, the Dutch East Indies, Singapore, the Solomon Islands, and the Bataan peninsula in the Philippines. The tidal wave of Japanese victories echoed that of Nazi Germany's blitzkrieg in Europe. Fearful that an invasion of Hawaii was eminent, a supreme effort was made to strengthen the islands' defenses. If captured, Hawaii could conceivably serve as Japan's staging area for attacking America's West coast. With each passing day, the Japanese occupation of the South Pacific islands mounted. On May 6, the U.S. Garrison at Corregidor in the Philippines surrendered.

In the short span of six months since America entered the war, her citizens had undergone a radical transformation. Equipping and sustaining the military was now the top priority. Government rationing boards were established to effect a fair distribution of scarce goods to the civilian population. Food, gasoline, and automobile tires were among the first items subject to strict rationing. The Japanese occupation of the Philippines cut off a third of America's sugar supply. Strict rationing of sugar, imposed on every citizen, averaged eight ounces per week. There were "eggless days" and "meatless days" at the markets. To conserve gasoline, a law was passed limiting speed to thirty-five-miles-per-hour. A twenty percent federal luxury tax on jewelry, furs, and cosmetics discouraged the purchase of these luxury items.

By government decree, men's suits made during the war appeared without cuffs on the trousers.

The morale of Americans was given a tremendous boost when, on April 18, Lt. Col. "Jimmy" Doolittle bombed Tokyo and Yokohama. Launched from the aircraft carrier, *Hornet*, sixteen B-25 bombers carried out the daring raid. Three flyers died in crash landings. The Japanese captured eleven crewmen and executed three as "war criminals." Eleven bombers landed safely in China. It was a remarkable accomplishment!

Americans were further encouraged by reports of the Japanese sustaining heavy losses of warships in the Battle of the Coral Sea.

February 1, 1942
Dear Dick,
Congratulations on your nineteenth birthday. I wish we could be together to celebrate the occasion. I'd bake you a cake like Matt did at Bremo Bluff on your thirteenth birthday! The best thing about my junior year at Thomas Jefferson High School is my art class. The Richmond Times Dispatch has published several of my drawings. Edith Linderman, editor of the Entertainment section, has taken an interest in my work. Hope all is well with you.
With love to my brother, Phil

Certificate of Registrar

This is to Certify that pursuant to the Rationing Orders and Regulations administered by the OFFICE OF PRICE ADMINISTRATION, an agency of the United States Government,

6 ft. 3½ in. 160 lbs. Brown Brown 19 yrs. Sex { Male ☒ / Female ☐

(Name, Address, and Description of person to whom the book is issued:)

has been issued the attached War Ration Stamps this 5th day of May, 1942, upon the basis of an application signed by himself ☒, herself ☐, or on his or her behalf by his or her husband ☐, wife ☐, father ☐, mother ☐, exception ☐. (Check one.)

Jefferies   Richard   Livingston
(Last name)   (First name)   (Middle name)

3207   Hanover   Ave.
(Street No. or P. O. Box No.)   (Street or R. F. D.)

Henry L. Wood _____ (Signature)
(Registrar)

Richmond   Henrico   Virginia
(City or town)   (County)   (State)

Local Board No. 61-2 County Montgomery State Virginia

Stamps must not be detached except in the presence of the retailer, his employee, or person authorized by him to make delivery.

UNITED STATES
OF AMERICA
War Ration Book One

WARNING

1 Punishments ranging as high as *Ten Years' Imprisonment or $10,000 Fine, or Both,* may be imposed under United States Statutes for violations thereof arising out of infractions of Rationing Orders and Regulations.

2 This book must not be transferred. It must be held and used only by or on behalf of the person to whom it has been issued, and anyone presenting it thereby represents to the Office of Price Administration, an agency of the United States Government, that it is being so held and so used. For any misuse of this book it may be taken from the holder by the Office of Price Administration.

3 In the event either of the departure from the United States of the person to whom this book is issued, or his or her death, the book must be surrendered in accordance with the Regulations.

4 Any person finding a lost book must deliver it promptly to the nearest Ration Board.

No. 271424 —160

OFFICE OF PRICE ADMINISTRATION

| WAR RATION STAMP 24 | WAR RATION STAMP 22 | WAR RATION STAMP 20 | WAR RATION STAMP 18 | WAR RATION STAMP 16 | WAR RATION STAMP 14 |
| WAR RATION STAMP 23 | WAR RATION STAMP 21 | WAR RATION STAMP 19 | | WAR RATION STAMP 15 | WAR RATION STAMP 13 |

War Ration Book One—
The missing stamps were used for the purchase of two tires for the 1937 Dodge.

Two-pairs-of-pants suits were forbidden. Silk hose and lingerie became extinct, as silk was needed for parachutes. Americans took these restrictions in stride. Each family member was allocated a war ration book. As the need arose, stamps were used as authorization to purchase sugar, butter, and other scarce items. Although prohibited by law, there were always buyers for unused stamps. The penalty for transferring stamps ranged as high as ten years' imprisonment, or a $10,000 fine. The scarcity of fresh produce brought about the planting of "victory gardens." Vacant lots, lawns, and flower beds were plowed up for growing vegetables. Collection centers were established for scrap metal. Every household was asked to donate their aluminum pots and pans for the manufacture of fighter planes and bombers. A walk down any street clearly revealed the transformation from a time of peace to that of war. Few cars were on the street. People were walking more or riding bicycles to conserve gasoline. Street lights were dimmed to conserve electricity. Women were taking on jobs formerly held by men: taxi drivers, elevator operators, streetcar conductors, and service station attendants. Industry was hiring women as welders, mechanics, crane operators, and machinists.

B-17 Flying Fortress—The B-17 built by Boeing Aircraft Company was a low-wing, high-altitude, long range bomber used for strategic heavy bombardment missions against enemy targets. The prototype flew successfully in July 1935. A total of 12,731 B-17s were built. Over 5,000 failed to return from their missions. Exhaust turbo-supercharging of the four 1200 horsepower radial engines allowed the plane to fly 300 miles per hour at an altitude of 30,000 feet. Normal bomb load was 6,000 pounds. A crew of ten manned the Fortress: pilot, copilot, navigator, bombardier, radio operator, engineer, tail gunner, waist gunner, chin turret and belly turret. In combat, the flight engineer also manned a machine gun in the top turret.

Dad accepted a position with Merck & Co. in Rahway, New Jersey. As Chief Engineer, he would oversee the expansion of the chemical company's power plant. The family moved to Rahway two weeks after Philip's graduation from Thomas Jefferson High School. Philip was very popular and enjoyed the warm friendship of many of his classmates who shared in his enthusiasm for art. Merck hired him as an office boy delivering messages throughout the complex. Twice a week he commuted to New York to attend the Grand Central School of Art.

In April, Matt was transferred to Geiger Field near Spokane, Washington. He wrote briefly to say that he could not have hoped for a better time to arrive in Spokane, a city in northeastern Washington comfortably situated between the Rocky Mountains and the Columbia River Basin. Days were refreshingly warm and sunny. Lilacs in full bloom graced lawns and parks, adding to the beauty of the city. However, the intense training program at Geiger Field allowed few opportunities to leave the base. He was assigned to the 301st Bombardment Group, a newly-activated group flying B-17 bombers. Matt's training at Keesler and Chanute Fields qualified him to serve as flight engineer. At long last, he had attained his goal, one of ten crewmen manning a B-17, America's "flying fortress."

On May 25, the 301st arrived at a remote location near Alamogordo, New Mexico. No air base existed. A concrete runway had been built to accommodate the heavy bombers. The B-17s flew submarine patrol missions over the Gulf of California to North Island, San Diego. These missions provided inexperienced crews with valuable flying experience.

The summer of 1942 was one of profound activity in both war zones.

Boeing B-17 on Antisubmarine Patrol

America signed a mutual aid pact with Russia who was in a desperate struggle to halt the German invasion. Great Britain was pounding Germany with massive bombing raids. The greatest air attack in history occurred when the R.A.F. sent a thousand bombers over Cologne and dropped six million pounds of bombs on the industrial city. In the Pacific, Japanese aggression continued. On June 12, a Japanese force landed in the Aleutians, and on June 22, a Japanese submarine shelled the Oregon coast. America's vulnerability to invasion was all too apparent, so measures were taken to defend our shores. The Air Force flew submarine patrols over the coastline and the Panama Canal. The Coast Guard and civilian spotters patrolled the waterways. Lights were required to be blacked out for a distance of fifteen miles inland. The only good news to come out of the Pacific was America's defeat of Japanese naval forces attacking Midway Island. The battle cost Japan four aircraft carriers.

On June 21, the 301st moved to the Richard E. Byrd Field in Richmond, Virginia, preparatory to a transatlantic crossing to England. Classroom instruction, flying practice, and aircraft maintenance continued at an accelerated

Alamogordo, New Mexico
June 10, 1942

Dear Mom, Dad, Phil, & Jack, I'm now assigned to the 301st Bomb Group and flying B-17's. This is what I have always wanted to do! Can't tell you more as we are instructed to discuss our missions with no one. Great living conditions here in southern New Mexico: tarpaper shacks, white sand, blistering sun, cacti, sage brush, lizards and road runners. I will keep you informed of our next move which should happen soon. Give my regards to Dick. Has he transferred to the Army Engineers yet?

Love to all,
—Matt

❋

North American Aviation began producing the P-51 Mustang fighter plane. It was powered with the 1,350 horsepower Packard Merlin engine, a copy of the Rolls Royce engine powering the British Spitfire. The P-51 fighters would escort B-17s on their bombing missions over enemy territory.

❋

Richard E. Byrd Field—Matt was thrilled when informed that the 301st was ordered to relocate to Richmond, his *hometown*. Upon arrival he made an effort to contact a few of his Richmond friends but most were in various branches of the military and away from home. Matt boarded a train for Rahway, New Jersey, arriving on his dad's birthday, June 30th.

rate. All personnel were allowed ten days away from the base to visit their families or to accept Richmond's hospitality. Private homes, churches, and the U.S.O. opened their doors and hearts to the airmen.

Matt had been away for sixteen months. Homecoming to Rahway was a new experience. He was pleased to see that his family was settled in a comfortable apartment at 2-D Alden Drive. The city was a beehive of commerce and activity. To keep up with the demand for wartime goods, the factories geared up and worked around-the-clock. Merck (chemicals), Wheatena (cereals), Eureka (vacuum cleaners), and a host of other major manufacturers added thousands to their payrolls. With many young men entering the military, employers were hard-pressed for workers. Even New Jersey's state prison, located within the city limits of Rahway, advertised for guards and clerical help. Unemployment was a thing of the past! Rahway was booming! American flags flew atop buildings, in store fronts, on light poles, and in the yards of private homes. Although factory smoke often blotted out the sun and dusted the city with soot and cinders, the citizens of Rahway graced their yards with shrubs and flowers in tune with New Jersey's reputation as the "Garden State."

Dad had a special treat in store for us, a visit to New York City to attend a musical, "This Is the Army," at the Broadway Theater. The show was staged by an all-soldier cast with music and lyrics by Irving Berlin. The romantic ballad, "I Left My Heart at the Stage Door Canteen," touched the heartstrings of the audience. The reviews stated that when the curtain dropped, "there wasn't a dry eye in the theater."

New Jersey—Standup comics often said: *"There's a stretch of land between New York City and Philadelphia that's called New Jersey."*

❋

General Foods of Hoboken, New Jersey, announced the development of a soluble coffee for the armed forces. Called "Instant Maxwell House," the powdered coffee would be included in the all K ration kits. It would not be available to the civilian population until after the war.

❋

Merck was constructing a new facility for the production of the wonder drug, *penicillin*. (As 100 percent of their production was allocated for the armed forces, the new plant would serve the civilian population as well.)

Mom and Matt

Atlantic Crossings—In the first six months of 1942, German U-boats accounted for the sinking of more than a million tons of Allied shipping. To better insure safe passage, the ships sailed in large convoys protected only by destroyers armed with depth charges and deck guns.

The 301st Bombardment Group consisted of four squadrons: 32nd, 352nd, 353rd, and 419th. The Group flew eight missions and 104 sorties over France, Belgium and Holland. One B-17 was lost.

Matt was assigned to the 352nd squadron consisting of nine B-17s. He flew on two missions as flight engineer.

Boeing produced 2,300 B-17F bombers. Douglas Aircraft and Vega built an additional 1,005 planes to Boeing specifications.

The day of Matt's departure was soon at hand. Everyone endeavored to remain upbeat although aware that it could well be many months or years before he would return. The fear of his never returning played heavily on our minds. "Don't worry, Mom," he said. "I'm just going flying. I always said that I would, remember?"

Matt returned to Byrd Field and was informed that the 301st had orders to move to Fort Dix, New Jersey, on July 19. A physical examination, shots, and a supply of incidentals for a sea voyage and overseas duty comprised the final preparations. Matt also received a directive stating that he was promoted to the rank of corporal.

On August 5, the 301st boarded the troop ship in New York. A former Grace Line cruise ship, the *Santa Rosa*, was refitted to carry three times as many troops as it could peacetime passengers during its cruising of the South America-Central America-Panama Canal-Atlantic Route. From the Port of New York, the *Santa Rosa* steamed to Halifax, Nova Scotia, where it lay at anchor for two days

Ocean liner, *Santa Rosa*

pending the arrival of escort naval vessels, other troop ships, and freighters, making up a large convoy for safe passage across the Atlantic. The crossing was made without incident. On August 18, the *Santa Rosa* docked at Swansea, Wales. The 301st boarded a train for Wellingbrough, northwest of London. British lorries transported the airmen to Podington Airfield which was in the process of reconstruction. Originally an R.A.F. command station, Podington was transferred to the newly formed Eighth U.S.A.A.F. The runway was being lengthened to accommodate the B-17F heavy bombers. Living conditions at Podington were miserable. Rusting Nissen huts served as barracks. It rained every day for three weeks. Mud was ankle-deep. Duckboards connected the barracks to the latrines, the mess, and briefing rooms. Meanwhile, the B-17s, ferried over from the States, arrived at nearby Chelveston Airfield, an operational Eighth Air Force base at Caldecott-cum-Chelveston. The 301st began bombing missions over France, Belgium, and Holland on September 5. Matt was a member of the ground crew as an electrical specialist.

Maintenance of the heavy bombers was a demanding task for the ground crews. Mechanical, electrical, and hydraulic systems required inspection and appropriate servicing following every mission.

On September 19–21, Matt journeyed to London for a little R&R. A v-mail letter stated that he "enjoyed a fine dinner at St. Martin's in the Field-Crypt restaurant."

Clubmobile—The mobile canteen began operation in Great Britain in late 1942. Eventually, thirty air bases were served. An oil fired *Primus* stove was installed for heating water for coffee which was prepared in 50-cup urns. Three American Red Cross girls were assigned to each *Clubmobile*.

Nissen Hut: Matt fifth from left.

Red Cross Clubmobile: Matt on right.

When he returned to base, he bought a bicycle from an airman who was transferred back to the States. Bicycles were invaluable for getting around the base and for an occasional foray to neighboring villages for a much deserved change in scenery. As winter set in, maintenance of the aircraft became extremely difficult. The work had to be performed in the open with no protection from the elements except for canvas tarps draped over engine cowlings. Coal fired stoves in the Nissen huts provided relief from the bitter cold. The American Red Cross served hot coffee and donuts from a *Clubmobile*. They also distributed cigarettes, candy, and chewing gum. A Victrola provided up-to-date music over a loud speaker.

In October, Matt volunteered to substitute for a flight engineer who was suddenly taken ill. He flew on two missions over enemy territory.

On December 8, the 301st ground crews departed Chelveston by train to Liverpool where they embarked on a steamship for Oran, Algeria.

The passage down the Irish Sea, the Atlantic to the Strait of Gibraltar and across the Mediterranean to Oran was long and exhausting. Disembarking on December 21, they boarded trucks for an overnight stay at the Oran Airdrome and then to the Biskre Airdrome where planes, equipment, and supplies arrived to support Operation Torch. On January 31, 1943, Matt was sent to La Senia Airdrome to replace faulty engines on a number of bombers. When they took to the air to check engine performance, Matt went along as flight engineer.

On May 8, 1943, he was officially transferred from the 301st BG to the Eleventh Air Depot Group stationed at the Oran Airdrome. The Eleventh ADG, attached to the Twelfth Air Force, were uncrating and reassembling B-25 and B-17 bombers and P-38 and P-40 fighters. Working under a blazing sun with temperatures over a hundred degrees and being frequently subjected to blinding sand storms and swarms of locusts, the specialist crews accomplished the impossible.

After landing in North Africa on November 8, 1942, General Eisenhower's "Operation Torch" sent the British First Army, supported by American elements, racing towards Tunisia, which was heavily defended by the Germans. The British and American forces shared a common objective, to drive the Germans and Italians out of Africa. The final outcome of the war could very well hinge on the Allies defeating the Germans in Africa. By the end of January 1943, all of Algeria had been cleared of the Axis armies, and they were in full retreat towards the Mediterranean seaport of Tunis, Tunisia. Determined to hold Tunisia, Hitler sent reinforcements to Rommel through Italy and Sicily. Rommel lost no time in launching a counterattack.

North Africa, May 29, 1943, V-Mail from Matt.

In the summer of 1941, Hitler sent General Erwin Rommel with his Afrika Korps into North Africa to capture the Suez Canal. The British fought him in the Libyan Desert for eighteen months. Rommel had captured Tobruk, Libya, and advanced within seventy miles of Alexandria, Egypt. Britain sent General Montgomery to halt Rommel's advance. The British Eighth Army struck the Afrika Korps at El Alamein in Egypt and sent Rommel's army back into Libya. To prevent him from regrouping, British and American forces landed at Oran and Algiers, Algeria, and Casablanca, Morocco, on the northwest coast of Africa. The bold invasion, commanded by General Dwight Eisenhower, was called *OPERATION TORCH.*

April 19, 1943—Richard was inducted into the Regular Army and stationed at Fort Leonard Wood, Missouri, for three months of basic training.

✳

The British and American press sharply criticized Eisenhower for allowing Rommel to retake the Kasserine Pass. In their first major engagement against the Axis forces, American forces had "come up short." Although he accepted full blame for the disaster, Eisenhower was well aware that the divisions involved had not been sufficiently trained. The British, on the other hand, had the advantage of having battle-seasoned troops who understood the determination of the Axis forces to resist and to fight back.

✳

Russian Front—The June 1941 German invasion of Russia was a bold undertaking. For two years, the German armies won battle after battle, reaching the Volga River near Stalingrad. The Russian defense of the city stopped the Germans from further penetration. The battle for Stalingrad stalemated as bitter winter weather arrived with a vengeance. January 31, 1943, the commander of Germany's Sixth Army surrendered. Germany would never recover from the defeats in North Africa and Stalingrad.

One of Rommel's objectives was to retake Kasserine Pass, a vital mountain pass connecting Algeria and Tunisia. Against overwhelming odds the American army which had previously captured the pass was forced to retreat. Rommel pursued the American divisions into Algeria for up to fifty miles. However, his inability to supply his army forced Rommel to halt the advance. The loss of American troops and materials was staggering. Eisenhower quickly brought up reinforcements and succeeded in forcing the Germans to retreat. Kasserine Pass was recaptured on February 25. The Allies pursued Rommel until the German and Italian armies were bottled up in a narrow Tunisian salient. On May 7, the Allies captured Tunis and Bizerte. All resistance ceased. Rommel escaped and left behind 275,000 troops of his prized Afrika Korps, who were taken prisoner.

On July 9, British paratroopers and American airborne troops invaded Sicily. In preparation for the invasion of Italy, 500 bombers blasted industrial targets in Rome. Benito Mussolini was arrested and imprisoned.

On July 12, 1943, the Eleventh ADG moved to a new base in occupied Tunis. Repair and inspection of aircraft con-

Tunis, Tunisia—Matt, in copilot's seat, preparing to flight test a B–17F.

In the North Pacific, the Japanese occupied Attu and Kiska in the Aleutian Islands. American forces landed at Attu on May 11, 1943, and within two weeks, had reclaimed the island. Late in July the Japanese were forced to withdraw from Kiska.

Richard—Following completion of basic training, former ROTC members who had transferred into the Regular Army from a selected number of colleges were ordered to return to their respective schools to resume their studies. Roosevelt felt it necessary to continue training engineers, doctors, teachers, and other professionals for the future needs of America. The Army Specialized Training Program (ASTP), also included advanced military training.

North Africa P-38 *Lightning*—Matt (Rt)

tinued at a furious pace in support of the Sicilian campaign. Matt, in the copilot's seat of a B-25, suffered facial lacerations and broken front teeth when the bomber crash-landed as a result of a jammed nose gear. The impact slammed his face into the control yoke. Landing in the dark of night, the pilot explained that he was "blinded by the runway lights." When the flight surgeon asked Matt about the crash landing, he replied, "It was a good landing!" Perplexed by his reply, the flight surgeon said, "What's good about a crash landing?" Matt managed a smile on his damaged face and said, "Any landing that you can walk away from is a good landing!" Within two days, Matt was back at work.

On September 3, the British Eighth Army established a beachhead on the Italian mainland near the city of Reggio on the heel of Italy's boot, and the First British Airborne Division captured Bari on the coast of the Adriatic Sea. Subsequently, the Italian government in Rome surrendered. Germany rushed several divisions into Italy. To support the British advance from the south, American amphibious forces stormed ashore at Salerno. They met unexpectedly strong resistance. Heavy losses of men and equipment were sustained. There was grave concern that the beachhead might have to be abandoned, leaving the British to fight alone until another American invasion could be launched. However, the USAF, flying from bases in North Africa and Sicily, conducted massive bombing raids on railroads, bridges, marshaling yards, and the hills surrounding Salerno. The Germans abandoned the city and retreated to Naples. On the first of October, facing annihilation, they left Naples. American and British forces linked up for a unified drive towards Rome. Critical to the support of the Allied armies was the effectiveness of the air forces. Allied air bases were relocated to Bari and Foggia in southern Italy to provide aerial support for the advancing Allied armies. At Tunis, the Fifteenth Air Force was formed from various forces in the Mediterranean. Commanded by Lt. Gen. James Doolittle, the Fifteenth operated twenty-one bombardment groups, of which the 301st was included. Matt was assigned to the Fifteenth Air Force Service Command and promoted to sergeant. He was delighted to be back with the 301st. In December, the Fifteenth USAF transferred to Bari, Italy. The Fifteenth Air Service Command was called upon to execute extraordinary missions. A variety of unarmed aircraft was placed at their disposal, the C-47 being the mainstay of the service. Matt was assigned to

In spite of their setbacks in North Africa and Russia, the Germans still controlled a vast empire reaching from the English Channel in the west to the interior of Russia.

B–17 F *ALL AMERICAN*
In January, 1943, the United States was electrified by a photograph taken in the air of a B-17 Flying Fortress which was almost cut in half but still flying after a midair collision with a German ME109 fighter. At first glance, All American was a doomed plane, even.though the pilot brought it back to base and landed with all of the crew safe. When the plane was hauled off the runway for damage assessment, representatives of Boeing Aircraft glowed with pride at the durability of the B-17. They recommended that the aircraft be junked. However, a service squadron of the 12th Air Force received permission to repair the plane. Eighteen enlisted men in thirty-seven days completed the repair. All American was flying again and sent to the Fifteenth Air Force in Bari, Italy.

Crew pictured Left to Right : Lt. Robert W. Lane, pilot, Sgt. Walter M. Jefferies, flight engineer, PFC Aeron Silverman, mechanic, and M. Sgt. Sam Chauency, radio operator and navigator.

Boeing B-17 "ALL AMERICAN" over North Africa

a B-17F, a veteran aircraft which had flown on a dozen bombing missions. Piloted by 1st Lt. Robert W. Lane of San Diego, California, the plane, stripped of its guns, turrets, and armor plate, was used for the transport of emergency equipment and personnel.

Because of its size, speed, and altitude capability, the *All-American* was utilized to the greatest extent. When word spread that the much publicized B-17 was stationed at Bari, everyone wanted to inspect the plane up close and talk to the crew. They felt a sense of pride that American ingenuity and determination saved one B-17 from the scrap heap. Boeing Aircraft had every reason to be proud.

On February 29, Matt copiloted a C-47 flight to a base at Foggia and to a base on Corsica. Both flights were uneventful. On May 30, a flight of four C-47s out of Bari was attacked by German fighters. Three C-47s were shot down. Matt's plane returned to Bari unharmed.

Two divisions of American seaborne forces landed behind Nazi lines at Anzio, twenty miles south of Rome. German troops were brought in to repel the invasion. For many weeks, the Germans contained the beachhead, exacting severe casualties on the American troops. Meanwhile, the Anglo-American armies advancing up the peninsula towards Rome were pinned down south of the town of Cassino. Winter set in with a vengeance. Food, water,

January 6, 1944—Richard begins Officer Candidate School at Fort Belvoir, Virginia.

❋

Reports from the Pacific were encouraging. U.S. Forces landed on Bougainvillea in the Solomon Islands, followed by the capture of Tarawa in the Gilbert Islands. The Japanese fought tenaciously to defend the islands. However, Japanese prospects were fading. The Allies dominated the air and the sea in the Pacific arena.

❋

On May 3, 1944, Richard graduated from Officer Candidate School and was assigned to the Engineer School's Mechanical and Technical Department as an instructor of Engineer equipment.

❋

Philip—Drafted into the army, Philip reported to Camp Gordon, Georgia, for basic training.

❋

Cassino, Italy—A sixth-century Monastery, the Abby of Monte Cassino, stood atop a mountain overlooking the town of Cassino. From the heights around the Abbey, German artillery and mortar fire rained down on the Allied armies. It was believed that the German army had outposts within the Abbey. A decision was made to destroy the monastery. Waves of American planes leveled the historic Abbey on February 14, 1944, with 500 tons of bombs. Only the tomb and cell of St. Benedict remained intact.

On the Russian front, the Soviet army, buoyed by its victory at Stalingrad and bolstered by a steady stream of trucks, food, and supplies from America, regained huge tracts of Russian territory.

✳

Richard was selected to establish a diesel engine school at Fort Belvoir. He was sent to Fort Benning, Georgia, in July to attend The Infantry School's Officer's Motor Course, one recognized as well organized and well taught.

✳

The U.S. First Army included the Twenty-Ninth Division, the former National Guard Division in which Matt and Richard served in 1939–40. The division sailed to England in September 1942 aboard the *Queen Mary*. The Twenty-Ninth landed on *Omaha Beach*, the most fortified beach on the coastline of France. Wading ashore under devastating fire, the first wave of troops suffered terrible losses of men and equipment.

and ammunition were parachuted to the troops who were dug into the frozen earth. It was May before the Germans withdrew from the heights.

The Allied plan to cross the English Channel and invade German-occupied France slowly materialized. Great quantities of war materiel, planes, tanks, gliders, and troops amassed in England. American and British navies stood by for the daring operation. Germany continued to fortify the French coast with concrete pillboxes, gun emplacements, mine fields, and miles of barbed wire and antitank obstacles. Hitler charged his favorite commander, Field Marshal Rommel, with the responsibility of defeating any attempt by the Allies to establish a beachhead along the vast French coastline. On June 6, 1944, German-occupied France was invaded by the Allied armies. Termed "D-Day," the cross-channel operation, under the supreme command of Gen. Eisenhower, was the greatest amphibious landing ever undertaken. The invasion took place on a crescent-shaped row of beaches along the northern coast of Normandy. The U.S. First Army landed at two strips, code-named Omaha Beach and Utah Beach. The

British Second Army and a Canadian division landed at three adjacent beaches, code named Gold, Juno, and Sword. Paratroopers from the U.S. Eighty-Second and 101st Airborne Divisions were dropped behind the beaches to prevent German counterattacks. German resistance to the invasion was terrifying.

Rome—When a G.I. saw the Coliseum for the first time he remarked, "Gee, I didn't know our bombers had done that much damage!"

❋

January 5, 1945—Fort Belvoir-Richard taught his first diesel engine class for Engineer Officers recently graduated from West Point. Classes that followed included officers from Canada, Russia, Brazil, Peru, and Venezuela.

❋

Philip—Following basic training, Philip was sent to Camp Campbell, Kentucky, for maneuvers. Somehow he found time to submit some of his cartoons to *YANK* magazine. Appearing in a number of issues, the cartoons depicted the life of a raw recruit on maneuvers.

❋

FDR—November 7, 1944, President Roosevelt was elected for a fourth term. With Senator Harry S. Truman as his running mate, he was easily reelected. For twelve years he had worked as president, chief executive, and commander-in-chief during the country's most difficult years. Americans wanted him *at the helm* until the war was won.

❋

Philip—After completion of the Tennessee maneuvers, Philip was granted two weeks furlough, after which he was ordered to report to Fort Dix, New Jersey.

Between April 1 and June 20, the *All-American* was sent on a series of dangerous missions over the Adriatic Sea to destinations heavily patrolled by the German *Luftwaffe*. For their performance, Brigadier General James A. Mollison, Commanding General of the Fifteenth Air Service Command, awarded the prestigious Air Medal to the crew.

"For meritorious achievement in aerial flight while participating in sustained operation against the enemy," the citation reads.

One less to worry about!

The Germans were gradually retreating from Italy. General Mark Clark's Fifth Army liberated Rome on June 4, 1944. Allied forces had fought their way across France, liberating Paris on August 25, and reaching the German frontier on September 2. Six Allied armies, numbering three million men, faced the great Siegfried Line extending the entire length of the German border. On the eastern front, the Russian armies pressed the Germans relentlessly. Although Germany was sandwiched between two invading forces, Hitler was more determined than ever. He had several aces up his sleeve which he believed would turn the tide. Robot bombs were hurled against England, killing thousands. Guided missiles with powerful warheads, launched from inside Germany, targeted greater London. A new "jet" fighter was faster than any Allied aircraft. However, the bombing of Germany gradually eliminated Hitler's ability to wage war. As many as five thousand Allied planes dropped bombs on Germany in a single day. On October 14, Britain invaded Greece and drove the Germans out of the country. These victories, coupled with Roosevelt's reelection on November 7, buoyed up the morale of the American people. Although many predicted that the war would be over by the end of the year, most Americans were well aware that Germany and Japan were prepared to defend their homelands to the bitter end. On December 16, Germany's General von Rondstedt's army staged a counterattack against the Allied armies through the Ardennes Forest in Belgium and Luxembourg. The retreating Allies suffered heavy casualties and the loss of huge quantities of military equipment. The weather turned bitterly cold. The sudden turn of events was of grave concern. Unless the German attack was halted there was a real possibility that the Allied retreat could evolve into a full-scale withdrawal from France.

Matt returned to New York aboard the Queen Mary on December 20 with orders to report to the Commander of Byrd Field in Richmond. He was granted a thirty-day furlough before reporting to Scott Field, Illinois.

Matt, Phil, and Dick met in Washington, D.C., on December 22 for a reunion at the Shoreham Hotel. They dined, toasted their good fortune to be reunited, and thanked God for Matt's safe return from the war.

April 12, 1945, President Roosevelt died of a cerebral hemorrhage at Warm Springs, Georgia. It was ironic that

Europe—"Battle of the Bulge" Weather on the western front cleared. Allied planes blasted Germany's sixty-mile penetration into Belgium and Luxembourg. The Nazis' drive was halted just short of the Muse River. The "Battle of the Bulge" continued with German armies gradually retreating towards the Rhine River. On January 18, Churchill urged Germany to surrender. He refused and boasted that Germany still had "millions of new soldiers and artillery," and declared, "Germany will never surrender!"

※

Russia—A new winter offensive placed the Russians within fifty-two miles of Berlin. On February 22, seven thousand Allied planes blasted German cities. On April 21, Russian troops entered Berlin and destroyed the city block-by-block. Hitler, residing in an underground bunker in the heart of the city, committed suicide on April 30. Two days later, the German capital fell to the Russian armies. With General Patton's third Army advancing from the west and Anglo-American armies approaching from the south, German commanders surrendered on all fronts. On May 7, a formal surrendered document was signed in Eisenhower's headquarters in Reims, France.

※

Pacific—General MacArthur's forces continued to make great progress. Fifteen hundred carrier planes bombed Tokyo. Corregidor was invaded. On February 27, Manilla was restored as the civil capital of the Philippines. The Japanese held island of Iwo Jima fell to the Americans. Fifteen square miles of Tokyo were destroyed by B–29 bombers. American forces raided the island of Okinawa on April 1. All of the island battles were won at a terrible loss of American lives.

Dick, Matt, and Phil

America's beloved president, having brilliantly led the nation in four years of war, was denied the opportunity to witness the end of the war in Europe which occurred on May 7. President Truman proclaimed May 8, 1945 as "V-E Day" for "Victory in Europe," and called on Japan to surrender in order to avoid destruction and the loss of thousands of lives. On July 26, President Truman met with Churchill and Stalin at Potsdam, Germany. A joint declaration called for Japan to surrender unconditionally or face complete destruction. Japan ignored the ultimatum.

On August 6, a B-29 bomber dropped an atomic bomb on Hiroshima, destroying the city and killing 80,000 inhabitants. On August 9, a second atomic bomb was dropped on Nagasaki, killing over 40,000. On August 14, Tokyo sued for peace. The surrender document was formerly signed September 2 on the deck of the battleship *Missouri*. The war was officially over. September 2, 1945 was proclaimed

Scott Field—Matt instructed classes in aircraft recognition and flight tests procedure. His work included routine checkup and maintenance of all aircraft assigned to Scott Field.

Matt was qualified as flight engineer and copilot on the following aircraft: B-17, B-24, B-25, B-26, C-47, C-53, C-46, C-54, AT-10, AT-11, & C-45.

Matt—Awarded the following commendations: Air Medal, Bronze Star, Afro-European Campaign Ribbon, and American Defense Ribbon.

Philip—European tour of duty took him across France and into southern Germany. His infantry battalion reached Berchtesgaden, Hitler's Bavarian retreat. He witnessed firsthand the ovens at Buchenwald, the Nazi death camp near Weimer, Germany.

❀

Richard—21 June 1946, Letter from the Commandant: *First Lt. Richard L. Jefferies, At this time, when the need for qualified and experienced officers is so great, it is with sincere appreciation that I note your action in voluntarily agreeing to remain for a time in the Military Service when discharge criteria permit your immediate separation.*

—*Willis E. Teale,*
Colonel Corps of Engineers

Phil, Dad, Jack, Matt, and Dick

"V-J Day." Three days later, Matt received his discharge from the Air Force and boarded a train for Rahway. After three years of active duty overseas, Matt was exhausted and apprehensive about his return to civilian life.

Mom and Dad urged him to take it easy and try to put all thoughts of the war behind him. Their loving support coupled with Mom's home cooking gradually returned Matt to good health, both emotionally and physically. In September 1945, Phil returned to the States and was stationed at Fort Lee, Virginia, pending a decision from the army as to the disposition of the thousands of troops no longer needed in Europe or Asia. He was given a furlough to visit his home.

Still on active duty at Fort Belvoir, I took time off from my teaching schedule to be present for the family reunion. It was an occasion for thanksgiving and appreciation for all of God's blessings.

CHAPTER EIGHT

etermined to pursue his interest in aviation and aviation art, Matt devoted his time to freelance drawing. He had long admired the work of aviation artist, William Heaslip, also a resident of Rahway. Matt visited Heaslip at his New York City studio. They became fast friends. Heaslip hired Matt as an understudy to carry out research on aviation-related subjects for his magazine illustrations. Learning that Matt was collecting photographs and drawings of aircraft of every description, Heaslip generously presented him with hundreds of prints from *Sportsman Pilot*, a publication that was going out of business. From William Heaslip, Matt acquired the techniques of advertising layout and composition. Matt's salary was $200 a month.

Matt learned that Erco, an aircraft manufacturer in Riverdale, Maryland, was seeking an illustrator for their Ercoupe monoplane parts catalog.

Matt—While working for William Heaslip, Matt created a technical aviation reference file covering over six hundred subjects, two thousand different aircraft, and over five thousand photographs.

John—At age 8, he attended Fork Union Military Academy in Fork Union, Virginia.

Richard—Discharged from the Army Engineers on December 26, 1946, Richard returned to Virginia Tech to complete his senior year in mechanical engineering.

Philip—Following his discharge from the Service at Fort Lewis, Washington, Philip moved to Hollywood. Hired by RKO as a sketch artist, he was assigned the job of painting background scenes for a movie starring Ginger Rogers.

William J. Heaslip—Born in Toronto, Canada, in 1898, Heaslip was an aviator in the Royal Flying Corps during WW-I. An accomplished artist, his aviation related illustrations appeared in *Saturday Evening Post, Collier's, and Boys' Life*. During WW-II, he illustrated war scenes for the *New York Times* Sunday Magazine, and the Associated Press.

"I Saw Three Ships Come Sailing In"

Artist—William J. Heaslip Holiday Card Collection Circa 1944.

ERCO—The Engineering and Research Corporation (ERCO) manufactured the Ercoupe, a twin-tailed, low wing monoplane equipped with a tricycle landing gear and a bubble canopy. The plane was advertised to be stallproof and spinproof. Easy and safe to fly, the Ercoupe appealed to the inexperienced pilot. Marketing the unconventional plane through unconventional outlets such as the men's department of Macy's department store proved to be a successful strategy. Sales were brisk. In 1946 alone, 4,000 planes came off Erco's assembly line in Riverdale.

❋

April 5, 1946, Matt attended the National Aviation Show held in Grand Central Palace, New York. An Ercoupe was on exhibit. Matt represented ERCO and remained with the show for its entire run to respond to questions from interested viewers.

❋

November 15–24, 1946, Matt attended the National Aircraft Show at the Municipal Airport in Cleveland, Ohio, where an Ercoupe was exhibited.

❋

Matt also represented ERCO at other shows and conventions where his expertise contributed to the ERCO sales pitch. The assignments allowed him to meet many aviation enthusiasts, pilots, artists, and writers. All contributed to his depth of knowledge.

His application was accepted and he reported to work eager to satisfy their requirements. As the Ercoupe parts manual materialized, Matt's artistic talents were quickly recognized by Erco's management.

He was moved into the sales department to illustrate sales promotional material and a brochure entitled "How to Fly the Ercoupe." His drawings of an improved version of the instrument panel brought about design modifications that made the instrumentation of the Ercoupe more acceptable to pilots of the aircraft.

Matt often speculated on what the next generation of the Ercoupe would look like. He did a rendering in watercolor of a futuristic plane with a retractable landing gear and tacked it to the wall of his office. A company photographer took a picture of the rendering and it appeared in a house publication. Erco's president, Fred Weick, was not at all pleased with the picture of a plane that closely matched one being developed by his experimental crew—one with a retractable landing gear. He all but accused Matt of spying on the top secret project. However, upon learning the facts, he apologized and complimented Matt for his vision of the future.

College Park Airport, considered the "cradle of aviation," was only a short distance from Riverdale. To acquire a civilian pilot's license, Matt signed up for flight training with Brinckerhoff Flying Service. The school's fleet of fifty horsepower, J-3 Cubs was a far cry from the planes Matt had flown in the Air Force. The G. I. Bill paid for his training.

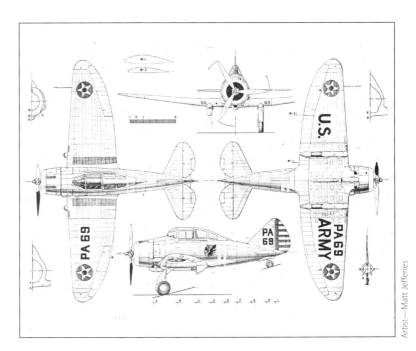

Matt's profile of the Seversky P-35.

Artist—Matt Jefferies

Matt in his '39 rag top.

Matt spent his leisure hours on the drawing board, turning out scale drawings of aircraft and submitting them to model airplane publications including *Air Trails-Hobbies for Young Men* and *American Modeler*.

Matt's aircraft profiles and cutaway drawings began to appear in *Flying* and *Air Progress*, both popular aviation magazines. Hobbyists and aviation enthusiasts acknowledged his work and asked the editors for more.

Up to this time, Matt had to rely on public transportation to take him to work and to the airport. All payday money was put aside to purchase a car, one that would not cost him an arm and a leg. Ultimately he found a reasonable bargain for a 1938 Plymouth convertible coupe in "reasonable condition."

One day Matt was having lunch in a Hot Shoppe in Hyattsville. Across the crowded room he saw a beautiful young lady seated at a table with several friends. Chatting, laughing, and obviously enjoying their lunch break, they were oblivious to the clamorous activity surrounding them. Matt wished that the object of his infatuation would pause in her animated conversation and cast her eyes in his direction so that he might convey his attraction to her.

She did, and their eyes met, not once, but repeatedly, a clear invitation for Matt to go on the offensive. He timed his departure to coincide with hers and introductions followed.

Mary Ann Benson, daughter of Sara and Howard Benson, was born in Colon, Panama, in 1927. *Mary Ann's maternal grandfather, Edmond Veysset, had arrived in Panama from France to work on the construction of the canal.* His daughter, Sara, married Howard Benson, an American banker whose work took him to various offices throughout Latin America, i.e. Panama, Costa Rica, and Mexico. In 1934, Mary Ann, age six, Doris, age nine, Flora, age twelve, and Estelle, age fifteen, sailed to Panama from Costa Rica, crossed the canal, and boarded the liner, *Santa Rosa,* for a six-day voyage to New York, arriving May 28, 1934. The girls, and a brother, Henry, who had arrived in the U.S. two years earlier, were raised by their grandmother, Margaret Benson, in Berwyn Heights, Maryland.

A date was made for lunch on the following day. This chance meeting led to a romance that was destined to last a lifetime. On June 15, 1946, Matt soloed. After receiving his private pilot's license he demonstrated the Ercoupe to potential customers. The increase in sales as a result of his demonstrations guaranteed Matt the job, one that was secure and rewarding. In February 1947, Erco again exhibited the Ercoupe at the National Aviation Show at Grand Central Palace on Lexington Avenue in New York City. Before having the plane trucked to Grand Central Palace from the Newark airport, Matt convinced Mom to take her first ride in an airplane. She was thrilled with the experience and praised Matt's capable handling of the plane. "I never dreamed," she said, "that I'd have the opportunity to look down Merck's smokestack!"

In May, Mary Ann accompanied Matt to Rahway to meet his parents. They heartily approved of Matt's "girlfriend" and felt instinctively that Mary Ann was one who could provide Matt with the love and support he so desperately needed in his purposeful life.

Matt, Ercoupe pilot demonstrator

Santa Rosa—Matt and Mary Ann discovered that they had both traveled the ocean on the *Santa Rosa* passenger liner. However, their voyages were separated by twelve years. The accommodations aboard the *Santa Rosa* in 1934 when Mary Ann and her sisters sailed to New York from Panama were undoubtedly very comfortable. When sailing on the converted troop ship, the passengers were packed in like sardines. Many of the troops slept on the deck.

Things were not going well for Erco. The boom in private flying declined at an alarming rate. Hundreds of Ercoupes languished in dealers' stocks. Erco's days were numbered. Regretfully, Matt resigned and accepted a job as a commercial illustrator for the Regal Neon Sign Company in Washington, D.C. His work entailed the design of neon signs and the cold cathode lighting for theater marquees and interior indirect lighting.

Although unrelated to the field of aviation, Matt saw the design of neon signs as a challenge. It entailed full color, graphic renderings and the presentation of his designs to clients. Originality of design was a key ingredient in producing signs which would assure acceptance. Most of his graphics were executed in airbrush. The technical side of the business comprised sheet metal work, electrical design, and lighting considerations. All contributed to Matt's knowledge of graphic arts.

Library of Congress, Washington, D.C.

Library of Congress—One of the most beautiful public buildings in Washington, or for that matter, in the United States, is the Thomas Jefferson Building of the Library of Congress. In the style of the Italian Renaissance, the architecture of the building is magnificent. It is the world's largest library, containing over thirty million books and fifty million manuscripts. Visitors entering the Great Hall encounter eight pairs of statues of the Roman Goddess Minerva, known as "a woman of great Wisdom."

Mary Ann Benson continued her secretarial career through a year's employment as secretary to the County Engineer in Hyattsville, followed by six months of self employment as a public stenographer. Her work included transcribing letters, legal papers, theses, manuscripts, specifications and estimates.

Richard—After earning a degree in mechanical engineering from Virginia Tech, Richard was hired by Allis Chalmers Manufacturing Company's Tractor Division in West Allis, Wisconsin. A-C was developing two new tractors, the Model WD and the Model G. Richard's first assignment was designing a clutch for the WD. His work included the design and construction of visual aids for his presentations to the sales and service departments.

On July 26, 1948, Matt was employed by the air research section of the Library of Congress. As a graphic presentation specialist, he answered directly to the chief draftsman. Much of his work involved the translation of governmental reports into visual aids which allowed him to make full use of his creative imagination. Within a short time he was promoted to the position of assistant chief of graphics.

Mary Ann was hired by the library's science division. As secretary to the chief of a science and technology project, she prepared highly classified, scientific memoranda, and reports.

Subscribing to the legendary theory that two can live cheaper than one, Matt and Mary Ann were married November 25 at St. James Catholic Church in Mt. Rainier, Maryland. "What better place to take my beautiful bride on our honeymoon," Matt thought, "than on a trip to Virginia." The newly married couple visited Shenandoah National Park and drove the 105-mile length of the scenic Skyline Drive that runs along the crest of the Blue Ridge Mountains. The vistas were spectacular! Someone was quoted as saying, "God lives here. You can tell by the

Reverend E. Albert Hughes with bride and groom.

scenery." Matt drove to Cumberland, to Richmond, and the Northern Neck to introduce Mary Ann to his many relatives and friends.

The newlyweds settled in an apartment in Riverdale and returned to their respective positions with the Library of Congress. Both were overwhelmed with an enormous volume of work related to the pressing requirements of the Congress for information. Weekends provided unlimited opportunities for them to enjoy the beautiful city of Washington, its monuments, parks, museums, and festivals. Matt used his camera not only to record their presence in the Capitol City, but to capture the aesthetic work of the masters of sculpture and artistry. The Chief Draftsman, recognizing Matt's versatility in design, assigned him special projects utilizing his aptitude for detail. One such project comprised the preparation of mosaics covering urban and industrial zones of a large metropolitan city. From the annotated mosaics, analytical reports and visual aids were prepared for Congressional use.

Matt's first cousins—Of the nine cousins who served in the armed forces in WW II, all nine returned home.

✳

L. B. Cottingham was a colonel with the Fifth Infantry Division. In July 1944 the Division relieved the First Division in France and became a part of General George S. Patton's Third Army after the St. Lo breakout at Normandy.

✳

Charles Mottrom Sanford—Mott entered the service as a Lieutenant in the Army Corps of Engineers. He served in the Eighty-sixth Engineer Heavy Pontoon Battalion. On March 7, 1945, the First Army reached the Rhine River. Major Sanford's battalion constructed pontoon bridges across the river under heavy German artillery fire.

✳

Library of Congress—The main purpose of the Library of Congress is to provide members of Congress with a source of reference material. James Madison is credited with suggesting the library when the federal government moved from Philadelphia to Washington. On April 24, 1800, President John Adams approved construction and the purchase of 750 books from a London bookseller. When the British invaded Washington in 1814, the Library of Congress went up in flames. Thomas Jefferson, retired at Monticello, sold his personal library consisting of 6,487 books to the government for $23,950. Of his library, Jefferson wrote, *"I do not know that it contains any branch of science which Congress would wish to exclude from their collection; there is, in fact, no subject to which a member of Congress may not have occasion to refer."*

In 1949, Matt was moved to the reference department of the library's aeronautics division. When he learned that the department was seeking to develop a photographic collection of racing aircraft, Matt requested that he be allowed, in September, to attend the National Air Races in Cleveland. "What better way," he suggested, "to acquire pictures of the very latest in racing aircraft!" His request was approved.

On June 30, 1949, Matt rented a plane and flew to Rahway for Dad's fiftieth birthday. Once airborne and leveled off, Matt sat back and said to Mary Ann, "It's all yours, fly the plane!" She grasped the controls and after a few deviations they sailed along smoothly towards their destination.

Mom and Dad acquired a building lot at a resort town called Barnegat Pines near Forked River, New Jersey. Close by, on Long Beach Island, Barnegat Lighthouse sits on the Atlantic shoreline. It was ultimately their plan to utilize weekends to build a home for retirement. Jack, age thirteen, was particularly excited about the idea as one of the main attractions of Barnegat Pines was a large, fresh water lake where he could swim and learn to sail. Dad looked forward to the day when he could devote his time to woodworking and fishing. However, with the demands of his work at Merck, Dad's time to accomplish the project was severely limited. Forked River was sixty miles from Rahway. Matt and Mary Ann, also enthused about the idea, suggested that they would drive or fly up whenever possible to help in the construction.

Over the next four years, the house at Barnegat Pines slowly became a reality. Matt and Mary Ann made frequent trips to lend a hand. A week's vacation found Matt

---

1949—The first nonstop flight around the world touched down at Fort Worth, Texas, on March 2. The B-50 Superfortress *Lucky Lady II*, flown by the Air Force and refueled in midair, allowed the plane to travel 23,452 miles in ninety-four hours.

❋

Richard accepted a position in the sales department of the Murphy Diesel Company in Milwaukee, Wisconsin. His experience with diesels and diesel-electric generators qualified him to conduct training sessions for dealers throughout the United States and Canada.

❋

"IT'S ALL YOURS, FLY THE PLANE!"

❋

Henry F. Benson, Mary Ann's brother, was killed in the crash of an RB57 jet bomber at Eglin Air Force Base, Florida. "Hank," age 34, was a captain in the Air Force. A veteran of thirty missions in Europe during WW II and fifty-five in Korea during the Korean War, he held the Distinguished Flying Cross, Air Medal with four Oak Leaf Clusters, E.A.M.E. Ribbon, and the World War II Victory Medal. His funeral services and a full military burial were held May 28, 1954, at Arlington National Cemetery.

Philip—In 1952, Philip was hired by Warner Brothers as an illustrator for a movie entitled *The Iron Mistress* starring Alan Ladd and Virginia Mayo. It told the life story of Jim Bowie and his famous knife.

❋

November 4, 1952—General Dwight D. Eisenhower was elected president of the United States. In his inaugural address he said, *"Whatever America hopes to pass in the world must first come to pass in the heart of America."*

❋

1953—Douglas Aircraft started production of their DC-7, a four-engine, propeller powered plane carrying ninety-five passengers at a top speed of 410 miles per hour. However, Boeing led in sales with their Model 707 jet plane carrying 181 passengers at a top speed of 600 miles per hour.

❋

John—Following his graduation from high school in 1954, John attended Newark College of Engineering in Newark, New Jersey.

❋

Barnegat Pines—A community in Ocean County located near Barnegat Light. The 161-foot tall lighthouse is on Long Beach Island. In 1944, the historic lighthouse was decommissioned when it was decided that the Barnegat Lightship was more effective.

glazing the windows and Mary Ann helping with the painting and the meals. On weekend visits they pitched in with the finishing of the floors, wainscoting, walls, and ceilings. By 1953, Dad, Mom, and Jack were enjoying the summer months at Whippoorwill Hill, their home away from home. Matt and Mary Ann drove up in December to spend a white Christmas in the comfort of a beautifully decorated, snug retreat.

Matt looked to Whippoorwill Hill as a place where he could perhaps have the peace and freedom to pursue his freelance drawings of aircraft for publication. He discussed the thought with Mom and Dad. They readily agreed that he and Mary Ann were more than welcome to share their home. Having great faith in his artistic ability, Mary Ann encouraged Matt to accept their hospitality. In July 1954, Dad, Mom, and Jack moved to Barnegat Pines. Matt and Mary Ann resigned from the Library of Congress and also took up residence at Whippoorwill Hill. Mary Ann was hired by the Ocean County Prosecutor's Office in the city of Toms River, New Jersey.

Whippoorwill Hill

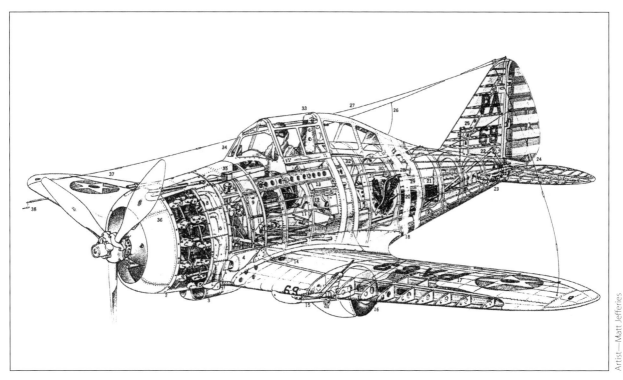

SEVERSKY P-35 Cutaway

Artist—Matt Jefferies

Matt—To share his interest in aviation with enthusiasts and broaden his contacts with those associations which could be beneficial to his work, Matt became a member of the American Aviation Historical Society, the Aviation Writers Association and the Air Force Association.

Matt attended the National Air Show held in Oklahoma City September 1-2-3, 1956. The Bendix Trophy Air Race was won by Capt. Pete Fernandez flying a North American F-100 at an average speed of 666.651 miles per hour over a course of 1,120 miles from George Air Force Base in California.

Matt soon realized that Whippoorwill Hill did indeed offer the environment he so desperately needed. His drawing board was set up in a den where natural sunlight brightened the room. Free from noise and distraction, he enjoyed a level of contentment conducive to turning out his best work. The photographic collection of aircraft and his research files were within easy reach. Books and manuscripts related to aviation, design, and art provided useful information for his ambitious projects. Magazines including *Air Progress*, *Flying*, and *American Modeler* published his scale profiles and structural cutaway drawings. Subscribers wrote in and asked for more of Matt's work. An issue of *Air Trails HOBBIES for Young Men*, featuring Matt's fine cutaway drawing of the Seversky P-35, received widespread recognition. Aviation enthusiasts prized copies of the detailed drawing.

Bell X-2 rocket powered aircraft

Aviation writers and historians became aware that Matt was a wellspring of information related to vintage aircraft. They turned to him to identify the remnants of planes found in barns, weed-covered fields, and abandoned hangars. On occasion, the skeletal frame of a fuselage was all that remained of a plane having no identifying markings. Matt's extensive collection of photographs, drawings, and specifications contributed to the identity of unknown aircraft. In 1956, Matt was approached by Warner Brothers Pictures in Hollywood to provide technical information on the X-2 Bell Aviation, rocket-powered, experimental aircraft. A movie, *Toward the Unknown*, starring William Holden and James Garner, was being filmed at Edwards Air Force Base in California. Interestingly, this film was James Garner's acting debut in a major motion picture. Likewise, it was Matt's first contribution to film making, one that also earned him a paycheck and encouraged him to seek similar employment in the film industry.

Canadian Aviation Museum, Ottawa, Canada—The museum possessed the fuselage of a twin-engine Delta aircraft which had been recovered from the site where it crashed in 1939. It was the first aircraft lost by the Royal Canadian Air Force in the Second World War. In addition to having several photographs, Matt had executed a scale drawing of the aircraft. He willingly provided the museum with data which would be useful on the plane's reconstruction.

August 26, 1954—The Bell X-2 rocket powered aircraft piloted by Capt. Iven Kincheloe Jr. reached an altitude of 126,000 feet. Powered by a double-barreled, Curtiss-Wright rocket engine, developing 15,000 pounds of thrust, the X-2 had a design speed of 2500 miles per hour.

Phil's steady employment at Warner Bros. clearly suggested that Hollywood welcomed young, talented artists. As Matt and Mary Ann weighed the thought of moving to California, a call from Phil convinced them to hesitate no longer. Several aviation films were in the planning stages, including *Bombers B-52*, a Warner Bros. production.

John—John joined the U.S. Air Force. He received his basic training at Sampson A.F. Base in Geneva, New York, and his multi-engine training at Sheppard A.F. Base in Wichita Falls, Texas. He was assigned to the 4060 Air Refueling Wing at Dow A.F. Base, Bangor, Maine. He was an inspector of Boeing KC-97 tankers which were utilized for the in-flight refueling of B-52 bombers. As a certified systems manager in flight, he performed the flight engineer's duties.

Philip—Color consultant credits went to Philip of four Warner Bros. films in 1954. In 1955, he received color consultant credit for *Battle Cry*. He was selected by Warner Bros. to utilize his talents as an illustrator on the film, *Bombers B-52*.

CHAPTER NINE

Matt and Mary Ann arrived in Hollywood on April 2, 1957. Although exhausted from their twenty-five-hundred-mile, cross-country trip in a sky blue, Plymouth station wagon, they lost no time in getting settled. An apartment was found on Edgecliff Drive within a short drive to the major movie studios. Matt accompanied Phil to Warner Bros. and was introduced to John Beckman, the *Bombers B-52* art director who had said that he was desperately in need of a set designer, "one with significant knowledge of military aircraft, or, more specifically, the B-52." The main character, he explained, is a U.S. Air Force flight engineer, played by Karl Malden, who is "proud of a job that keeps American bombers in the air." Phil recommended Matt!

In response to questions about his qualifications for the job, Matt presented his résumé, letters of recommendations, and a summary of his wartime experiences on the B-17 and other heavy bombers.

"Your credentials are certainly impressive, Matt, but what do you know about the B-52?"

"Well, I have a complete set of B-52 manuals so I feel that I know the aircraft quite well!"

Matt was hired on the spot and told to report to work the following morning. To move from a novice in the industry to set designer for a major film was indeed a quantum leap. Although overjoyed in landing the job, Matt wondered how he had been selected over other experienced set designers.

Sputnik I—The Soviet Union launched the first man-made Earth satellite October 4, 1957. In November **Sputnik II** was launched. The 1,000 pound sphere had a live dog aboard. The satellite orbited the Earth every ninety minutes in an elliptical orbit.

SAC—Following the Soviet Union's launching of Sputnik, America's Strategic Air Command (SAC) was placed on *high alert*. B-52 bombers, armed with nuclear weapons, were in the air *around the clock, twenty-four hours a day.*

Bombers B-52—The leading roles were played by Karl Malden, Marsha Hunt, and Natalie Wood. The film was released November 21, 1957.

Boeing B-52 Stratofortress—A long-range, heavy bomber capable of subsonic speeds at an altitude of 50,000 feet. The first B-52 flew in 1954. The bomber has a combat range of 8,800 miles. Eight jet engines, each delivering 17,000 pounds of thrust, power the 185,000 pound aircraft. Cruising speed is 650 miles per hour. A crew of five mans the bomber.

Mary Ann was employed as a secretary for Rexall Drug and Chemical Company. In 1959, Rexall was acquired by Dart Industries. Mary Ann was appointed secretary to the president's assistant.

John—Discharged from the Air Force, John moved to Los Angeles. He was employed in Lockheed's Missiles and Space Division as a design engineer on the Discovery, Mercury, and Apollo projects.

The Untouchables—The long-running TV series had its first showing in October 1959. Starring Robert Stack as Eliot Ness and narrated by Walter Winchell, the columnist, the show was extremely popular with viewers.

Ford Tri-motor—A high wing monoplane powered with three 450 horsepower radial engines. After introducing it in 1926, Ford built a total of 195 planes. The all-metal cabin plane carried eight passengers. It was dubbed the "Tin Goose" because of its corrugated metal fuselage.

Phil explained that the Designer Guild members were all busy on other projects. Determined to validate his being selected, Matt threw himself wholeheartedly into the job. The film depicts the Strategic Air Command's test of the Air Force's "newest flying fortress," the B-52.

The film was a challenge for Gordon Douglas, the director, in that it had to be technically accurate and had to satisfy the Air Force. Matt's expertise in designing the sets and working within the limitations imposed by the Air Force earned him high praise. Karl Malden had only to turn to Matt to learn how to portray a flight engineer. Unfortunately, the film's implausible plot maligned the quality of the final production.

Another Warner Bros. film, *The Old Man and the Sea*, starring Spencer Tracy and Felip Pazos, utilized the combined services of the Jefferies brothers. Matt executed technical illustrations for the construction of a twenty-foot long mechanical shark while Phil turned out the sketches and storyboards for the film's production. (It would be the last time Matt and Phil would work on the same film.)

Midnight to Breakfast
Matt's painting of a United Airlines Ford Tri-Motor en route between Chicago and New York, circa 1934.

Ben Casey—A medical drama that aired weekly on ABC from October 1961 to May 1966. The series was produced by Bing Crosby Productions. For the first two years *Ben Casey* was rated in the top twenty.

USS *Enterprise*—America's first nuclear-powered aircraft carrier launched in 1960 at Newport News, Virginia.

New York World's Fair—The theme of the 1964–1965 World's Fair, "Peace Through Understanding." The theme center was a 12-story high, stainless steel, model of the earth called *Unisphere*. The orbital tracks of three satellites encircled the giant globe.

Philip—1960, Philip was appointed assistant art director on the movie, *The Devil at Four O'clock*, a Columbia Pictures release starring Spencer Tracy, Frank Sinatra, Barbara Luna, and Kerwin Mathews.

Metro Goldwin Mayer hired Matt as a set designer on a seaborne mystery film, *The Wreck of the Mary Deare*. The saga relates the story of a salvage boat colliding with a derelict freighter, the *Mary Deare*, during a violent storm. The captain of the salvage boat, played by Charlton Heston, boards the apparently deserted freighter to discover that the half-crazed captain, played by Gary Cooper, is still aboard. The freighter is scuttled and the two survivors make for shore in a lifeboat to face a court of inquiry. The film was highly praised for the visual effects.

Desilu Studios turned to Matt to design a set of the Ford Tri-motor's eight-passenger cabin for an episode of *The Untouchables*. He had the advantage of having photographs of the plane's interior along with dimensional data. *Ben Casey,* another series for ABC Television, was also in production at Desilu Studios. The fictional Ben Casey, played by Vince Edwards, was a neurosurgeon at County General Hospital. The medical drama appealed to the viewing public as it dealt with the sufferings of contemporary society. Matt's reputation as a talented set designer preceded him, and he was given the job. One of his first assignments was the design of the hospital's operating room, one representative of the latest in medical technology. In the interest of expediency, Matt visited Los Angeles County Medical Center and painstakingly measured the operating room and photographed the array of sophisticated medical devices. Within a short time the detailed plans that emerged from his drawing board became a reality. The finished set was realistic and portrayed a sense of high tech professionalism in a sterile environment.

During a lull in the shooting, Matt and Mary Ann took a month's vacation and journeyed to the East Coast to visit family, friends, and the New York World's Fair. When he returned to Desilu Studios he found that his cubicle was empty. His drawing board, reference files, instruments, and art supplies were missing. Taken aback, he concluded that his taking an extended vacation had cost him his job. To clear up the matter he went to his boss and asked, "Where's my stuff . . . and where's the next *Ben Casey* script?"

"Matt, you're not on the show any more. We've moved your things to the big drafting room. There's a writer-producer by the name of Roddenberry who is on the way to meet with you. He's going to do a space show. You'll be working with him."

Having spoken, he turned and walked away with no further explanation. As Matt went about the task of setting up his drawing board, he looked up to behold a tall, stalwart, unkempt person approaching at a leisurely pace. Casually attired in an open collar shirt and rumpled corduroy trousers, his appearance suggested that he was unpretentious. He was accompanied by Herb Solow, assistant to Oscar Katz, vice president of Desilu Studios. "Matt," Herb said, "I want you to meet Gene Roddenberry. He's a writer. We want to make a pilot of one of his science fiction adventures. If the pilot sells it could lead to a series to be called *Star Trek*. Gene will tell you what he wants you to do. I'll leave you two alone to get acquainted."

(Throughout this text, all quoted statements of Gene Roddenberry and Herb Solow are those related to the author by Matt Jefferies.)

Matt's first impression of Gene Roddenberry was a positive one. They found that they had much in common. Both had volunteered for service in the Air Corps and had flown in B-17s in the war. Both were aviation buffs.

Gene Roddenberry—Born in El Paso, Texas, Roddenberry grew up in Los Angeles where his father was a policeman. During the Second World War, Gene Roddenberry piloted a B-17 in the South Pacific. Following his discharge from the Air Force he became a pilot for Pan American Airways. After surviving a crash in the Middle East, he followed in his father's footsteps and joined the Los Angeles Police Department. It was during this time that he began to write scripts for TV. He wrote twenty-seven episodes of *Have Gun-Will Travel*. Ten scripts were accepted for *West Point*, a 1956 series. Other shows for which he wrote scripts include, *Dr. Kildare* and *Dragnet*. Prior to *Star Trek*, he was best known as a writer for a series called *The Lieutenant*, an MGM production relating the experiences of a Marine Corps Lieutenant. Gene Roddenberry has been described as "a seemingly ordinary man with an extraordinary vision."

Herb Solow—Following the departure of Oscar Katz from Desilu Studios, Herb Solow was promoted to Vice President of Television Production.

Matt studied Rodenberry's demeanor as he began to explain the concept of *Star Trek*. Spoken softly, his words suggested that he was one with extraordinary vision and a driving determination to produce a space saga unlike any other in science-fiction history. "He told me what he wanted," Matt said. "Two hundred years into the future, a space ship with a crew of several hundred to go on a five-year mission into deep space to 'find out what's out there.' He explained that the ship would have 'warp drive.' I thought, *What the hell is warp drive?* He said that it was 'something he was working on.'"

Roddenberry went on to tell Matt that the space ship had to appear powerful but was to have no visible rocket exhausts or jet streams. "Its physical shape," he insisted, "must be unlike anything that appeared in 'Flash Gordon,' 'Buck Rogers,' or 'Amazing Stories.'" Before Matt could ask for more information, Roddenberry said, "See what you can come up with, Matt," and walked away. Matt watched his retreat, reached for pencil and paper, and began to sketch space ships as they emerged from his creative imagination. It was a time-consuming and challenging assignment.

Over a period of weeks hundreds of ideas were translated into rough sketches and tacked to the wall for Rodden-berry's scrutiny. With each viewing Roddenberry revealed more of what he expected of his "starship," as he now called the spacecraft. It would travel at three times the speed of light. A pressurized cabin and artificial gravity would allow the crew to function uninhibited as they would on earth. Matt recognized that a space craft designed to meet these criteria must be scientifically plausible. This would require consultation with engineers and space scientists.

Matt contacted representatives of NASA (National Aeronautics and Space Administration) and the Rand Corporation in Santa Monica, California.

Science Fiction Publications—Matt visited several used book stores and purchased copies of *Buck Rogers*, *Flash Gordon*, and *Amazing Stories*. All of the space ships depicted were rocket powered with visible exhausts. All were cigar-shaped and equipped with fins.

Warp Drive—Albert Einstein, in 1905, theorized that space could be *warped*. In nautical terms a vessel is *warped* into a desired position. In *Star Trek* jargon, warp drive enables a spaceship to travel faster than the speed of light.

U. S. S. *Enterprise*—The final sketch has been referred to as the "birth" of the *Enterprise*. It was this drawing that allowed Herb Solow to proceed with the filming of *Star Trek*. Drawn to a scale of a quarter-inch to the foot, Matt proposed a model having an overall length of sixty inches. However, the Anderson Co., a model builder, produced one which was eleven feet long. It was this model that was used in filming the early episodes of *Star Trek*.

U. S. S. *Enterprise*—A second model, only four feet long, was also used in the production of all *Star Trek* episodes. Paramount Pictures donated both the eleven foot and the four foot *Enterprise* model to the Air & Space Museum in Washington, D.C.

They concluded that with the continuing rapid advances in technology over the next two centuries, a spaceship like that envisioned by Roddenberry and Matt would conceivably be feasible. They offered their support.

After hundreds of ideas were translated into rough sketches, an intriguing design began to take shape. During each viewing, sketches were pulled from the wall and discarded. Others were left in place for further evaluation. Finally, one captured the attention of everyone involved in the painstaking selection process. "That's it, Matt!" Roddenberry shouted. "That's our Starship *Enterprise!*" Herb Solow smiled and said, "Congratulations, Matt! Now we have something to show to the people at NBC."

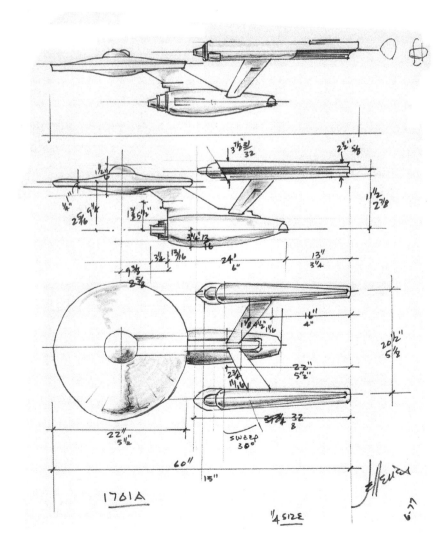

Fearful that Roddenberry and Solow might have second thoughts about the design, Matt duplicated the sketch, added dimensions, and rushed down to the mill to have a balsa wood model built. The dish and the lower hull were easily made, but turning of the engine pods had to await the availability of a lathe. Matt substituted birch dowels and the makeshift assembly was complete A string was attached for hanging the model from the ceiling. He also prepared a full-color rendering of the *Enterprise* to impress the NBC executives.

When a group arrived and applauded Matt's full-color rendering, Gene Roddenberry reached for the model, picking it up by the string. Because of the heavy, quarter-inch, wood dowels, the model flipped upside down. With his full attention directed towards the group, Roddenberry was unaware of the inversion. Matt had a difficult time convinc-

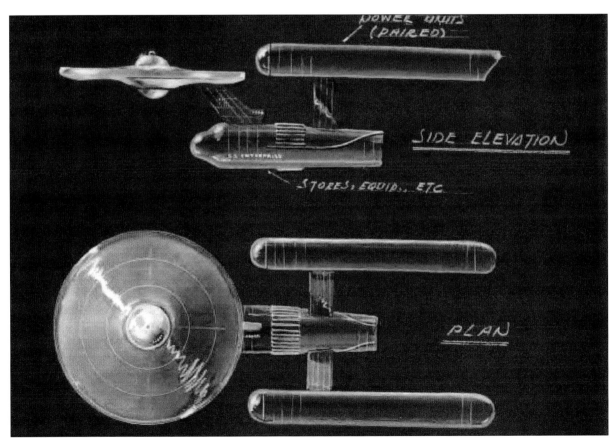

Matt's full-color rendering of the *U.S.S. ENTERPRISE*

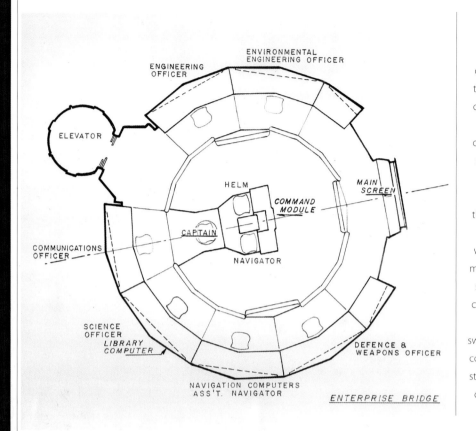

ENVIRONMENTAL ENGINEERING OFFICER

ENGINEERING OFFICER

ELEVATOR

HELM

COMMAND MODULE

MAIN SCREEN

CAPTAIN

COMMUNICATIONS OFFICER

NAVIGATOR

SCIENCE OFFICER
LIBRARY COMPUTER

DEFENCE & WEAPONS OFFICER

NAVIGATION COMPUTERS ASS'T. NAVIGATOR

ENTERPRISE BRIDGE

The Bridge—The bridge on the U. S. S. *Enterprise* is located atop the saucer-shaped primary hull. Its circular configuration allows convenient access to vital rooms from the centrally located command center. Around the periphery of the bridge are the laboratories, officers' quarters, sick bay, briefing room, navigation room and computer rooms. Access to the bridge is by an elevator from the primary hull. The location of the command center allows the captain, navigator, and helmsman to view the wall-mounted display monitors and the main screen without having to leave their stations. Construction of the bridge set challenged the ingenuity of the builders. Electrical automated indicator lights, switches, and sequential instruments were controlled from the command center, the stations, and from a remote panel located off-stage. The electrical wiring could be measured in miles.

ing everyone present that the ship had to be turned over to fly right side up. The enthusiastic response to Matt's *Enterprise* was a clear indication that NBC was reassured that a right decision had been made when they agreed to invest in a pilot episode.

Matt was acutely aware that the creation of the *Enterprise* in its basic configuration represented only the beginning of the set design work that lay ahead. The interior of the giant spaceship must serve every facet of operation: command center, engineering, navigation, communications, defense systems, crew accommodations, medical facilities, science labs, cargo, and environmental support. First priority was the design of the bridge which served as the ship's command center. The bridge required extraordinary attention to detail. It was on the bridge that the great ship would be operated and its complex systems monitored. Contemplating where to begin, Matt remembered that as a boy, he had often seen his father in the control room of a power plant, where he stood and faced an immense switchboard resplendent with colored indicator lights, switches, and gauges. Having to keep a watchful eye on the performance of all of the plant's systems, he had little opportunity to move away from his station.

Matt was determined to design a bridge which would allow the crew to sit comfortably, have the advantage of remote control, and have a clear view of the display monitors. To make the command center a model of high-tech efficiency, he used a hands-on approach to attain the desired results.

Matt enlisted the assistance of brother Jack. After arriving at the overall size of the bridge and each station, the size, shape, and location of the consoles and display monitors were decided. A full cut-out of each screen was pinned to the wall for viewing from a chair. Matt and Jack devoted many hours working together to arrive at the most effective location of monitors and consoles. Scale drawings were prepared and sent to the construction department for fabrication of the elaborate set.

The design of a futuristic sick bay presented Matt with another challenge.

Captain Kirk and officers in the Command Center

John Jefferies—In 1962, John left the aerospace industry to design sets for Columbia, Disney, Warner Bros, and Fox. Feature films included *King Rat* with George Segal, *Cat Ballou*, with Jane Fonda and Lee Marvin, *Marooned* with Gregory Peck, *Funny Girl* with Barbra Streisand, and *Hello Dolly* with Barbra Streisand and Walter Matthau. John also designed sets for the TV series, *I Dream of Jeannie*. In 1964, following his work as set designer on *Darling Lili*, he was hired by Matt to assist in the design of sets for **Star Trek**.

Star Trek—NBC rejected "The Menagerie" and requested a second pilot which was titled, "Where No Man Has Gone Before." Based on their acceptance of the pilot, NBC made a commitment to invest in *Star Trek*. The first episode, "The Man Trap" aired on NBC September 8, 1966.

Roddenberry predicted that with the extraordinary advances in scientific and medical technology, sick and injured members of the *Enterprise* would be diagnosed, treated, and cured quickly. He envisioned a full body, diagnostic scanner, a handheld scanner, and a hospital bed providing continuous monitoring of all bodily functions. Likewise, the medical instruments would be unlike any in present day existence. Working from Matt's original sketches, Jack proceeded to design the sick bay sets. Matt moved ahead with the sets required for the pilot episode entitled "The Cage," which was scheduled to start filming in late November 1964.

As the set designs emerged from Matt's drawing board, Roddenberry, script in hand, stopped by, studied the

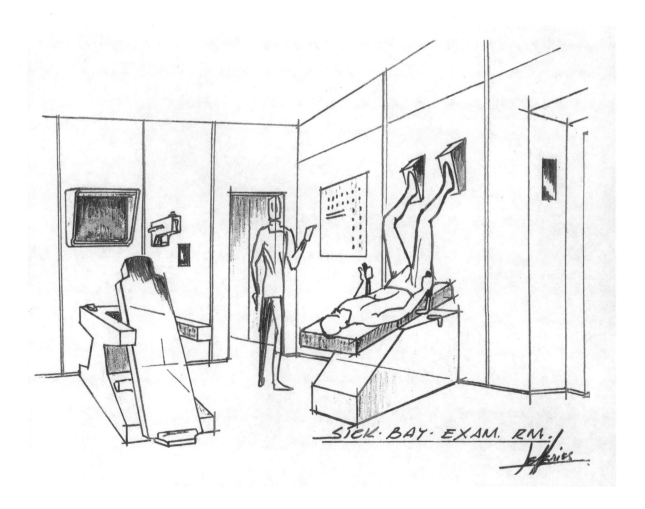

SICK·BAY·EXAM·RM.

Matt—For the two pilots, Matt had the title "set designer." For the first two episodes he was "production designer." For the remaining original series, he was "art director."

✻

August 9, 1965—Letter to Matt from Gene Roddenberry:
"I was enormously pleased by your unusual creativity and flexibility in meeting constantly changing problems in time, budget, and dramatic needs of the show."

✻

Star Trek—"Most TV shows can use their sets over and over. We can't. Except for the *Enterprise*, we make our sets one week and throw them away the next! It's an insanely difficult proposition!"

—Matt Jefferies

Dear Dick,
Be sure to watch your NBC station Thursday nights at 8:30. Your brother, Matt, is production designer on a space program called Star Trek.
Love, Mom

✻

Herb Solow—"Necessity made Matt Jefferies the absolute mother of *Star Trek* invention."

✻

Jefferies Tube—Access to mechanical and electrical components on the Enterprise is through a series of tubes located internally, behind, and beneath the compartments. To credit Matt with the innovation, the tubes were named for him.

✻

Star Trek Opening Narration—
"Space . . . the final frontier. These are the voyages of the Starship Enterprise, *its five-year mission: to explore strange new worlds . . . to seek new life and new civilizations. To boldly go where no man has gone before."*

✻

Enterprise—Matt designed the doors on the *Enterprise* to be triangular or trapezoidal. The doors never swung open. Rather, they slid sideways or upward. *Star Trek* Fans were curious as to how the doors opened and closed so rapidly. It remained a guarded secret.

sketches, and voiced his opinions. Suggested additions, omissions, or total rejection were debated, with Roddenberry having the final word. However, mutual respect frequently convinced either one to rethink his opinion and compromise. Matt explained their relationship when he said, "Coming up with ideas was the biggest problem. I liked Gene but he was a dreamer. I was a nuts and bolts man. I guess we were a good balance!"

Robert "Bob" Justman, co-producer of *Star Trek*, is quoted as saying, "Matt Jefferies was the most decent and devoted human being on the production team. He never lost his cool; never lost his temper. He would find it difficult to speak when our over-budget show forced me to take away half his construction money. I'd demand the

Courtesy Susan Sackett

Roddenberry and Matt

Matt's *Enterprise* painting

impossible, that he still provide us with believable sets for less money. He'd gulp a bit and finally say, in a very throaty voice, 'Well . . . let me see what I can do. I'll give it a try.' So Matt would try harder, and he always came through for us."

NBC had committed to sixteen *Star Trek* episodes for the 1966–67 season. Episode one, "The Man Trap," was scheduled to be aired on September 8, 1966. The pressure on the producers, directors, writers, designers, and film and construction crews was withering. Only components comprising the *Enterprise* were constructed as permanent sets. All others were built for single episodes and subsequently discarded. Having limited construction funds, Matt improvised, using every imaginable prop to simulate whatever the script required. Landscapes varied from one planet in the galaxy to another. Alien civilizations living

Gene Roddenberry—The staff nicknamed Gene Roddenberry, "Great Bird of the Galaxy." The expression was taken from the episode, "The Man Trap" and intended as a humorous blessing. The name stuck!

July 28, 1966
To: Matt Jefferies
Subject: SET SKETCHES

Dear Matt:
If I don't get the preliminary set sketches for "Mudd's Women," the Great Bird of the Galaxy is going to do something nasty on you!
Your former friend,
Bob Justman

July, 1967—Second season of *Star Trek* in production. Desilu and Paramount Studios sold to Gulf & Western Corp. Operations continue under the name, Paramount Studios.

U.S.S. *Enterprise* Engineering

Star Trek—The second season of *Star Trek* ended in January 1968. Ratings were mediocre. It was widely believed that NBC would cancel the series. However, an unprecedented groundswell of protest by the fans convinced NBC to continue the series for a third season.

***Galileo* Shuttlecraft**—The shuttlecraft bears the name of the Italian mathematician and astronomer, Galileo Galilei. As the first to explore the universe with a telescope, Galileo is credited with the discovery of many new facts related to astronomy. He was firm in conviction that the earth moves around the sun.

in Earth-Mars environments were as varied as those on planet earth. To produce a weekly, one-hour episode with limited funds and unsatisfactory working conditions in a deteriorating Desilu studio was a daunting undertaking.

The *Galileo* Shuttlecraft did not exist in the first fifteen episodes of *Star Trek*. The script of episode sixteen, titled "The *Galileo* Seven," called for a landing party to physically step foot on a planet's surface. As the U. S. S. *Enterprise* was not designed to land on a planet, a small, short-ranged craft was needed to serve as a shuttle vessel. Matt worked up sketches for a teardrop-shaped craft and submitted them to AMT Corporation who was contracted to build a miniature model for filming. Much to Matt's bitter disappointment, AMT decided that his curved hull design was beyond their capabilities and too costly to build. In exchange for the right to market a model of the U. S. S. *Enterprise* and the *Galileo* Shuttlecraft, AMT was allowed to construct a shuttlecraft of their own design. Box-like and without the nacelles configuration of the *Enterprise*, the AMT *Galileo*-7 shuttlecraft was accepted by the studio. Matt designed the interior, which accommodated seven crew members. The control console was designed with a minimum of basic instrumentation. It was never clear how many shuttlecraft were docked in the *Enterprise's* shuttle bay. Matt suggested that perhaps there were seven, as the *Galileo* shuttlecraft was assigned the number NCC-1701-7.

The *Enterprise* was on a peaceful mission to explore outer space. However, as earthly explorers throughout history often encountered hostility, so it was with the *Enterprise*. The Klingon Empire from an unknown planet challenged the Starship to engage in battle. Their ships were comparable in size and capability to those of the Starfleet. To capture the

Matt's original sketch of the *Galileo* Shuttlecraft depicts a small ship which could take-off and land vertically. Other variations illustrate twin landing pads mounted beneath the propulsion units. All of his hull designs are of the teardrop configuration. Matt's reasoning was that the shuttlecraft may land on a planet having an atmosphere similar in density to that of earth. Therefore, he concluded, the hull should be aerodynamically shaped. It is interesting to note that the model constructed by AMT incorporated the landing pad concept rather than vertical take-off and landing power units.

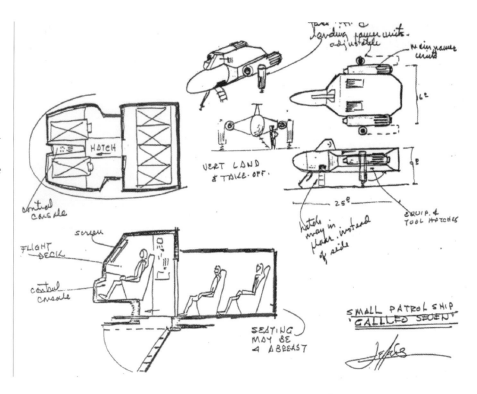

sequence of events on film necessitated the construction of a miniaturized model of a Klingon battle cruiser. As with the evolution of the *Enterprise*, Matt again used his imagination to render sketches of a vessel which in appearance would reflect the hostile nature of the Klingons. The final configuration was overwhelmingly approved by the studio and by AMT who were contracted to build the model.

One day, Roddenberry, appearing worn and perplexed, cornered Matt and asked, "Matt, what do you know about thermodynamics?"

"Only the basics, but I remember it's about the conversion of energy from one form to another. I believe that the first law of thermodynamics states that 'the energy going into a system, minus the energy coming out of a system, equals the change in the energy stored in the system.'"

Klingon battle cruiser—Matt designed the battle cruiser for an episode entitled "Elaan of Troyius" which aired in the third series. He prepared dimensional drawings of the ship for AMT Corp, who built two 28.5 inch models; one as a studio model for filming and the other as a prototype for producing a plastic model kit for marketing by Paramount. Following the final episode of *Star Trek*, AMT gave Matt the studio model. He donated the model to the Air and Space Museum in Washington, D.C. The second model was given to Gene Roddenberry.

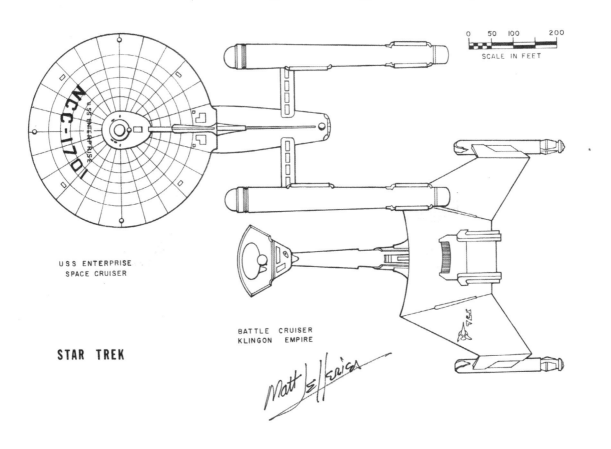

0   50   100   200
SCALE IN FEET

USS ENTERPRISE
SPACE CRUISER

STAR TREK

BATTLE   CRUISER
KLINGON   EMPIRE

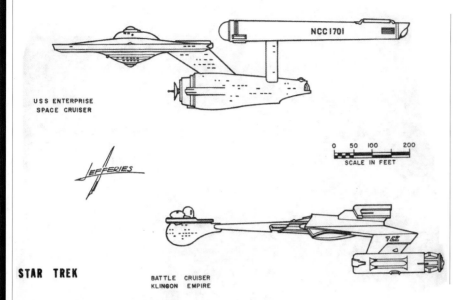

USS ENTERPRISE
SPACE CRUISER

JEFFERIES

0   50   100   200
SCALE IN FEET

STAR TREK

BATTLE CRUISER
KLINGON EMPIRE

When asked how he conjured up such a bizarre configuration for an alien space ship, Matt replied: "Given the belligerent nature of the Klingons, I imagined their warships to appear formidable. The sting ray and manta ray came to mind. Both aquatic creatures impart fear when sighted."

Roddenberry gave his model of the Klingon battle cruiser to a friend who in turn sold it at auction in 1998 for $11,500. The buyer later resold the model at a second auction in 2004 for $64,900.

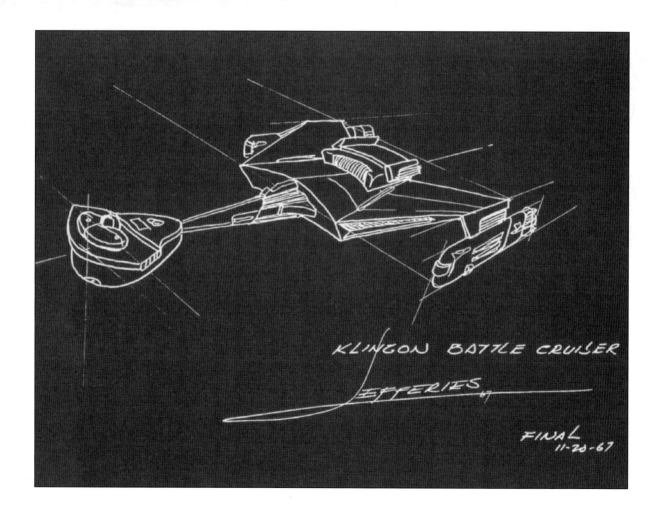

KLINGON BATTLE CRUISER

JEFFERIES

FINAL
11-20-67

Matt with model of Klingon Battle Cruiser

Dorothy C. Fontana—Dorothy was Roddenberry's secretary during the planning and filming of the two pilots. Following the September 8, 1966 airing of "Man Trap", the first episode of *Star Trek*, she was promoted to the position of story editor. Dorothy was an accomplished writer but had never written a screenplay. Her ultimate goal was to work as a film writer. She wrote a *Star Trek* episode titled "*Tomorrow is Yesterday*" and showed it to Roddenberry. Pleased with the story concept and the dialogue, he approved the script. The episode was aired on January 26, 1967. When Matt donated the model of the Klingon battle cruiser to the Smithsonian's National Air and Space Museum, Dorothy offered to take it with her as carry-on luggage on a trip she had previously planned. They discussed how best to prepare the model for the journey and decided to merely wrap it in clear plastic and place it in a garbage bag. On boarding the plane she found that the three-foot model could not be placed in an overhead bin so a flight attendant decided to put it in a coat closet in back of the plane. As the garbage bag was not deep enough to cover the whole model, the 'head' was exposed. Some passengers recognized the Klingon battle cruiser and asked that they be allowed to see it. Following take-off, the model was unwrapped and walked down the aisle of the airliner to the applause of everyone on board.

※

Romulan Star Empire—An alien, militaristic empire from the outer edges of the galaxy. Through an alliance with the Klingon Empire, the Romulans copied their fleet design. The Klingon battle cruiser (as a Romulan ship) was used in the "Enterprise Incident" episode.

"You've got it right, Matt! I've been reading up on the subject. It's about the properties of stored energy in an object, such as velocity, temperature, pressure and other characteristics."

"Why do you ask, Gene?"

"I've been awake all night trying to come up with a hand-carried weapon for the crew of the *Enterprise*. I have decided that it must be an all-purpose, stored energy weapon with multiple capabilities."

"Meaning what?"

"Well, it should be capable of emitting a beam of energy similar to a laser but one that can also be adjusted to inter-

April 26, 1966—Memo from Gene Roddenberry to Matt:

Subject: **Phaser Weapons**
Reference the mating of various components of the phaser weapons, the point I was trying to make in my original sketch (if you can call my scribbling "sketching") is that when the hand phaser is mated to the pistol, they should appear as *one weapon*. Same with the pistol mating into the future rifle. This not only has good dramatic logic behind it but would have much greater toy advantages that way too.

Gene Roddenberry

When the maximum power phase is utilized, a human target can be made to disappear entirely in a flash of light.

The phaser can be set to disintegrate rock or to heat it into a molten state.

The phaser can be set to hit a man with such force that he will be hurled through the air.

"THE ENEMY WITHIN"
Episode #5 on October 6, 1966.
Sulu, the weapons officer on the *Enterprise*, uses hand-held phaser to heat solid rock.

act with the wave pattern of any molecular form. In other words, the beam can be steady, intermittent or pulsating. The particular energy phase selected will depend on the nature of the target. For example, it may be used as a thermal device to convert matter into energy or a pulsating weapon to stun or disintegrate. I have decided to call it a *phaser* for obvious reasons, and it must be small enough to be held in the palm of the hand. So, my friend, put your magic to work. See what you can come up with so that I can get a full night's sleep!"

"OK, boss! You'll have your little gizmo phaser design tomorrow, and if you don't like it, I'll dream up another one for the day after that and then again, the day after that . . . just as we did when we decided on the design of the *Enterprise* and the Klingon battle cruiser."

"Thanks, Matt. I knew that we could count on you. I'll owe you one!"

After numerous ideas were consigned to paper, it occurred to Matt that designing something as simple as a hand-held

SULU HEATS ROCK
"THE ENEMY WITHIN"

phaser was in some respects more difficult than designing a space ship. The weapon would have to be of a design unlike anything seen in any science fiction publication or film. In all respects it had to be original. Gradually, by his usual tedious process of observation and elimination, he prepared a conceptual sketch and presented it to Roddenberry. Pleased with the design, Gene informed Matt that he had more work to do before he could return to what he was doing before the matter of a phaser came up. The hand-held weapon, he explained, must fit comfortably into a pistol having a handle, which serves as a power pack to increase the energy. Likewise, the pistol must mate with a rifle, having even greater range and accuracy. With these requirements in mind, Matt again tackled the innovative project with his usual determination.

The genesis of an episode for television is the story. Nothing in the manner of production can move forward until the art director/set designer has been briefed by the script writer and made aware of the environment of each scene. Matt had the daunting task of not only designing new sets every week but he was painfully aware that no two planets visited by the *Enterprise* were alike. His unique designs earned the respect of the cast, the crew, and the viewing public.

"Squire of Gothos," Episode #18

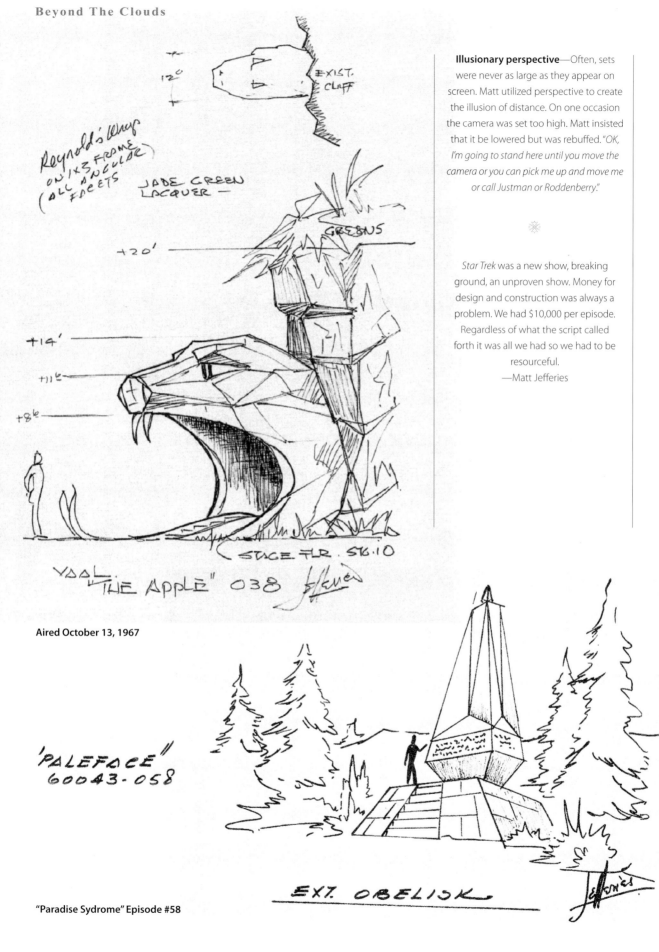

12°
EXIST. CLIFF

Reynold's Ruys
ON 1X3 FRAME
(ALL ANGULOR
FACETS)

JADE GREEN
LACQUER —

+20'

GREENS

+14'

+11⁶

+8⁶

STAGE FLR. 516.10

YOAL
"THE APPLE" 038

Aired October 13, 1967

Illusionary perspective—Often, sets were never as large as they appear on screen. Matt utilized perspective to create the illusion of distance. On one occasion the camera was set too high. Matt insisted that it be lowered but was rebuffed. *"OK, I'm going to stand here until you move the camera or you can pick me up and move me or call Justman or Roddenberry."*

❊

Star Trek was a new show, breaking ground, an unproven show. Money for design and construction was always a problem. We had $10,000 per episode. Regardless of what the script called forth it was all we had so we had to be resourceful.
—Matt Jefferies

'PALEFACE"
60043·058

EXT. OBELISK

"Paradise Sydrome" Episode #58

Bob Justman, Matt Jefferies, and Herb Solow.

Final Season—After seventy-nine episodes of *Star Trek*, spanning three seasons, NBC dropped the show. In its wake were millions of fans around the world who memorialized the show by attending *Star Trek* conventions. Anything connected with the show was prized. Pieces of the original sets, costumes, scripts, props, and even office memos were collected by loyal "trekkers." The model of the *Enterprise* set pictured sold in 2001 for $43,000. Matt donated the proceeds to The Motion Picture and Television Fund, a charity for the entertainment industry.

During the filming of the first episodes of *Star Trek* in 1966, Matt was frequently interrupted in his work by directors who asked him to accompany them to the stage to see the sets. The request was a valid one in that a director must plan the filming of an episode well in advance of the shooting date. Unfortunately, there was no way that Matt could comply in a satisfactory manner, as the permanent sets were not left in place due to the crowded and limited space on Desilu's Stage 9. To solve the problem and at the same time maintain a good rapport with the directors, Matt constructed a four-foot square, three-dimensional model depicting all of the *Enterprise* permanent sets. The project was accomplished in his home on evenings and weekends. When it was completed, he carried it to the studio and hung it up on the wall of the art department for viewing. The directors were elated! The scale model allowed them to be thoroughly acquainted with the layout of the sets prior to the deadlines.

Filming of the final episode of the second season was concluded on January 10, 1968. Viewers complained that the episodes no longer resembled the successful *Star Trek* format. There was serious doubt that NBC would agree to a third season. However, loyal fans convinced NBC to return to the air in the fall.

Although the daily grind of designing sets for *Star Trek* consumed most of his time, Matt continued to pursue his interest in aviation art. His paintings attracted an admiring audience of aviation artists and historians. "When I am researching or painting a plane," he said, "I am oblivious to the relentless pressure of creating new sets for futuristic, outer space episodes. My paintings are meant to portray aviation as it was in the dawn of flight."

Matt's painting of "Hi Hats"

"HI HATS" PAINTING

The U.S. Navy's Fighter Squadron One "HI HATS" Aerobatic Team performed at the 1921 Cleveland Air Races. Three Boeing F3B biplanes, (tied together with 30-foot ropes), thrilled the crowd with their daring maneuvers.

June 9, 1988
Dear Walt,
I am pleased to inform you that the membership of the AAHS has chosen your painting, *High Hats*, to receive the 1986 Annual Artist Award. A plaque with a suitable inscription has been mailed to you. I wish to personally congratulate you and to thank you for your superb contribution to the society.

Harry Gann, President

American Aviation Historical Society—Established in 1956, the society provides mutual support to members dedicated to the preservation of recorded aviation history. The society fosters the development and dissemination of aeronautical knowledge. Matt, designated Life Member # 1, served two terms as a director of AAHS. He was also technical editor of *Journal*, the society's quarterly publication.

"Walt Jefferies has made many valuable contributions to the operation of the Society and to the content of the *Journal*. His art has enlivened the rear covers of several AAHS *Journals*. In addition, his inboard scale profiles and other technical illustrations have further dramatized AAHS articles."

1995 AAHS Journal

Matt and Mary Ann took advantage of every opportunity to explore the wonders of Southern California. Of particular interest were the missions established by Padre Junipero Serra along the El Camino Real, the "King's Highway." Known for his energetic determination, the devout Franciscan priest accomplished wonders despite ill health, hostile natives, and a harsh environment The beautifully restored missions of Santa Barbara, San Miguel, and San Gabriel were often visited because of their close proximity to Los Angeles. On the day that migratory swallows were expected to return to the Mission of San Juan Capistrano, Matt and Mary Ann were there to witness the miraculous phenomenon. Visits to Yosemite National Park were awe-inspiring. The majestic granite sentinel, El Capitan, the cascading, mist-enshrouded, Bridalveil Fall, Cathedral Spires, and the towering giant sequoias were reminders of God's creativity. "Yosemite," Matt said, "is a photographer's paradise!" He always took his camera to record the scenic panorama of Yosemite.

Padre Junipero Serra—Sent to New Spain as a Franciscan missionary, Serra arrived at Vera Cruz, in 1749. Emulating St. Francis, he traveled on foot. On his journey to Mexico City he was bitten on the leg by a snake, which left him lame for the rest of his life. During the fifteen years of ecclesiastical jurisdiction, he established nine missions. In 1784 he died at Carmel Mission and is buried in the sanctuary of its Church.

✳

Yosemite National Park—The monolith known as El Capitan is said to be the largest single granite formation in the world. It rises 3,604 feet above the Yosemite Valley. Waterfalls in the Park are numerous. Perhaps the most famous is Yosemite Falls, which cascades from three elevations, the height of one elevation being eight times the height of Niagara Falls.

✳

Giant sequoias—These trees are the largest living things in the world. Some are over 300 feet tall with base trunks thirty-five feet in diameter. Tree rings indicate that many are over 3,000 years old.

Matt's 1961 Chryslter 300

Mary Ann and W.M. Jefferies Sr. atop a fallen giant Sequoia during visit to Yosemite.

Love, American Style—The anthology comedy series, aired on the ABC network, ran for four seasons. The last of 108 episodes was January 11, 1974.

John—In 1972, John left *Love, American Style* and went with Columbia as assistant art director for a six-hour mini-series, *QB VII*. In 1973, Universal Studios appointed John set designer for a feature film, *W. C. Fields and Me*, starring Rod Steiger and Valerie Perrine. This film led to Universal's appointing John as assistant art director on *The Rockford Files*, a one-hour TV series which would enjoy a popular run.

Philip—In 1968, Philip was art director on *Butch Cassidy and the Sundance Kid*, a feature film starring Paul Newman, Robert Redford, and Katherine Ross. The film won an Academy Award for music and lyrics with "Raindrops Keep Fallin' on My Head." The picture was also nominated for best picture, but the award went to *Midnight Cowboy*.

Excursions to the remote corners of California were particularly enjoyable after Matt acquired a beautiful 1961 Chrysler 300 convertible. The classic car was a joy to own and drive.

Following the demise of *Star Trek*, Paramount was not about to allow Matt and Jack to take their combined talents elsewhere. Matt was appointed art director and John, set designer, for a comedic weekly TV series called *Love, American Style*. When Matt inquired about the general scope of the new series he was told, "Bedrooms, Matt, bedrooms! You will have to come up with a new bedroom set for almost every episode. Each one-hour show may contain one, two, three, or four vignettes. Most will most assuredly include a bedroom scene. Many writers will contribute to the series. All will be instructed to include a bedroom in their stories. You can count on it, Matt!" To design as many as four bedroom sets every week, with no two alike, would tax Matt's aptitude and patience, but he was up to the challenge. Matt rolled up his sleeves and tackled the job with as much enthusiasm as he could muster. Several weeks into the project, Matt and Jack could not pass a furniture store window without looking in to see how the bedrooms were displayed. The show premiered September 29, 1969. It was an immediate success! The viewing public welcomed a show which required little or no concentration in order to follow a story line or to decipher a plot. *Love, American Style* was pure entertainment, providing an escape from the daily grind of working Americans. Although many of the episodes bordered on the ridiculous, they explored the lighter side of ordinary people in their quest for love and romance. For example, "Love and the Bed," an episode aired December 29, 1969,

1935 Waco YOC Cabin Plane was originally the property of the adjutant general of the State of Indiana. Its calling sign was NS40Y. The plane was manufactured by the Weaver Airplane Company of Lorain, Ohio, hence the name, WACO. Matt and Mary Ann purchased a hangar at the Santa Paula Airport where the Waco was parked for restoration. Weekends and holidays often found Matt hard at work on the disassembly, repair, and replacement of components. The plane was painted black with a white stripe running the length of the fuselage. Wing and tail surfaces were white. The plane was given a new calling sign, NC17740.

Santa Paula is located in the Santa Clara River Valley, sixty-five miles northwest of Los Angeles. Known as the "citrus capital of the world," Santa Paula is surrounded by lemon, orange, and avocado orchards. In 1928 the city was all but wiped out by a twenty-five-foot wall of water. Forty-two miles upstream on the Santa Clara River, a 205-foot high concrete dam failed, sending millions of gallons of water racing toward the Pacific Ocean, fifty miles away. The St. Francis Dam disaster took over 500 lives and laid waste to thousands of acres of ranch land and farms. In 1929–1930, local ranchers, Ralph Dickenson and Dan Emmet, decided to build an airport on an area adjacent to the river. Dedicated in August 1930, the airport is known for its array of antique, classic, and experimental aircraft owned and flown by retired airline and military pilots, Hollywood personalities, ranchers, and local businessmen.

told of the battle of two neighbors for ownership of a brass bed. The episode explained the Colonial courtship custom of "bundling," where sweethearts would lie on the same bed fully-clothed. The brass bed in this episode became as popular as Spock's ears in *Star Trek*. Every bedroom set thereafter included the brass bed.

The proverb, "All work and no play makes Jack a dull boy," was not in any way applicable to Matt. His interest in aviation never diminished. When not at the studio concentrating on the next episode, he continued with his drawings and research of vintage aircraft. To someday own a plane was an objective that never left his mind. One day he saw a 1935 Waco YOC Custom cabin plane advertised in an aviation magazine. Although he was looking for an open-cockpit model, he decided to fly to Reno, Nevada, to inspect the plane. When Matt and writer/photographer, Bob O'Hara, boarded a commercial airliner for Reno, they carried parachutes in their carry-on baggage, much to the consternation of the stewardess and fellow passengers. They found the Waco parked in a remote corner of the airport. Judging from its appearance and the height of the weeds in the field, the plane had not been flown for many months. Permission was obtained to start the engine and check the controls to determine if it was air-worthy. Satisfied that they could fly safely to the airport at Santa Paula, California, they made a deal with the owner, and they took off in a burst of power. Matt finally had the airplane he had talked about since he was a boy.

Matt's Waco shared a hangar with Bob Hathaway's 1941 LCA Culver Cadet, a low-wing monoplane. Bob had flown B-26 bombers and C-54 transports for the Air Force in World War II. He was manager of Disney Studio's sound department.

WACO YOC 'Custom' Cabin Plane before restoration.

"Good morning! Looks like that old Waco has seen better days!"

Matt, occupied with disassembly of the plane's Jacobs engine, turned to see who was speaking. "No doubt about it," Matt replied as he wiped his oily hands, studied the stranger, and reached out to shake hands.

"Name's Gurney. They call me Bud. And yours?"

"Matt Jefferies. I've heard of you. You're Lindbergh's friend."

"Right, Slim and I barnstormed together."

"I'm told that you fly a Gypsy Moth."

"Yep, great bird, the Gypsy Moth! I'm heading over to the sandwich shop for a bite. Care to come along?"

"Thanks. I could use a break. Give me a minute to clean up a bit."

From that first casual meeting, Bud Gurney and Matt became good friends. Bud was a retired United Airlines pilot. He and Matt had much in common. Their love of flying started when they were youngsters. Bud was sixteen and doing odd jobs for the Nebraska Aircraft Company in Lincoln when he met twenty-year-old Charles Lindbergh, who was taking flying lessons. After buying a war surplus

Harlan "Bud" Gurney—Bud Gurney was technical director on the feature film, *Spirit of St. Louis*. The role of Charles A. Lindbergh was played by Jimmy Stewart. In 1972, Lindbergh visited his friend, Bud Gurney, at the Santa Paula airport. With Lindbergh at the controls, they went aloft in Bud's Gypsy Moth biplane. Gurney reminded Lindbergh that he was the first to call him "Slim."

Logsdon's Restaurant—Shirley Logsdon's eatery replaced the old sandwich shop. Good food, moderate prices, and friendly service attracted a loyal clientele. It was a place for pilots and aviation enthusiasts to gather and *shoot the breeze*. They talked about flying and airplanes. They talked about air speed, lift, drag, thrust, torque, dihedral, manifold pressures, gyros, and altimeters. And they talked about the weather. Flying was their obsession. Talking about flying was second only to flying. Many of the tales were tall ones, but no one minded when it was all about flying.

Cliff Robertson—Famed movie actor, accomplished pilot, and collector of antique aircraft, Cliff Robertson was a well known figure around the Santa Paula airport. Two *Tiger Moth* biplanes occupied his hangar. He also owned one of the few remaining British *Spitfire* fighter planes of World War II fame. When flying over the Santa Paula airport, he was known to fly low and wave to his admirers.

Curtiss Jenny biplane, Lindbergh teamed up with Gurney to barnstorm around the Midwest. Lindbergh flew the plane, and Gurney parachuted to entertain at state fairs and livestock shows. Gurney also became a pilot, and both flew U.S. Post Office mail routes. Their friendship has been well-documented.

Ralph Dickenson was manager of the Santa Paula airport, a position he had held since it opened in 1930. The airport, small in comparison to most privately held airports, had a single, 1,700 foot runway, a wind sock, and no control tower. Pilots knew the rules: No straight-in approaches allowed. Pilots must circle to make certain that the runway was clear for landing. Flying over the city must be above 1,500 feet altitude. Only daylight flying permitted. No touch-and-go on weekends and holidays. Any violation of these rules would guarantee the guilty pilot a thorough chewing out by Ralph Dickenson. He was adamant about keeping the airport a safe one.

To limit the frequency of commuting between Hollywood and Santa Paula, Matt and Mary Ann had living quarters constructed on a level above the hangar. The addition

Matt in hangar's "FLIGHT LOUNGE."

Apollo 11 Spacecraft—Launched from the Kennedy Space Center in Florida, the Apollo 11 spacecraft arrived at the moon four days later. From a moon orbit, the lunar module descended from the spacecraft and landed on the moon July 20, 1969. Commander Neil A. Armstrong informed Mission Control in Houston, Texas, "the Eagle has landed." As he stepped out onto the "Sea of Tranquility," he spoke these words: "That's one small step for man, one giant leap for mankind." Edwin E. Aldrin, pilot of the lunar module, was the second astronaut to walk on the surface of the moon.

Richard—Construction, oil field, and mining equipment sales in Western United States and Alberta, Canada, allowed Richard frequent visits to Hollywood to visit his mother, (now residing in Hollywood), and his brothers.

John—1968–69, Set designer for a film, *Paint Your Wagon*, starring Lee Marvin, Clint Eastwood, and Jean Seberg.

Philip—1969–70, Art Director on *WUSA*, a feature Paramount film starring Paul Newman and Joanne Woodward.

Matt—The bed pictured was from the *Star Trek Enterprise* set. It was occupied in the original series by Captain Kirk. Not pictured is Mr. Spock's bed. Both were sold at auction and the proceeds donated to The Motion Picture and Television Fund, an entertainment industry charity.

Curtiss JN-4 Jenny, a two seat biplane built for training American and Canadian pilots in WW-I. It is powered by the Curtiss-built, OX-5, V-8, 90 hp liquid cooled engine. The plane has a cruising speed of 60 mph. During the war 6,070 JN series aircraft were delivered to the U.S. Air Service. After the war the Jenny became the most popular plane for barnstormers who performed death-defying stunts for an admiring public. Five dollars would buy a ride in a Jenny. Considered the most famous of all antique airplanes, the Jenny has captured the imagination of aviation enthusiasts around the world.

Logsdon's Restaurant—Logsdon invited Matt to exhibit his paintings on the walls of the popular restaurant. Patrons who asked about the artist were surprised to learn that he was the art director on *Star Trek*, *Love, American Style*, and *Little House on the Prairie*.

U.S. Air Force Art Program—Another of Matt's paintings depicting three Curtiss JN-4 "Jennies" flying over Love Field in celebration of the Armistice was donated to the Air Force for display on the walls of the Pentagon.

allowed them to devote more time to restoration of the Waco and more opportunities to enjoy the camaraderie of their friends. Called the "Flight Lounge," the accommodation provided a place to relax, sleep, prepare meals, dine, and entertain. Furnishings salvaged from *Star Trek* sets were utilized to good advantage. Beds were those used by Captain Kirk and Mr. Spock on the U. S. S. *Enterprise*. A gallery of Matt's framed paintings graced the walls. An American flag displayed above the hangar door announced that the Jefferies were "in residence." Word got around that coffee and "fly talk" were always available at the Jefferies's hangar. Many stopped by to see the artist at work. Although his aviation art was for the sheer joy of painting, Matt eventually succumbed to the urgings of others to exhibit his work on special occasions.

Matt's manifest penchant for painting vintage aircraft undoubtedly derived from his childhood fascination with planes having fabric-covered wings and wooden props. Called "tail draggers," the flimsy planes were veterans of the First World War era. They were flown by the mail pilots who passed over the Sanford farm in Ottoman, Virginia. They were the planes favored by the barnstormers to entertain thousands across the country. They were the planes used by flying bootleggers to transport illegal

Matt's painting *Flying Frolic*

whiskey during Prohibition. Matt and I had constructed balsa wood models of the Curtiss JN-4 Jenny, the Pitcairn PA-5 *Mailwing*, the Sopwith *Camel*, and other tail draggers. Owners of vintage aircraft at Santa Paula marveled at the attention given to detail in Matt's paintings. A number of pilots commissioned him to render paintings of their privately owned planes. However, he usually declined to paint modern aircraft. "I don't really enjoy doing modern aircraft," he explained. "Now, if someone has a classic or an antique and wants a painting—that's another story! They can reach me at the Santa Paula Airport, and then we'll take a good look at the project."

The TV show, *Little House on the Prairie*, made its debut on NBC in 1974. Michael Landon, executive producer, brought Matt to the show to design the sets. Filming the life and adventures of the Ingalls family in the nineteenth century in the prairie town of Walnut Grove provided a vast array of opportunities for Michael Landon to capture an audience of millions, both young and old. The migration of adventuresome and determined settlers to America's western frontier was epic in proportion. The hardships they endured challenged their staying power. Prairie fires, drought, pestilence, floods, and lawlessness threatened their very existence. But they remained! They broke the sod and tilled the soil. They raised crops and livestock.

They built communities like that of Walnut Grove. Buildings were erected to house a bank, town hall, post office, school, restaurants, doctor's office, and mercantile establishments with false fronts to achieve a sense of elegance. The Walnut Grove movie set was located in a remote Simi Valley site on the edge of the Angeles National Forest. Hills, valleys, trees, streams, rocks, and the open sky provided natural backdrops for the film makers. Cast and

John Hawkins, writer and historian, was the executive story consultant on *Little House on the Prairie*. He wrote eleven episodes. His career included stints as a story consultant on *Bonanza* and *The Cowboys*. He created the series, *Manhunt*, and *Boots and Saddles*. He was a writer for numerous dramatic films including *The Virginian* and *Voyage to the Bottom of the Sea*. John Hawkins worked closely with Matt in the interest of historical accuracy.

Walnut Grove—In the final episode, "The Last Farewell," Walnut Grove was blown up by the town's residents. The set no longer exists.

Walnut Grove Set: Aerial view of Walnut Grove set taken from Matt's Waco on its first flight, April 24, 1977.

LITTLE HOUSE ON THE PRAIRIE CAST
(Clockwise from top left)—Melissa Gilbert as Laura Ingalls, Michael Landon as
Charles Ingalls, Karen Grassle as Caroline Ingalls, Lindsay/Sidney Greenbush as
Carrie Ingalls, Melissa Sue Anderson as Mary Ingalls.

TUCSON CITIZEN
SEPTEMBER 12, 1977

For art director Matt Jefferies, a sunny, dusty street in Old Tucson is only a brush away from the Starship Enterprise. Jefferies, on location with Little House on the Prairie, *was focused on an old, black barn in the little world that is Old Tucson. Inside, director, Michael Landon and the rest of the* Little House *cast and crew were sweltering through a fight scene in which farmer Charles Ingalls (Landon) is matched with a traveling boxer.*

When scripts called for a lumber mill, the exterior of the grist mill was magically converted to Hanson's lumber mill by the simple act of stacking logs adjacent to the mill and displaying a lettered sign reading **LUMBER.**

crew united in a family-like atmosphere to transform the stories into living episodes. The casting of a church bell by a mute craftsman had to be realistic. When Charles Ingalls, played by Michael Landon, drilled and blasted in a mine shaft in search of gold or rode horseback to stop a train from crashing into a runaway caboose, the action had to be accurate and believable. When told that a working grist mill was to be a permanent structure on the Walnut Grove set, Matt researched the subject in great depth. Every detail related to the design, construction, and operation of the mill received careful attention. Matt reached back in time and recalled the old grist mill at Sports Lake in Virginia. The mill had fallen into disrepair many years past. Although the overshot water wheel had long-since disappeared, the working components were still in place beneath the aging structure. Iron drive shaft, wooden pillow blocks, toothed gears, and vertical shafts were as they existed when the mill was functional. From

Milling proverb—A lot of water runs by the mill while the miller soundly sleeps, meaning, *"water over the dam."*

Seconds—Intermediate quality. The coarser particles of ground wheat mingled with bran. Also called middling. Hence the common expression: "Fair and middling"—meaning, "in fairly good health."

Matt remembered that a grist mill is always in danger of an explosion. Fine, pulverized flour dust generated by the grinding process could ignite and explode if the millstones are set too close and spark on contact. The gases generated from the decomposition of flour are another source of explosion. To avoid the potential danger, shovels, scoops, forks, and other tools were made of wood. So it was in Mr. Hanson's grist mill.

Pioneer millers constructed their mills by hand. Millstones were cut from local sources. Shafts, gears and pulleys were carved from hickory. Belts were made from home-tanned cowhide.

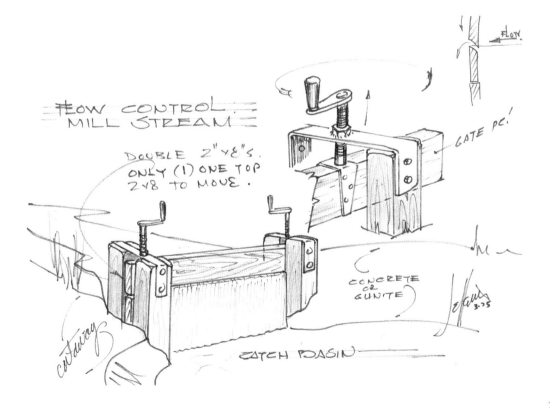

FLOW CONTROL MILL STREAM

DOUBLE 2" x 8"s. ONLY (1) ONE TOP 2x8 to MOVE.

GATE PC.!

CONCRETE OR GUNITE

cutaway

CATCH BASIN

his recollection of the old grist mill and his research material, Matt designed a mill which would grind grain between matching mill stones and produce flour. Construction of Hanson's mill replicated his drawings in every detail.

Authenticity was paramount in Matt's designs. His plans for Hanson's grist mill comprised over a hundred sketches beginning with one depicting the flow control gate on a mill stream. A second illustrates the mill race and a third the mill proper and overshot waterwheel. Drawings of the interior trace the transmission of power from the waterwheel to the rotating mill stone. Hoppers, chutes, bucket elevators, sifters, and bolsters are accurately illustrated. With Matt's sketches and dimensional drawings in hand, the construction crew built Hanson's grist mill. It performed beautifully! Grain received on the second floor was ground and processed to produce flour, seconds, and bran. Water, power, and gravity worked together in noble symphony not unlike the workings of a clock.

To broaden his knowledge of grist mill construction, Matt visited several old mills in Virginia. One, the Muddy Creek Mill, in Cumberland County near the home of his grandparents, served the surrounding area for over two hundred years. February 26, 1753, a patent was granted to Nicholas Davies to build the mill on Muddy Creek, a mile from the James River. The mill ground corn meal and flour until the late 1960s. Matt's visit to the

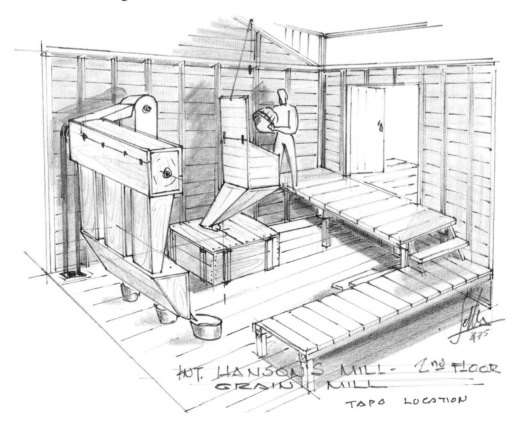

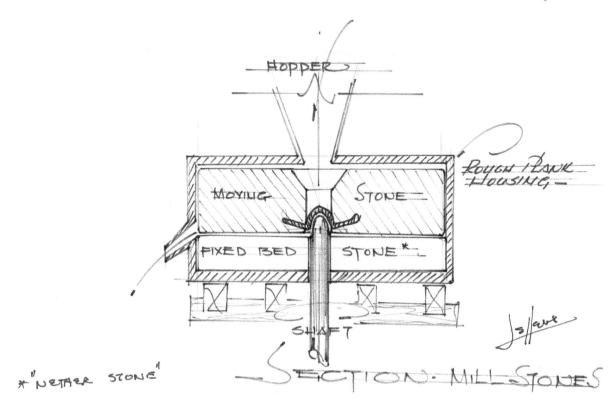

HOPPER

MOVING STONE

ROUGH PLANK HOUSING

FIXED BED STONE *

SHAFT

* "NETHER STONE"

SECTION · MILL STONES

Millstones—The top, rotating stone is also called the "runner stone." The stationary bottom stone is also called the bed or Nether stone, i.e. the "lower stone." The average thickness of a stone is eight inches and each weighs up to fifteen hundred pounds. The best millstones—known as "French burr"—were imported from a quarry near Paris. The American equivalent of the French burr is the raccoon mill stone. Few pioneers could afford these high quality stones.

Stone dressing—The grinding surfaces are dressed to shape radial grooves or furrows so that the grain is sheared rather than crushed. The furrows carry the flour away from the center of the stones and serve as channels to dissipate the heat generated by the grinding.

mill occurred on a day when a millwright was present to demonstrate the picking and trimming of a millstone. The millwright explained that dull grooving of the millstones drastically affected the quality of the flour. In days long past, itinerant millwrights performed this tedious task.

Matt often said that he enjoyed his work on *Little House on the Prairie* more than anything he had done in the film industry. Matt was a history buff. He derived great pleasure from remembrances of days and events of the past. He marveled at the entrepreneurial zeal of the pioneers. The men and women who settled in the great plains and in the West were a sturdy and resourceful lot. Matt admired their spirit of adventure. Designing the sets for the mythical town of Walnut Grove brought to mind their ominous hardships. Michael Landon and John Hawkins shared Matt's passion for bringing to the screen a true representation of family life on the prairie.

Mike (Mickey La Clair) and Melissa Sue Anderson. "Bully Boys" Episode.

Under the leadership of Michael Landon, cast and crew worked together in harmony to produce each episode with a sense of truthfulness. Pa Ingalls, his wife, Caroline, and daughters, Mary, Carrie, Laura, and Grace became known to viewers around the globe. Fans, young and old alike, wrote in to praise the family-oriented series.

Laura Ingalls Wilder wrote eight *Little House* books. In accepting the position of art director for the television series, Matt obtained copies in order to acquire a feeling of what life was like in a prairie town in the late 1800s. Childhood memories of his grandparents' farms in Virginia provided an insight into the harsh conditions endured by the pioneers. The Jefferies and Sanford farms had no electricity or running water. A horse-drawn plow and harrow tilled the soil. Wood for heating, cooking, and washing was hand-cut. Crops were threatened by drought, slashing rain, hail, or hordes of grasshoppers. Water was drawn from a well. The "necessary room" was an outhouse. Wild game was hunted for food. Youngsters were taught to respect

Little House on the Prairie—
One-hundred eighy-three episodes of *Little House* were aired September 11, 1974, to March 21, 1983.

Laura Ingalls Wilder, author of the *Little House* books, wrote of her first view of the Kansas plains: "In a perfect circle, the sky curved down to the level land and the wagon was in the circle's exact middle. There was only the enormous, empty prairie with grasses blowing in waves of light and shadow across it, and the great blue sky above it, and birds flying up from it and singing with joy because the sun was rising."

In Laura Ingalls Wilder's book, *The Long Winter*, she wrote: "No one who has not homesteaded can understand the fascination and terror of it."

Dear Dick,
I'm working on an episode of *Little House* in which Charles is building a house. What do you have in your files on nails? In the late 1880s, were the nails square or round? Were claw hammers available? Your help appreciated.
Love to all,
Matt

Walnut Grove is actually in Minnesota. Charles and Caroline Ingalls left Wisconsin to homestead on the plains of Kansas. When the farm failed, they moved to Minnesota and then to Dakota Territory. They had four daughters, Mary, Carrie, Laura, and Grace. Pa Ingalls had two burning ambitions: to seek his fortune in the western frontier and to do what was best for his family.

(Top) Mary Ann and Matt (bottom) Jack, Dick, Matt, and Phil

PILOT'S ADVICE

"Keep the blue side up and the green side down."

"There is not a word in all the dictionaries that can serve as an alibi if your airplane runs out of fuel while in flight."

"Don't run out of ideas and altitude at the same time."

"Cactus Fly-In"—Matt flew the Waco to Casa Grande, Arizona for the annual "Cactus Fly-In." On the trip back to Santa Paula, they ran into a storm front east of the Colorado River. "You can't hear the rain in the cockpit of the Waco, as the windshield is quarter-inch plate glass," Matt said. "However, the rainstorm was heavy enough to remove some paint from the leading edges of the wings. We finally landed at Agua Dulce, just fifty miles from home, and we went back a week later to pick up the ship."

their parents and elders. Grace was said before meals and Sunday was a day of rest. None of his grandparents ever wrested prosperity from the land, but they survived and raised their children in an atmosphere of love and thanksgiving. It was Matt's good fortune to have this storehouse of memories to draw from for his work.

May 29, 1977, was a bright, sunny day in Santa Paula, California—ideal for the enjoyment of those who were present for the christening of Matt's Waco. Beautifully restored, the plane captured the eye of everyone who crossed the tarmac to see the result of Matt's nine-and-a-half years of painstaking labor. The glistening black fuselage and contrasting black-and-white color schemes on the wing and tail surfaces reflected his artistic bent. The vintage Waco was a bird of great beauty, preened and ready to return to the air. Matt was deservedly proud! His trademark signature, one pierced by an artist's pen, graced the engine cowling. Mary Ann, always supportive of Matt's projects, performed the custom-

Spacelab 1—America's first space station was launched into orbit on May 14, 1973, by a Saturn V booster rocket. It was unmanned.

❊

Skylab 2—America's first manned mission, carrying three astronauts, was launched into orbit on May 25, 1973. The crew rendezvoused with Skylab on the fifth orbit and remained aboard for twenty-eight days, fifty minutes.

❊

Skylab 3—America's second manned mission, carrying three astronauts, was launched into orbit on July 28, 1973. The crew remained aboard the Skylab space station for fifty-nine days, eleven hours.

❊

Skylab 4—Launched November 16, 1973, with three astronauts. The crew remained aboard for eighty-four days, one hour. They completed 1,214 Earth orbits.

❊

Note—It was concluded that all three crews demonstrated the ability to stay in space under weightless conditions for long periods without jeopardizing their health.

❊

July 11, 1979—All engineering tests completed, Skylab was placed in a stable attitude and all systems shut down. On July 11, 1979, Skylab impacted the Earth. Debris stretched from the Southern Indian Ocean to a section of Western Australia.

❊

NASA's USS Enterprise—Following five manned, free-flight tests, the shuttle was ferried between several NASA facilities for further static tests. The shuttle was then sent on a world tour with visits to Italy, France, Germany, Canada, and England. When returned to the United States, the space shuttle was donated to the Smithsonian Institution. It is on display at the Air and Space Museum's Center at Washington Dulles International Airport.

ary ritual of sprinkling champagne on the polished prop. Matt graciously invited those who wished to accompany him on short flights over the Santa Paula landscape. The powerful 245-horsepower engine roared to life, and with three passengers aboard, Matt lifted off the runway for the first of many flights.

NASA'S USS *Enterprise* shuttle atop Boeing 747

Matt took a keen interest in NASA's space program. He was particularly interested in the development of a manned shuttle vehicle to be carried into space on a rocket. After separation from the rocket, the shuttle would dock on an orbiting space station and have the capability of returning to earth. A test vehicle, *Constitution*, was scheduled for unmanned flight testing in February 1977. *Star Trek* fans waged a write-in campaign to have the shuttle renamed *Enterprise*. NASA acceded and the space shuttle was officially designated the USS *Enterprise*. On February 18, a Boeing 747 carrying the unmanned *Enterprise* piggyback lifted off from Edwards Air Force Base. "The purpose of the test," NASA explained, "is to measure the flight characteristics of the mated combination." NASA

Philip—Production designer on a feature film adaptation of H.G. Wells' *The Island of Dr. Moreau*, with Burt Lancaster, Michael York, Barbara Carrera, and Richard Basehart. Filmed on location at St. Croix, Virgin Islands, the film tells the tale of shipwrecked sailors on a Pacific island where a mad doctor experiments with animal mutations.

John—Set designer on a feature film, *The Hindenburg*, with George C. Scott, Gig Young, Anne Bancroft, and Burgess Meredith. The film suggests that the 1937 disaster was caused by sabotage. The special effects were highly praised.

Richard—Assigned drilling equipment sales on 800-mile Trans-Alaska oil pipeline from the North Slope's Prudhoe Bay to the port of Valdez.

Kohoutek—Described as the "comet of the century" by astronomers, Kohoutek was believed to be the largest comet ever to be seen by man. Its fiery tail stretched millions of miles across the sky. Skylab's presence during the passage of Kohoutek was an exciting event for the scientific community. Seneca, a Roman philosopher, wrote: "Some day there will arise a man who will demonstrate in what regions of the heavens the comets take their way; why they journey so far apart from other planets; what their size, their nature."

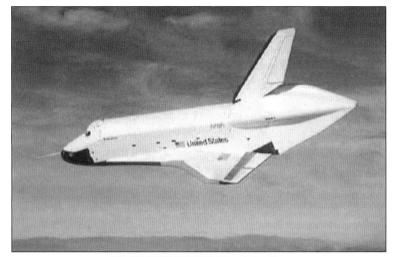

NASA'S *USS ENTERPRISE* Shuttle landing

kept Matt informed of the day the shuttle, manned by two astronauts, would be free-flight tested. At four o'clock on the morning of August 12, Matt roused Mary Ann from a deep sleep to drive to Edwards to witness the historic event. They watched as the 747, carrying the *Enterprise,* roared down the runway and climbed into the early morning sky. And they remained until the shuttle came into view and glided to a flawless touchdown.

The free-flight shuttle test represented an enormous step towards the future construction of a permanent space station. The shuttle's cargo bay would haul individual modules for assembly in space. The space station would be pressurized to provide working quarters for six to eight astronauts. Matt recalled another NASA milestone which had occurred previously. He had received an invitation from Col. William R. Pogue, a NASA astronaut, to visit the Kennedy Space Center in Florida to observe the launching of Skylab 3 on or about November 11, 1973. In his letter, Col. Pogue stated: "*Skylab 3 will continue the program of scientific investigation. Briefly, the effort is aimed toward observations of the sun, the earth, man, plus a variety of corollary experiments. In addition, the launch will permit orbital observations of the comet, Kohoutek, which is predicted to reach its closest approach to the sun on December 28. This comet is anticipated to be brighter than Halley's Comet, and astronomers worldwide consider this the "astronomical event of the century." If you cannot see the launch at the Cape, you can share with us the spirit of inquiry, quest for knowledge, and personal involvement in pursuing the exploration of space."*

January 1977, Michael Landon informed Matt that Gene Roddenberry had asked to "borrow" his art director for a few days. Paramount Studios was committed to produce a new series entitled *Star Trek II*. Matt was asked to provide technical assistance and redesign the *Enterprise* to reflect more powerful engines. Engine nacelles were changed from tubular structures to flat-sided modules with tapered struts. Distinctive *photon* torpedo ports were added to the saucer connector. By July 1977, *Star Trek II* was in full production. However, the episodes were never telecast as Paramount made the decision to convert what had been accomplished to a *Star Trek* movie.

Star Trek's U.S.S. *ENTERPRISE*.

Paramount Studios released *Star Trek: The Motion Picture* on December 7, 1979. It was an instant success with dedicated fans queued up in long lines to view the first new *Star Trek* production in over ten years.

U. S. S. *Enterprise*—In the *Star Trek III* movie, the *Starship Enterprise* was destroyed. In later movies, the space ship was enlarged and designated as NCC-1701-C & NCC-1701-D. However, it continued to bear the name *Enterprise*.

Gene Roddenberry—First writer to receive a sidewalk star on Hollywood's Walk of Fame.

Star Trek—The original series which debuted on September 8, 1966, lasted only seventy-nine episodes, but spawned the phenomenal success of the movies and the TV series which followed. The original series is the most successful show in syndication history. It is seen in over one-hundred domestic markets and over eighty countries.

Sierra Railway

Little House on the Prairie **Episode #38**—"The Runaway Caboose," was written and directed by John Hawkins. It tells the story of Mary and Laura Ingalls and their friend, Carl Edwards, who wandered into an empty caboose. The caboose unexpectedly began to roll backwards towards a speeding train headed towards them on the same track. Pa Ingalls raced on horseback to catch up with the train just in time to avert a tragic head-on collision. The episode was filmed on the Sierra Railroad.

※

Caboose—Derived from the Dutch word "kabuis," meaning, ship's galley. Originally a refuge for the train's crew, the caboose provided a place where they could eat and sleep. The interior was heated by a coal-burning stove and illuminated by a kerosene lantern. Later, an observation cupola was added which allowed the conductor to do his paper work and the brakeman to watch for "hot boxes," the overheated axles that often caused derailments.

Having satisfied Roddenberry's need for a more powerful *Enterprise,* Matt resumed his work on *Little House on the Prairie.* Several episodes were filmed in Northern California's Mother Lode country where the Sierra Railroad provides film makers and tourists alike with an operational, steam powered, train. Matt's fascination with early transportation was not limited to airplanes. Antique automobiles and steam locomotives also captured his attention. The roundhouse at Jamestown housed three turn-of-the-century Baldwin locomotives. Passenger cars, caboose, depot, foundry, machine shop, and car repair shop was authentic and operational. After a long day of filming, Matt and Mary Ann delighted in riding the "Twilight Limited," a relaxing excursion to Cooperstown through Dry Creek Canyon. The shrill steam whistle and chugging engine accompanied by the clatter of wheels on the rails provided a welcome respite. A favorite place for the film crew to congregate was the roundhouse. Lou, the conductor, Al, the brakeman, and Ed, the engineer, all former railroaders, welcomed the attention and

Matt & Mary Ann—Model T Ford equipped with flanged wheels for riding on the rails.

Jamestown Roundhouse

willingly shared their experiences. As is generally the case, the cast and crew of *Little House* formed friendships, which led to groups spending their leisure time together. One of the most popular places to dine was the City Hotel in Columbia. Established in 1856, the hotel had a long and illustrious past. A typical evening would find Matt and Mary Ann in the company of director John Hawkins, set designer Bill Newman, and Marion Anderson, mother of Melissa Sue Anderson, who portrayed Mary in the Little House series. Topics of discussion reflected their mutual interest in the lore of the Mother Lode. The building of railroads through the High Sierras, the prospector's tenacious quest for gold, and the brutal hardships endured by the early settlers in a hostile environment captured their imagination. Matt said of the area, "A great place to relive history!"

CHAPTER TEN

olden rays of sunrise spread over the Santa Clara valley. Santa Paula Airport awakened for another day of flying. Crisp morning air and crystal clear skies inspired flyers to hasten their pre-flight checks before going aloft to chase the few scattered clouds scudding towards the wide Pacific. Matt put a shoulder to the heavy hangar door and slid it open. Shafts of light penetrated the dark interior to reveal the glistening Waco which had been thoroughly serviced the previous evening. With Matt manhandling the tail wheel tow bar and Mary Ann pushing on a wing strut, the plane was rolled out onto the tarmac. They clambered aboard. The engine was started and allowed to warm up before the plane taxied towards the far end of the runway. With a deep-throated roar, the Waco rushed down the runway and lifted off into the open skies. As it gained altitude and banked to circle the airport, spectators on the ground applauded the sight of the beautifully restored plane.

For the traditional "First Sunday in the Month" event when the airport was open for visitors to see vintage aircraft displayed on the

China Lake (dry) is located in the Mojave Desert near Death Valley, California. The area is surrounded by the China Lake Naval Weapons Center. The nearest city, Ridgecrest, hosts annual fly-ins at its airport. An aviation museum displays many vintage aircraft.

Other "fly-ins" at private and regional airports catering to owners of antique, classic, and sports planes, were annual events attracting hundreds of recreational flyers. China Lake and Watsonville, California, and Casa Grande, Arizona, hosted "fly-ins" which Matt and Mary Ann attended regularly. The Waco was parked wingtip-to-wingtip alongside Fairchild, Beech, Stinson, and Stearman tail-dragging biplanes.

Mr. Mulligan—In the 1930s, Benny Howard built racing airplanes. His DGA-6 mono plane, Mr. Mulligan, won the 1935 Bendix Air Race and the Thompson Trophy Race. It is the only airplane to capture both races in the same year. Mr. Mulligan was a four-place, strut-braced, high wing racer powered with a Pratt & Whitney 750 hp Wasp radial engine. When questioned about the "DGA" designation, Benny Howard replied: "Damn good airplane." Benny entered Mr. Mulligan in the 1936 Bendix Race. With his wife as copilot, he was two hours short of the Los Angeles finish line when the propeller broke apart and he crashed in the mountains of New Mexico. Although injured, both survived the disaster. A replica of the plane was built at the Santa Paula Airport. It took to the air in 1977. The Mr. Mulligan painting was initially exhibited at the EAA Aviation Museum in Oshkosh, Wisconsin. It is currently owned by Mr. and Mrs. Bruce Dickenson of Santa Paula, CA.

ground, the plane was parked in front of the hangar. On other occasions, Matt took friends on flights over the rolling Santa Ynez Mountain range and the ranches and citrus fruit groves of the beautiful, Santa Clara Valley.

Matt was a member of the Experimental Aircraft Association. In the spring of 1978, the EAA held its second-annual Sport Aviation National Art Competition at Carmel, California. Matt's painting of Benny Howard's legendary DGA-6 Mr. Mulligan placed third in a field of 300 entries. Judges of the competition praised Matt for his rendering of the famed monoplane lifting off from a dimly lit runway against a backdrop of dark mountains and star-studded skies. Streaks of light from a distant city added depth and perspective to the remarkable painting.

Matt's painting of the WACO YOC over Santa Ynez Mountain Range

Mr. Mulligan

Matt's reputation as one of America's foremost aviation artists spread rapidly. Prestigious art galleries in Scottsdale, Arizona, and Carmel, California, exhibited his work. Paintings were loaned to the Smithsonian National Air and Space Museum and EAA's aviation museum in Oshkosh, Wisconsin. Douglas Aircraft and Boeing acquired his paintings of their respective aircraft. The U.S. Air Force established an Air Force Art Program at the Pentagon. Six of Matt's paintings contributed to the program and are rotated from various locations: the Air Force Memorial Foundation in Arlington, Virginia, the Air Force Museum at Wright Patterson Air Force Base in Ohio, the Air Force Academy in Colorado, and in offices throughout the Pentagon. Many members of the Air Force have voiced praise of his artistic talents in portraying vintage military aircraft. Matt subscribed to the notion that one should paint only what the eyes can see. Vision, he said, must be reproduced with precise accuracy. Realism was paramount in all of his paintings. His craftsmanship evolved from a thorough understanding of light, shadows, and color. His systematic approach to starting a new canvas was deliberate and functional. He began by defining the perspective in soft, penciled lines, followed by sketching the overall patterns of the subject: landscape, structures, and sky. An uncluttered background enhanced the beauty of the central and foremost object, the aircraft. Color was introduced to define the subjects in terms of composition, proportion, and reflected light. His skill as a draftsman enabled him to balance scale and geometric design.

The hundreds of hours flying below and beyond the clouds during his military and civilian career as an aviator served to provide him with a grasp of realism pertaining to cloud formations. He recognized that rare are the days when one can say, "It's a clear day! Not a cloud in the sky!" One expects to see clouds: fluffy, white cumulus clouds floating lazily across the sky, or

Matt, at work in his Hollywood studio. File cabinets contained over ten thousand photographs, prints, and drawings of aircraft and automobiles.

silky stratus clouds streaking across the distant reaches of space. The inclusion of cloud formations in his paintings was scientifically and artfully depicted. "*Better to leave the clouds out entirely,*" Matt suggested, "*than to corrupt the rendition of a fine aircraft with clouds which are unnatural or overpowering.*"

Throughout his career Matt had worked with every medium: pen and ink, watercolors, oils, and acrylics. It was with acrylics that he was the most comfortable and proficient. More versatile than other mediums, the fast-drying acrylics enabled him to instantly transfer artistic images to his canvas. The smooth viscosity of acrylics allowed effortless glazing. Matt made full use of the tools of the trade, all placed within easy reach as he sat or stood before his easel. Round and square tipped brushes, palette knives, sponges for dabbing, and splayed brushes for stippling were carefully selected to achieve the proper effect. A wide range of colors allowed him to replicate the hues and tones cached in his vivid imagination. Cobalt blue,

Richard—He was on assignment in San Francisco to provide underground rock drilling equipment and technical support for the Bay Area Rapid Transit System project. In the spring of 1978, Richard was relocated to Jeddah, Saudi Arabia, to manage construction, mining, oil, gas pipeline, and water well drilling equipment sales.

Philip—He was the production designer for Paramount's feature film, *Grease*, starring John Travolta and Olivia Newton-John.

John—He was the production designer on twenty-nine episodes of *Baa Baa Black Sheep* starring Robert Conrad. This was a World War II epic relating the performance of an air squadron over the Solomon Islands in the South Pacific.

Betty Mae Woolsey—Warsaw, Virginia:
Ned Woolsey was the plane's ground Crew Chief.

B17F "Holey Joe" on bombing mission over France.

cadmium yellow, crimson, burnt umber, and titanium white comprised only a few of the colors spaced around the edge of his palette. As if by magic, painted images emerged from the flat surface of his canvas to reveal an aircraft, accurately and artistically portrayed in its entire splendor. His skill in achieving flawless results was recognized as extraordinary.

Matt artfully applied his brush to the outlined wing of a plane he was painting. Satisfied with the burnt orange tone of the canvas, he stood back and observed his work with a critical eye.

"Unless I'm mistaken," an onlooker said, "the biplane is a UPF-7 Waco coming in for a landing at sundown."

"It is, indeed. You know your Wacos!"

"I should! I own a UPF-7. Been taking it to the fly-ins in the Midwest for the past ten years. Great airplane! You're Matt Jefferies. I've seen your paintings in several of the aviation magazines and have wanted to meet you. I'm Phil Coulson, president of the American Waco Club."

"HOLEY JOE"—September 5, 1942. B-17F S/N 41-24352 took off from the Eighth Air Force Base at Chelveston, England, to bomb the Marshalling Yards at Rouen, France. It was the first combat mission of the 301st Bomb Group. Subsequent missions were carried out to Rotterdam in the Netherlands and to Mesuite and Lille in France. During a second mission to Lille, the German Luftwaffe sent a squadron of FW-190s to intercept the bombers. Although severely damaged and with two engines shot out, B-17F S/N 41-24352 made it back to England where it landed on an emergency strip near the Cliffs of Dover. When the crew deplaned and saw the extent of the damage, one was heard to exclaim, "Holey Joe!" So that is how S/N 41-24352 got its name.

WACO—The original Advance Aircraft Company was started in Lorain, Ohio. A partner in the company, Buck Weaver, was a local barnstorming pilot. *The Weaver Airplane Company* (WACO) was named for Buck to interest the flying public in a new plane, the WACO-7. The first WACO-7 was produced in 1923. As new models were introduced, the factory was relocated to Troy, Ohio.

Return to Terra Firma—WACO UPF-7 on a landing approach at sunset.

WACO—Factory in Troy, Ohio, produced 600 *UPF-7s* for the Civil Pilot Training Program in the 1940s. Many future pilots learned to fly in the UPF-7. A WACO museum is located in downtown Troy.

✴

WACO developed a code to designate each model.
U—Engine Type
P—Basic Wing Design
F—Basic Fuselage Design
7—The 7th Improved Version.

✴

AMERICAN WACO CLUB—Formed by Phil Coulson in 1958, having split off from the NATIONAL WACO CLUB. Members of both clubs attend one another's Fly-Ins and share the same camaraderie. Some are members of both clubs. Matt attended the 1982 NATIONAL WACO CLUB Fly-In at Mt. Vernon, Ohio. Although he did not bring his 1935 YOC "bird," he brought several of his WACO paintings, including the UPF-7 pictured. While in Ohio, Matt visited the WACO museum in Troy, the Air Force Museum at Wright-Patterson Air Force Base at Dayton, and the Wright State University where the Wright Brothers' papers are stored in their archives.

"Glad to meet you, Phil. I'm a member of your club."

"I know. I've seen your name on the roster. Your easel is most unusual, Matt. Looks familiar."

"It's a Stearman engine mount dolly. Works for me."

"Have you a title for the painting?"

"*Return to Terra Firma.*"

"I like it! An appropriate name!"

"Give me a moment, Phil, and I'll show you my 1935 YOC."

During a lull in the filming of *Little House*, Michael Landon asked Matt to provide art direction for a pilot episode of a new TV series entitled *Father Murphy*. As with *Little House*, the proposed show was family-oriented, one mirroring the qualities that appealed to the faithful followers of the *Little House* series. Acutely aware of the slipping ratings of *Little House*, Landon was determined in his new series to recreate the homespun appeal of the early

FATHER MURPHY—The first episode aired November 3, 1981. After twenty-two episodes comprising the first season, the series was approved by NBC for a second season. Episode twenty-five, titled "Stopover in a One-Horse Town," relates a visit to the mining town by Samuel Clemens (Mark Twain) during his itinerant travels to the gold mines of California. Two characters in the episode become Twain's inspiration for Tom Sawyer and Huck Finn. Episode thirty-five, the final episode, aired on September 18, 1983. The series failed to duplicate the success of *Little House on the Prairie*.

✳

WRIGHT BROTHERS—On December 17, 1903, at Kitty Hawk, North Carolina, Wright Flyer No. I, piloted by Orville Wright, was airborne for twelve seconds. The plane covered a distance of 120 feet. It attained an altitude of eight to ten feet and an air speed of thirty to thirty-five miles per hour. It was the first powered aircraft to successfully fly. Twin propellers, rotating in opposite directions, were powered by a four-cylinder, twelve horsepower, gasoline engine. The 600-pound aircraft had a wingspan of more than forty feet. Flyerfeet. Flyer No. 1 made three more flights, the longest covering 859 feet in fifty-nine seconds.

Little House episodes. After all, he reasoned, in the span of eight years, the little Ingalls girls had grown up. The cast of *Father Murphy* would introduce a new set of faces and personalities. Placed in the Old West of the 1870s, the premise of the *Father Murphy* series was elemental but powerful in its creation. John Michael Murphy, a kindly frontiersman, appears in a mining camp that has been destroyed by a despicable gang.

Murphy, disguised as a friar, assists a pretty schoolmarm in establishing a home for orphans. The format allowed Landon to share his love of children with the viewing public. As with *Little House,* the innocence of children in an era of hardship and deprivation would appeal to the imaginations of young and old alike. Landon knew only too well that the key to selling *Father Murphy* to a network was a pilot that would convince media executives that their investment was justified. It was for that reason that he again called on Matt to design the sets for the pilot episode. Filmed at the Big Sky Ranch in Simi Valley, the pilot was well received by NBC and the series went into production. Matt resumed his work on *Little House.*

Matt continued to paint, to fly his plane, and to broaden his knowledge of aviation history. He was cognizant of the role Southern California played in the early development of aviation in America. It was in Santa Ana that Glen L. Martin began the manufacture of airplanes in 1909. Los Angeles became the home of Donald Douglas' airplane factory, later to become the Douglas Aircraft Company. In 1916, Alan and Malcolm Loughead built airplanes in a garage in Santa Barbara. They changed their name to Lockheed and moved to a facility in Burbank. In 1925, Claude Ryan, an army pilot in World War I, established the first airline passenger

service with flights between San Diego and Los Angeles. This led to the forming of his manufacturing firm, Ryan Aeronautical Company located in San Diego. However, these entrepreneurs were preceded by earlier aviation pioneers who chose Southern California to exhibit their flying machines. In 1910, America's first international air show was held at a remote place called Dominguez Hill, between Compton and Los Angeles. Sponsored by William Randolph Hearst's Los Angeles *Examiner*, the ten-day meet attracted more than 226,000 spectators. A primitive field, *Aviation Field,* was prepared on the native soil of what was known as the Dominguez Ranch, originally part of a Spanish land grant. A French aviator, Louis Paulhan, piloting a Farman biplane, set an altitude record of 4,164 feet. (The altitude attained was verified by an Examiner balloon.) He also won the cross-country prize by flying to Santa Anita and back, a distance of forty-five miles. Glenn Curtis took second place in a Reims Racer. The Wright Brothers declined to attend.

In 1924, the adobe home on the Dominguez Ranch was deeded to the Claretian Missionaries, a Catholic Order. The Claretians established a seminary on the property for the training of candidates for the priesthood.

Matt learned that a museum dedicated to the memory of the Dominguez family had been established at the ranch. A room had been set aside to display memorabilia from the 1910 air meet. He visited the Ranch and met Father "Pat" McPolin, former superior of the seminary. Father "Pat," as he was affectionately called, was responsible for the restoration of the home and the establishment of the museum. Matt designed a diorama depict-

Father "Pat" McPolin & Matt

ing the grounds and structures which existed at the time of the historic event. Old photographs of the Air Meet were used in executing his sketches. An artist associate of Matt's utilized MGM's carpenter shop to construct the glass encased diorama. Father Pat was overjoyed with the reproduction of the original Dominguez Ranch. A scale model of the Glenn Curtiss Reims Racer was suspended from the ceiling of the aviation museum.

Top view of dirorama.

In 1983, TV viewers saw the final episodes of *Little House on the Prairie* and *Father Murphy*. An era had passed. The ratings of one-hour shows and sitcoms clearly indi-

JIMMY DOOLITTLE—In an *American Heritage* interview, Lt. Gen. Jimmy Doolittle was asked: *"How did you become interested in aviation?"* His response: *"In the winter of 1909–1910, I saw the first air show that took place on the West Coast at Old Dominguez Field near my home in Los Angeles. I was very impressed with the airplanes of that day, even though they were quite frail and of very little performance."*

FATHER "PAT" McPOLIN—Matt and Father "Pat" became very good friends. Matt and Mary Ann celebrated their fiftieth wedding anniversary in the chapel of the Dominguez Rancho. They renewed their marriage vows with Father "'Pat'" officiating as celebrant.

JOHN—Production designer and art director on twelve episodes of *Hardcastle & McCormick* and sixteen one-hour episodes of *Greatest American Hero*. For his flying pleasure, John purchased a 1958 Bellanca Cruise Master monoplane.

PHILIP—Production designer of Part II of a variety show titled *Alice in Wonderland*. Nominated for an Emmy Award.

RICHARD—Relocated to Dallas, Texas, to manage the sale of heavy construction and oil field equipment.

cated that America's taste for TV entertainment was as changeable as the weather. The networks were frantic for new shows which would retain the old devotees and also capture new audiences. Many shows were canceled following the airing of well-publicized pilots. Studios suffered from actors' strikes, poor scripts, rising production costs, and fierce competition for viewers. However, one prime-time show, *Dallas*, had consistently attracted huge audiences since its first airing in 1978. It featured a fictional scoundrel, J. R. Ewing, who broke all the rules to further his Ewing Oil empire. *Time Magazine* dubbed J. R., "the human oil slick." The show dealt with greed, alcoholism, drug addiction, abortion, and financial shenanigans—issues that were commonplace and accepted as the reality of the '80s. Cohabiting the sprawling South Fork Ranch were two generations of Ewings. In addition

Merced, California—During the 1985 "Merced Antique Fly-In," Matt's Waco YOC won the trophy for a Classic Age (1935-1941) cabin biplane.

Matt's Recipe—For preflight lunches: Peanut Butter and Hot Dog Sandwich—Spread peanut butter on toast of your choice. Boil an all-beef hot dog, slice it lengthwise, and lay on top of peanut butter for an open-face sandwich.

Star Trek Convention—Matt attended one more *Star Trek* convention. Held in Las Vegas, the guests included astronauts Neil Armstrong and Buzz Aldrin. Matt could not pass up the opportunity to sit on the same panel as these renowned figures. He was astonished to learn that they, too, were *Star Trek* fans and just as eager to make his acquaintance.

George Pal—A pioneer in the production of live-action films. In 1949 George Pal produced *Destination Moon* and *When Worlds Collide*. The success of the futuristic films encouraged George Pal to produce H. G. Wells' *The War of the Worlds* and *The Time Machine*. He then produced The *Wonderful World of the Brothers Grimm*, *7 Faces of Dr. Lao*, and *Tom Thumb*.

PHILIP JEFFERIES—1987 Philip died of cancer at age. sixty-two.

to the ranch, location sites included oil fields, bars, high rise offices, hospitals, shopping centers, restaurants, and airports. A critical need arose for innovative art direction. Matt was hired for two seasons of the widely acclaimed series. Larry Hagman (who played J. R.), the directors, and many members of the cast and crew created a working atmosphere of togetherness that made the filming of Dallas a pleasurable experience.

Matt was frequently invited to attend Star Trek conventions. Thousands of Trekkers flock to cities around the world to see *Star Trek* memorabilia, buy *Star Trek* collectibles and merchandise, and to share in the camaraderie of dedicated fans. Members of the cast: William Shatner

(Captain Kirk), Leonard Nimoy (Spock), DeForest Kelley (Dr. McCoy), and James Doohan (Scotty), were often present to promote *Star Trek* and to further their careers. Gene Roddenberry, Bob Justman, and Herb Solow were equally popular and willingly participated in question-and-answer panels. Although appreciative of the adulation, Matt scrupulously shunned these events. However, when urged by Paramount to attend a highly-publicized *Star Trek* convention in Pasadena, he reluctantly consented. From the moment he arrived at the convention center, mobs of devotees and the ever-invasive press swarmed around to shake his hand. As the number of admirers swelled, police were summoned to maintain some semblance of order and to protect the *Star Trek* notables. Exhausted from the experience, Matt informed Mary Ann that he would decline all future invitations!

One day Matt received a call from George Pal who produced and directed *War of the Worlds* and *The Time Machine* for Paramount Studios. Matt and George had become good friends. He asked Matt to attend a science fiction and fantasy convention in Los Angeles where models of futuristic spacecraft would be judged. Because of Matt's reputation as the designer of the *Enterprise,* George felt that no one was better qualified to judge the entries. Matt accepted Pal's invitation. The models placed before him were crafted by highly professional model builders. They were all beautifully designed and flawlessly finished, that is, except for one, which was of inferior quality. However, the one model of inferior quality was distinctly original in design. All of the other entries were variations of the *Enterprise*. After careful scrutiny, Matt awarded first prize to the young man who had crafted a spaceship unlike any other. George Pal had questioned the decision until Matt explained, "Originality must count for something!"

In June 1989, Matt returned to Dayton to attend the American Society of Aviation Artists' art exhibit at Wright-Patterson Field. He received high praise for his painting, *Safe Harbor,* depicting Lindberg's Lockheed *Sirius* taxiing into the harbor at Angmagssalik, Greenland.

Matt was asked why he chose to paint the *Sirius* rather than the *Spirit of St. Louis*. "All aviation artists have painted the *Spirit,*" he replied. "It is perhaps the most recognized plane to be rendered on canvas. The *Sirius* represented a giant step in the evolution of the monoplane, an aircraft of great beauty and reliability. Its cantilevered, low-wing design became the norm for future aircraft." Matt also visited the U. S. A. F. museum at Wright-

Safe Harbor, Matt's painting of Lindbergh's Lockheed SIRUS

Patterson where his painting of the Boeing P-26A was on display. He was asked why he selected the P-26A rather than other pursuit planes of the same era. "That's an easy one," he replied. "Probably one of the most humiliating defeats suffered by the Army Air Corps came in 1929 when a civilian pilot, flying a low-wing monoplane, trounced an Army *Curtiss Hawk* pursuit during the Pulitzer Races at Cleveland, conclusively proving that the biplane days were over. Thus the P-26A ushered in a new era of low-wing pursuit planes. Entering service in 1932, the P-26A was still in use by some squadrons at the time of Pearl Harbor. Like the *Sirius*, the P-26A represented a significant turning point in aircraft design."

"I have one last question, Matt," a reporter said. "Have you retired?"

"Retired from what?"

"You know, the film industry . . . designing and directing for TV shows."

"Yes, in that regard, I have been retired . . . since 1986, following *Dallas*."

SIRIUS—Named for the Dog Star, Sirius, the brightest star in the heavens. Designed by John K. Northrop and Gerard Vultee, the monoplane was built by Lockheed Aircraft in 1929. Lindbergh and his wife, Anne, flew from North Haven, Maine, to the Orient via Canada and Alaska in 1931. Equipped with floats and powered by a 680-hp Wright Cyclone engine, the plane performed well, but Lindbergh felt that it needed more horsepower. A 710-hp Wright Cyclone engine was installed. In the summer of 1933, the Lindberghs took off from New York to establish and plot a transatlantic route for Pan American Airways. They flew north to Hopedale, Labrador, refueled, and left for Greenland, a distance of 650 miles. The plane's name was changed to *Tingmissartoq*, which, in Eskimo, means "one who flies like a bird." From Greenland they flew to Iceland, Europe, Russia, Africa, and across the South Atlantic to South America. Having traveled 30,000 miles, they returned to New York.
Note: *The Sirius is now on display at the Air and Space Museum in Washington, D.C.*

P–26 Peashooter

"Do you miss the excitement of making *Star Trek* or *Mission Impossible?*"

"Not at all! It entailed a lot of hard work, long hours, and having to endure poor scripts, tight budgets, and nay sayers . . . these I can well do without! It's the wonderful people I worked with all those many years whom I shall dearly miss."

"So, what are your future plans?"

"Same as I'm doing now . . . traveling with my wife, Mary Ann, flying our Waco, attending aviation forums, and continuing with my paintings and aviation research."

Forums held by the ASAA provided Matt with the opportunity to associate with artists whose work he admired. In keeping with the association's objective to stimulate and

Anne Lindbergh authored a book, *North to the Orient.* Published in 1935, it quickly became a best seller. She wrote eloquently of their 1931 flight in the Sirius to the Far East:

"One could look at life from the air . . . conscious of the magic of flying . . . .a magic that has kinship with standing in front of serene madonnas . . . listening to cool chorales, or reading one of those clear passages in a book . . . so illuminating that one feels the writer has given the reader a glass-bottomed bucket with which to view the world."

Morning Mission P–26 A's

inspire both professional and amateur artists, he shared his artistic techniques in open sessions. He strongly advocated constructive criticism of one another's work. "Don't let your ego get in the way of learning from others!" he declared. "Your best paintings are those based on a story, as opposed to just a picture of an airplane," he said. To emphasize this point, a workshop in Dallas included a scenario from which the participants were instructed to produce a drawing representative of a story line.

"Now, get your creative juices flowing and draw the image that comes quickly to your mind—We have all heard about the kid who rode a bicycle to the airport, leans it against a fence, and looks goggle-eyed at the airplanes. The kid is wondering if today is the day someone might offer him a ride. Nearby a pilot is preflighting an airplane . . . wiggles the ailerons and flaps, looks at the engine, kicks the tires, peeks in the gas tank, checks how much of that stuff was

AMERICAN SOCIETY OF AVIATION ARTISTS—Founded in 1986, the ASAA brings together artists who are dedicated to professionalism, authenticity, and artistic quality in aviation art. Forums held in major cities throughout the country enable members to discuss painting techniques, exchange information, and critique one another's work. Matt readily gained the respect of America's best known and admired aviation artists: Nixon Galloway, Keith Ferris, Robert McCall, R.G. Smith, Andrew Whyte, and others. Matt often contributed technical data and photographs to the ASAA newsletter, "Aero Brush."

NIXON GALLOWAY—"Nick" Galloway's interest in aviation dated from his early childhood. His father and his grandfather were pilots in the '20s and '30s. As a freelance artist he was commissioned by Lockheed, Boeing, Northrop, and Hughes to produce art for advertising their products. The major airlines also utilized his talents in their promotions.

Boeing P-26A fighter plane known as the "Peashooter."
Delivered to the U.S. Air Corps in 1934, the monoplane was powered with a 600 horsepower Pratt & Whitney radial engine.
Maximum speed: 235 mph.
Armament: Two half-inch machine guns.
Bomb load: 200 pounds.

❋

ASAA FORUMS—Matt and Mary Ann attended forums in Pensacola, Dayton, San Diego, Dallas/Fort Worth, Wichita, and other cities. Matt set up the *Walter M. Jefferies* Fund to reward artists, both established and neophyte. The entries are judged by popular vote of the ASAA membership.

on the dipstick in the oil tank, pulled the prop through, and cleaned the windshield. The pilot was aware of the eager young face looking over the top of the fence. He remembered when he too was just a kid and stood at a fence and wished the same thing. So he calls and says: "Come on, kid, let's go flying and chase some clouds! I don't know how this story comes out because, you see, I am not there. You are! You have ten minutes!"

One could have well questioned the benefit of such an exercise, but no one did. They knew Matt's work and wished to emulate him. They left with a better understanding of the relationship of a painting to a story line.

gerald asher
© 2006

Artist—Gerry Asher, Fort Worth, TX

Dallas/Fort Worth Forum-Gerry Asher, a president of ASAA stated in an issue of their newsletter, *Aero Brush*: "Matt was sitting in a chair in the motel lobby. A handful of other artists were listening intently to what he had to say. I was sitting at his feet. The occasion had all the earmarks of a modern-day Plato or Aristotle, surrounded by his students, hanging on every word. There was never a moment that I did not enjoy being around Matt Jefferies."

Rick Ruhman related the following story about Matt: "At an ASAA forum Matt was questioned by a modeler about the accurate colors of WW II aircraft. Matt replied: "The International Plastic Modelers Society" crowd is always so fanatically concerned about accurate, authentic, historically correct color. They refer to military specs, Munsen color codes, and paint chips. Let me tell you about how we painted our bombers in North Africa. The planes always needed painting and touch-up because of the harsh sand and weather conditions. We were running out of our paint so we grabbed some captured German and Italian paint and mixed it with what we had to get close to the color we needed. Sometimes we just slopped it on with brooms and with cut-down brushes. That's the way we did it in the field, so try and match that to a chip chart! The modelers will have to make 1/48 inch scale brooms to do it right!'"

ASAA Forum— (L-R) Art & Pamela Lumley, Gerry Asher, Matt

For many years Matt and Mary Ann hosted annual "Artober Fests" at the Santa Paula airport. Rick and Denise Ruhman were always in attendance. Rick, a charter member of ASAA, had this to say about the experience: "These gatherings were some of the most fun, valuable and interesting parties and events I have ever attended. We had a star-studded group of aviation artists, aviators, and historians mixing with a wide array of fascinating fans. I loved it when Matt would 'hold court.' It usually started with someone asking our favorite walking encyclopedia about some aspect of an aircraft or aviation-related subject. Off Matt would go in precise detail, delivering the information in his wonderfully colorful and animated style. One by one, an audience would begin to form a circle, which eventually became a crowd. These impromptu seminars usually involved a stack of Matt's drawings or sketches, and often he would address the personal anecdotes and stories behind the creation of these works. Matt usually accumulated a very educated, tough crowd, members of which were always spellbound by his knowledge. Matt always addressed his lecture to the person who had asked the question and was usually surprised when he finally looked up to a crowd of smiling, admiring faces surrounding him. 'What the hell is this?' he once asked. 'A party?'

"Without a doubt, Matt was the heart and soul of the ASAA. He was the spiritual leader of the group. He constantly reminded us that painting should tell a story—evoke an emotional response—and that painting a pretty portrait of an airplane was not enough. He challenged all of us to raise the bar and to push personal limits."

Rick went on to say that the Artober Fests at Santa Paula were not only instructive, but enjoyable. At the end of a day of flying, painting, and viewing vintage aircraft on display, Matt and Mary Ann would open the hangar doors and invite everyone to enter and partake in refreshments, chatter, music, singing, and dancing. Rick and Mike Machat, ASAA's first president, formed a band which they appropriately called the "Revell-a-tions."

"Artober Fest," Santa Paula airport—On one occasion, a dedicated "Trekkie" arrived and asked Rick Ruhman if "the guy over there is related to Walter M. Jefferies, the art director for *Star Trek*." Recognizing a good chance to pull the kid's leg, Rick replied: "I don't know. Let's go ask." "Hey, Matt," Rick said. "This guy wants to know if you're related to, or know of a Walter M. Jefferies. Something about a science fiction show." "Yeah, I met the guy. He's no big deal! What about him?" The kid went on and on about how talented Walter Jefferies was and gave Matt his own history lesson about his TV career. "Rick," Matt suggested, "why don't you take this man upstairs to our Flight Lounge and make yourselves a drink. I'll be up in a minute." The first thing that caught the kid's attention was the F-104 sculpture which was used in Captain Kirk's stateroom in the original series. As he looked around, other *Star Trek* items were seen. Just as he turned to Rick for an explanation, Matt entered the room. Rick then introduced Matt and informed the kid that he was indeed the former art director on the original series of *Star Trek*. The kid turned pale and then red, truly stunned at having been in the presence of Matt Jefferies.

❉

Rick Ruhman—"Late one night in the hangar after most of the gang had left, Matt and I were having a night cap. We were discussing our wives and how fortunate we were to have such wonderful gals that put up with us *artists*. Matt said that if it wasn't for Mary Ann he would be nothing, that she was the glue that held everything together, and she was the greatest gal in the world."

"Artober Fest" event at Santa Paula airport hangar—standing
(l-r) Rick Ruhman, John Cvek, Steve Smith, Matt Jefferies—kneeling
(l-r) Joshua Townsand, Mike Machat

In an issue of *Aero Brush,* Rick Ruhman wrote: "Flying was the central theme of every Artober Fest. The Santa Paula airport sits in a beautiful agricultural valley between two long mountain ranges leading to the Pacific Ocean. The pilots carried passengers throughout the day and racked up lots of takeoffs and landings. The flights through crisp, clean air with light to moderate clouds, were especially beautiful—especially the coastline views. Virtually all the flights included formation flying, so the passengers got lots of nice air-to-air-to-air photos as well as just taking in the views and sights of the beautifully restored classic aircraft just off the wings. The best part of these events is the camaraderie and friendships, enhanced during these "family" reunions. The sharing of art and ideas and genuine mutual interest and appreciation of each other makes the Jefferies' Artober Fest special!"

WW II BOMBER PLANT—B-24 Liberators were produced in this Fort Worth facility. The twin tail bomber was powered with four, Pratt and Whitney, 1,200 horsepower, air-cooled radial engines. The maximum speed was 303 mph. Its bomb capacity was 8,800 lbs. Armed with ten .50 cal. machine guns.

F–16 "FIGHTING FALCON"—The Lockheed F-16 fighter jet is a single seat plane having a maximum speed of 1320 mph at an altitude of 40,000 feet. Powered with a 25,000-lb thrust Pratt & Whitney or a 25,200-lb thrust GE afterburning turbojet.

SERGEI SIKORSKY—Son of Igor Sikorsky who designed the helicopters used exclusively by the USAAF during World War II. Sergei Sikorsky, vice president of Sikorsky Corporation, was a highly respected lecturer on helicopter aviation.

ASAA members who attended the Dallas/Fort Worth forum were invited to visit the American Airlines C.R. Smith Museum. A beautifully restored DC-3, the *Flagship Knoxville,* was the centerpiece attraction. As was his usual practice, Matt snapped many pictures of the artifacts and memorabilia for inclusion in his aviation reference files. This was followed by a tour of the Lockheed/Martin plant in Fort Worth where the F-16, 'Fighting Falcon' fighter jets were being assembled. Golf carts were provided for ease in traversing the length of the mile-long facility. Sharing Matt's cart was Sergei Sikorsky, son of Igor Sikorsky, who built the first successful single-rotor helicopter. At the conclusion of the tour, the visitors were informed that an aviation art exhibit was being held in the Future Projects Division. Upon entering the spacious graphics department, they were met by scores of paint-splattered artists who were eager to show off their paintings. Someone had spread the word that Matt Jefferies, designer of the *Starship Enterprise,* was present. He was quickly surrounded and plied with questions. A neatly attired man threaded his way through the crowd, reached out to shake Matt's hand, and said, "I feel honored to meet you. I have admired your work since I was a boy. I am head of this department. It is because of you and your extraordinary work that I became an engineer." Needless to say, Matt was overcome by the adulation. He later remarked that never in his wildest dreams did he think that his work would inspire one to choose engineering as a profession.

August 12, 1996, Jack guided his Ballanca Cruise Master to a smooth landing at Santa Paula's airport. Disguised as a World War I aviator, I occupied the right seat. Jack taxied the orange and blue monoplane across the tarmac to a location that was out of sight of Matt's hangar. I left the plane, paused to don a helmet, goggles, a scarf, and a false mustache, and proceeded on foot. The sound of the approaching aircraft compelled Matt to look up from working on the Waco.

1958 Bellanca Cruise Master with 230-hp engine and a cruising speed of 185 mph.

"Flying is the second greatest thrill known to man. Landing is the first."

Artist—John Amendola

He stood, waved, and waited as Jack maneuvered the plane to the hangar and then killed the engine. Emerging from the plane, Jack informed Matt that he had observed a "strange character" walking in their direction.

"What do you mean by 'strange'?" Matt asked.

"Looked like the ghost of a WWI aviator—there he comes now!"

Leaning on a cane for added deception, I ambled up to within inches of where Matt was standing. No words were exchanged until Matt broke the silence and said: "Hi, stranger! May I be of any help to you?"

Unresponsive, I continued to scrutinize Matt's countenance.

Jim Bender, publisher and editor of *Aviation Illustrated*, attended Matt's seventy-fifth birthday celebration. The December 1996 issue of this publication featured "Mr. Starship," Walter "Matt" Jefferies.

Wendell Dowling, aviation artist and creator of "The Adventures of Nick Blade" cartoon strip also attended.

Aviation artist **John Amendola** contributed a caricature of Matt.

"Don't know who you are or what you want, stranger," Matt said, "but I suggest that you blow your nose!" (Without the advantage of having a mirror, I had carelessly smeared spirit gum to my upper lip to hold the fake mustache in place.) Ignoring Matt's admonition, I reached out with my cane to tap the Waco's sparkling propeller.

"Don't touch the airplane!" Matt shouted. "Stay as long as you like, but don't touch the airplane!"

The chicanery could well have lasted for hours, but I finally revealed my identity and said: "Matt, you invited me to your seventy-fifth birthday celebration, so I came properly attired and eager to take to the sky in your beautiful bird. By the way, congratulations!"

"Thanks, Dick. Glad you could come, but you sure had me fooled! Keep the outfit on and let's see how well you can fool Mary Ann. She's shopping for a party at Logsdon's. We're expecting about a hundred guests, including our many airport friends, aviation artists, and some of the Hollywood crowd. A few vintage aircraft owners are flying in and will join us at Logsdon's."

When Mary Ann arrived, I approached her and repeated the charade. Taken aback by my aggressive attitude, she nervously glanced at Matt and Jack for some sign that they recognized the unknown stranger. Finally she laughed and said, "I know who you are! You're that guy who fooled us last week dressed like Abraham Lincoln!"

The birthday party was a resounding success. Live music, food and drink, and the camaraderie of friends and relatives provided an atmosphere of celebration for the honoring of Matt's seventy-fifth birthday.

Thirty years had elapsed since Matt concluded his work on the original series of *Star Trek*. Although he was grateful for the worldwide acclaim of his iconic *Enterprise,* he was not an avid science fiction fan.

STAR TREK—The original series is the most successful show in syndication history. It has been seen in more than one hundred domestic markets and in more than eighty countries.

❋

PENNY JUDAY—Penny got her start in the film industry as an assistant set designer for the highly-acclaimed 1990 film, *The Hunt for Red October*. The film received an Academy Award for best sound effects.

❋

WILLIAM CAMPBELL—A former *Star Trek* actor, William Campbell, is the founder of Fantasticon V 2K, a charity for the benefit of the Motion Picture and Television Fund. The fund maintains a hospital, residences, and four health centers for members of the film industry.

Matt receiving the "Shooting Star" award

Star Trek's universe lay "beyond the clouds." However, his art never ventured further into the realm of futuristic space travel. "Perhaps," he once stated, "my design of the *Enterprise* encouraged other imaginative artists to create *more* sophisticated ships to explore the far reaches of outer space." He turned down countless invitations to attend science fiction conventions. An exception was made when Penny Juday, Paramount art department coordinator, asked him to attend William Campbell's *Fantasticon V 2K* convention in Los Angeles. Much to his surprise, Matt was the recipient of the prestigious "Shooting Star" award. In making the presentation, Penny congratulated Matt and read aloud the adulatory inscription on the plaque: *"In Recognition and Appreciation of your Timeless Artistic Talents Which Helped to Create the American Icon that is* STAR TREK."

CHAPTER ELEVEN

anta Paula Airport—October 9, 1999. Flyers and friends assembled for a hangar party to bid farewell to Matt and Mary Ann's Waco YOC. For some months Matt was painfully aware that his vision was declining. Steering his bird on final approach to narrow runways had become more tedious. The time had come for him to face up to the realization that his piloting days were over. In a call to his boyhood friend, Neil November, cofounder of the Virginia Aviation Museum in Richmond, Matt offered to donate the plane to the museum. Neil graciously accepted the generous offer. "Your Waco," he said, "will be proudly displayed for generations to admire. There is only one condition! You are to be at the controls when the plane makes its final landing at Byrd Field!" Matt readily agreed. To make the flight, a close friend, Fred Chisholm, a corporate pilot, occupied the pilot's seat. Jo Anne Vest joined him as copilot and navigator. A crowd of onlookers lined the tarmac as Waco YOC NC17740 roared down the runway and lifted off. As the plane gained altitude and leveled off, Fred did a one-eighty and passed over the airport. The wings dipped as a final salute to the Santa Paula Airport and the loyal crowd of well-wishers. Matt took a commercial flight to Richmond to be present when Fred touched down at Byrd Airport three days later. Matt, Neil November, and members of the museum's Board of Directors waited on the tarmac as the plane landed and taxied to where they were standing. Fred and Jo Anne alighted and were welcomed by a hearty applause. It was now Matt's turn to pilot the plane. Accompanied by Neil, he took off, circled the field, and brought his bird in for a picture perfect landing. "Mission accomplished!" he said as he taxied towards the museum. Neil arranged for the Waco to be located adjacent to Commander Richard Byrd's Fairchild FC-2W2.

VIRGINIA AVIATION MUSEUM—*The Golden Age of Aviation* is represented by a collection of historic, vintage aircraft. A 1936 **Vultee V1-A**, owned by William Randolph Hearst, flew Hollywood notables to the ornate Hearst castle *San Simeon*. The V-1A is powered with a 1,000 hp Wright "Cyclone" R-1850 radial engine.

Pitcairn PA-5 Mailwing—The open cockpit biplane flew the mail routes from New York to Atlanta to Miami. Pitcairn Aviation manufactured its own airplanes. Richmond's Byrd Field was selected as the center base for its two divisions: Hadley, New Jersey, to Richmond, Virginia, and Richmond to Atlanta.

1928 Bellanca CH-400 Skyrocket was salvaged off an Alaskan glacier in 1962. It is powered with a 450 hp Pratt and Whitney WASP Jr. radial.

1938 Stinson SR-10G Reliant—The Reliant was originally owned by American Airlines. It is powered with a 300 hp radial engine. Known for its ease of handling and reliability, the plane was popular for charter services. Its gull wing design made the Reliant a strikingly beautiful aircraft.

Fairchild FC-2W2—Piloted by Commander Richard Byrd, the *Stars and Stripes* monoplane was the first aircraft to fly over the South Pole. For transporting the plane aboard ship, the wings were hinged for folding.

RICHARD E. BYRD FIELD—Casually called *Byrd Field*, the airport is now designated as the *Richmond International Airport*.

❋

Lockheed SR-71 Blackbird—The SR-71 can sustain a speed of 2,100 mph (Mach3+) at altitudes of 80,000 feet and above. Its flying range is 2,300 miles without refueling. The wingspan of the SR-71 is fifty-five feet. With a full load of fuel, it weighs 140,000 lbs. Two Pratt & Whitney J58 turbo-ramjets deliver 32,500 pounds of thrust each. To withstand the heat generated at Mach three-speeds, ninety percent of the airframe is made of a titanium alloy. A two-man crew occupies separate cockpits. The Blackbird was designed for high-flying reconnaissance. The Air Force retired the SR-71 in the 1990s.

WACO YOC Exhibit—Richmond Virginia Aviation Museum

As the Waco was rolled into place, Matt and Neil reminisced about their love of aviation since they were boys, building and selling model airplane kits in Eddie Galeski's garage. Sixty years had elapsed since they had bicycled to Byrd Field to watch airplanes land and take off. Flying had become a passion and aviation lore a reflection of the brave deeds of the pioneers of flight. The Waco was in good company: Commander Richard Byrd's 1927 Fairchild, a 1927 Travel Air 2000, a 1931 Curtiss A-14D, a 1928 Bellanca *Skyrocket*, a Pitcairn PA-5 *Mailwing* and many other historic, vintage aircraft. Suspended overhead were replicas of three Wright Brothers gliders. A painted line across the floor of the vast museum duplicated the 120-foot distance Orville Wright flew in the *Wright Flyer* in 1903. It was the world's first flight of a powered aircraft. Commanding the museum's entrance was a Lockheed *SR-71 Blackbird,* the fastest turbojet aircraft ever built. A Hall of Fame plaque honors prominent Virginians who have contributed to the advancement of aviation. One, Vincent "Squeek" Burnett, caught Matt's eye. He turned to Neil and said, "Squeek was one of my first flying instructors at College Park, Maryland. He knew more about seat-of-the pants flying than anyone I have ever known! Many who watched him perform in the Flying Aces Air Circus concluded that 'Squeek' Burnett was either insane or flew with his guardian angel in the cockpit."

Practice Time, painting by Matt Jefferies

FLYING ACES AIR CIRCUS—Jimmy Woods and his wife, Jessie, founded the Flying Aces Air Circus in 1929. The show featured aerobatic flying, wing-walking, and parachute jumps. Flying Stearman and Travel Air biplanes, Jimmy Woods and "Squeek" Burnett staged aerial dogfights. The show's finale was Burnett's daring inverted flight under a fifteen-foot high ribbon. Jessie performed as a "wing walker," in which she stood atop the wing as the plane executed barrel rolls and other aerobatic maneuvers. After a ten-year run, the Flying Aces disbanded in 1939.

In WWII, prior to the invasion of North Africa, the reputation of the Martin B-26 twin-engine bomber was tarnished as a result of an inordinate series of training accidents during takeoffs and landings. At Mac Dill Field in Florida, the common lament was "One a Day in Tampa Bay." However, experienced pilots found no problem with the bomber. In 1942, Gen. James Doolittle, commander of the 4th Medium Bombardment Wing, sent Capt. Vincent W "Squeek" Burnett, his technical advisor, to teach and demonstrate how to safely fly the B-26.

"No doubt about it, Matt, he was a daredevil. His famous stunt of flying an inverted biplane under a fifteen-foot high ribbon is one for the books!"

"I recently completed a painting of that stunt."

"I'd like to have it for the museum. Would you consider selling it?"

"Sorry, Neil. It's not for sale! But on second thought, I'll donate the painting to the museum as my own personal tribute to a great aviator."

From the Neilson J. November Observation Deck, visitors can look down the barrels of two machine guns mounted on a French 1916 SPAD, open–cockpit fighter plane. In 1918, Captain Eddie Rickenbacker, commander of the 94th Aero Pursuit Squadron, became America's ace-of-aces, accounting for the downing of twenty-six enemy planes and four observation balloons. The guns were mechanically timed to fire between the rotating propeller blades. Of the hundreds produced during World War I, only a few SPADS remain. It is indeed a rare fighter.

The French SPAD VII went into war service with fighter squadrons in 1916. A 150 hp. Hispano-Suiza V-8, liquid-cooled engine gave the plane a good rate of climb and a service ceiling of 18,000 feet.

Captain Eddie Rickenbacker In 1916 Spad

In the ensuing months, Matt and Mary Ann traveled extensively. They visited Panama, Guatemala, and Mexico. Deep-sea fishing off Acapulco, Matt landed a magnificent sailfish which was subsequently mounted for display in their Hollywood home. A cruise to Alaska from Vancouver, British Columbia, followed the inside passage to Ketchikan, Juneau, and Sitka. An auto tour of England included a visit to five-thousand-year-old Stonehenge in the Cottswalds and the sites of several World War II air bases. Of particular interest was a return visit to the site of the Chelveston Air Base where the 301st Bomb Group was stationed from August to November 1942. Very little remained of the once active Eighth Air Force base. Only the control tower, a few rusting hangars, and Nissen huts survived.

Standing on a crumbling section of Chelveston's old concrete runway, Matt reflected on the bitter winter of '42 when the 301st Bombardment Group flew missions over Continental Europe. He recalled the frigid mornings, arising before dawn in a poorly heated Nissen hut, hastily dressing, and trudging across frozen ground to the relative warmth of the mess hall. Powdered scrambled eggs, bacon, and dry toast were washed down with countless cups of coffee to fortify mind and body for the tasks awaiting the ground crews. Preflight servicing of the heavy bombers on the flight line was often hampered by dense fog or vicious winds and extreme cold.

Preflight at Chelveston, Matt's painting of B-17F "Dicky Doodle II"

As Matt conjured up memories of those miserably cold winter days at Chelveston, wind gusts rattled the rusting remnants of the control tower, now skeletal, abandoned and exposed to the elements. No longer heard was the deep-throated roar of powerful Wright-Cyclone engines as B-17 Fortresses lined up and took off on their bombing missions over enemy territory. Now, only the melodious songbirds and the pealing of a distant church bell disturbed the silence of the pristine English countryside.

Over the years, Matt enjoyed an abiding affinity with the 301st Bomb Group. Whenever time and circumstance allowed, he attended the 301st Bomb Group/Wings Association's reunions. A Seattle reunion afforded the Air Force veterans an opportunity to visit the enormous Boeing Aircraft plant where modern day jet transports were manufactured. A family of aircraft from the 737 to the 767 rolled off the same assembly lines where in the war years, thousands of B-17 were mass produced. Matt's paintings of the B-17 *Holey Joe* and *Preflight at Chelveston* were placed on exhibit and received wide acclaim. He derived great pleasure from the camaraderie of his fellow Air

Chelveston Air Base—The WW II, Eighth USAAF base was located near the village of Caldecott-cum-Chelveston, NW of London. After the war the church of St. James in the nearby village of Thrapston was given the pews which had been previously installed in the Chelveston Base chapel.

❋

Twelve O'clock High, a 1949 motion picture, was filmed at the former Chelveston Air Base. Gregory Peck played the starring role of a base commander who began to crack under the strain of sending USAAF, B-17 bombers over Europe in World War II.

❋

Most of the fifty-seven U.S. Eighth AIR FORCE BASES in England were built and maintained by the U.S. Army Corps of Engineers. Others were former Royal Air Force bases having runways incapable of handling the heavy U.S. bombers. Runways were extended and resurfaced by the engineers. Often when crushed aggregate for making concrete was not available, cement mixed with the native soil and water was fine-graded and compacted to build runways of sufficient strength to accommodate the bombers. Portable metal landing mats were also utilized until more permanent runways were constructed.

JOHN—From 1986 to 1995, John was production designer & art director on the weekly, one-hour TV Series *Matlock*. Andy Griffith portrayed Ben Matlock, an old-fashioned Atlanta lawyer who never lost a murder case. Filmed in and around Wilmington, North Carolina, *Matlock* received high ratings. The series was followed by a two-hour "Movie of the Week."

✤

RICHARD—Responsible for construction equipment sales to governmental agencies in the greater Dallas/Fort Worth area. Major projects included the Dallas-Fort Worth Airport and Dallas Love Field. Both airports were expanding and improving their runways and facilities.

✤

301st Bombardment Group—During its entire World War II service, the 301st claimed 395 enemy aircraft shot down. While in the Fifteenth Air Force, it flew 8,581 sorties and dropped 19,491 tons of bombs on targets in Italy, Germany, Romania, Czechoslovakia, Austria, Poland, Yugoslavia, Bulgaria, France, and Greece. The 301st lost 133 of its planes in combat and accidents.

✤

B-17 Flying Fortress—Crews of heavily damaged planes which returned to base safely could not say enough about the B-17. Many a Fort came back on only two engines. Others continued to fly with severed hydraulic lines and control cables. The fuselage, wings, rudder, and tail surfaces often suffered severe flak damage, but the planes continued to fly.

Force friends. They shared tales of daring, fortitude, and fright during the years they were based in England, North Africa, and Italy. They spoke with reverence of those who never returned from their missions. And they praised the reliability of the B-17 Flying Fortress. "The Fort," one exclaimed, "was indeed a remarkable bird!" A Spokane reunion brought the members back to Geiger Field (now Spokane International Airport) where the 301st originated in 1942. Little remained of the 1942 Air Corps base as they remembered it.

Matt's failing vision soon became a matter of grave concern. He underwent extensive testing to determine the cause. Ophthalmologists concluded that he was a victim of macular degeneration, an age-related disease which would eventually lead to blindness. For one who depended on good, keen eyesight to paint, or for that matter, to drive, or fly an airplane, the diagnosis was a crushing revelation. However, he bravely accepted the inevitable and vowed to make good use of the time remaining to conclude projects which were dear to his heart. He had long ago decided that his vast collection of aircraft drawings, photographs, and technical data would best be donated to Wright State University in Dayton, Ohio. The University is a repository of aviation history including a collection of the Wright brothers' papers documenting their aeronautical experiments. Matt's offer of his voluminous aviation collection was graciously accepted. Although aircraft were Matt's primary focus, classic race cars also captured his interest. His scale drawings appeared in *American Modeler* and various automotive publications. Each line drawing was accompanied by design specifications and a history of the car. The flaming red, 4.5 liter, Type 375 Ferrari was particularly famous. In the 1950s, the car had won virtually every road race—the twenty-four-hour Le Mans, the grueling 2,000-mile Mexican road race, and the Grand Prix. Powered by a V-12, 295 horsepower engine, the 1954 Italian "Rocket" had a top speed of 174 miles per hour. From a standstill, the car's acceleration (100 miles per hour in fifteen seconds) has been described as "neck snapping." Sports car fans wrote in and asked for more of Matt's illustrations of the aerodynamic, low-slung, European racers.

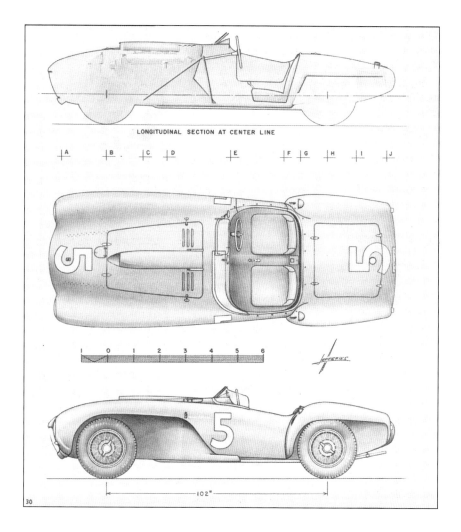

LONGITUDINAL SECTION AT CENTER LINE

Daybreak gradually illuminated the Santa Clara valley. Forecasters had predicted another hot, sultry day. It was Sunday, August 12, 2001.

Santa Paula pilots arrived early at the airport and rolled their planes out onto the tarmac for preflight run-up before queuing up on the taxi way to await their turn for takeoff. Incoming traffic further delayed those eager to take to the skies before the sun's rays dispersed the cool, misty morning air.

A special event was scheduled to take place at Logsdon's restaurant, where aviation enthusiasts gathered daily to talk airplanes. Preparations were underway for an afternoon party in the dining hall. It was Matt's eightieth birthday. Many guests were expected and Mary Ann was determined to throw a party that all would long remember. Throughout the morning they arrived and congregated at the Jefferies hangar. Some had flown in from distant places and taxied their planes up to the open hangar for all to admire. Mary Ann served refreshments in the upstairs "Flight Lounge," while Matt welcomed the new arrivals and chatted with his many friends.

Fellow pilots, aviation artists and historians, movie and television people, and "trekkers" comprised the bulk of those in attendance. The party was a resounding success! Matt was applauded and honored for his contributions to aviation, to the film industry, and to the community.

At sundown, as the celebration came to a close, a biplane took to the air towing a streaming banner which read: **"MATT WALT JEFF HAPPY 80TH!"**

WHY HERE?
by Matt Jefferies

By some strange phenomena, aviation types seek out one another. Any two in a room full of strangers will by some unknown means discover each other and their interest in flying. Aviation types, those who are completely involved in aviation for a living, or those who dabble in it just for fun . . . the "airplane nuts." The latter must be included lest the writer be excluded. Once these types find each other, the topic goes to flying and airplanes.
"You have an airplane?
Where do you keep it?"
"Santa Paula."
"Where in Heaven's name is Santa Paula?
Now the reasons begin to tumble forth in my mind. It is such a beautiful drive down the valley to get there once you are out of the city. It is a nice little airport with no control tower and all the complicated stuff that goes with big airports. It's a very friendly airport. Friends, so many over the years that we have gotten to know.
It is such a beautiful area to fly in with its citrus groves, flower farms, the ocean, and the nearby mountains . . . the pleasure of visitors who come by the hangar peering in with beady eyes to see what fascinating ships are there. They have heard that Santa Paula is a haven for such flying machines. Our guest book lists names and places from all over the globe: Australia, Alaska, England, France, Czechoslovakia, Norway, Sweden, New Zealand, South Africa, Mexico, and many, many more . . .
The pride in being a hangar owner which means being a part of one of the world's most unusual airports.
"Yeah, well . . . it's a long way out of town, but our birds have their own roof in Santa Paula."

From the Santa Paula Airport 50th year anniversary program.
August 9–10, 1980.

Friends who arrived in their planes departed before the dark of night blanketed the airport. Others stayed and accompanied Matt and Mary Ann to the hangar's "Flight Lounge" for more talk of airplanes and flying. They passed around congratulatory messages received from friends, family, and admirers throughout the world. One, beautifully crafted, was a poem by Janice Dickenson. As she was present, Janice was asked to read the poem aloud. Her words asserted Matt's accomplishments in a manner that touched his heart. When asked to say a few words, Matt choked up and wiped tears from his eyes before responding. He expressed his gratitude to Janice and to the Dickenson family who had been dear friends for so many years. He reminisced about Ralph Dickenson's foresight in founding the Santa Paula airport and how his legacy endured by those he left behind after his departure from this life, his son, Don; daughter-in-law, Patty; grandson, Bruce; and his wife, Janice. "Santa Paula," Matt said, "our home away from home. Here Mary Ann and I can sit back, relax, and enjoy the camaraderie of good friends."

July 15, 2003, Matt visited Paramount Studio to discuss the production of a video chronicling the origin of *Star Trek*. However, upon entering the screening room, he was greeted by many friends and family members who had assembled to honor the designer of the *Starship Enterprise*. Paramount's Penny Juday hosted the tribute and praised Matt for his unique contribution to the success of *Star Trek*. Her congratulatory words were echoed by others who had worked with him on the

You designed a man-eating shark
For the *Old Man and the Sea*
And an operating room
For the good Dr. Ben Casey.

The limits of your talents
Are assuredly Untouchable
And you took on many Missions
That to most would seem impossible.

For what other art director
Can it at all be said,
Has made four-hundred different bedrooms
Using just one old brass bed?

From the sinful *Dallas* Ewings
To the humble prairie Ingalls
You showed us *Love, American Style*,
Be they married, divorced, or single.

And with gifted hand and vision
Came what all the world does recognize,
As the most famous spacecraft ever built . . .
The Starship U. S. S. *Enterprise*.

That along with other planets
You created and much more,
You have boldly taken all mankind
To where no man has gone before.

You have shared the world your talents
And of those there are no end,
But the greatest gift you've given us
Is that you are our friend.

So we lift our glass to toast you, Matt
On this special day we roar,
You've blessed us all for eighty years
And may you bless us with many more!

—-Janice Dickenson

Herb Zimmerman—production designer on *Enterprise*, a spin-off series of *Star Trek*: "Matt Jefferies is a gentle soul. He has put his stamp on everything we have done since his brilliant *Enterprise*."

Bob Justman—Producer of the original *Star Trek* series: "Throughout the numerous trials and tribulations that Matt and I underwent during the production of the series, he never once wavered. He was positive and supporting."

Majel Barret Roddenberry—"He was inspiring yet humble, his art and feel giving form to Gene's dream. So much of what made *Star Trek* beloved came *from his pen* . . . the look and dynamic of the show, being timeless and futuristic and yet still logical. It was just what Gene wanted: to be inspiring and yet believable."

William Shatner—*Star Trek* actor in the role, Captain Kirk: "I love Matt Jefferies. He was a good friend all during the years of *Star Trek*. I often consulted him for the books I wrote. Matt was a true source of knowledge about *Star Trek*."

Doug Drexler—Paramount Studio's senior illustrator: "Matt Jefferies was my initial inspiration to become an artist in Hollywood. He inspired me to work hard and not be afraid to dream the big dream."

original series. Matt, thoroughly humbled, expressed his appreciation for the surprise tribute and said: "I find it very difficult to comprehend, honestly, how design work that I did oh-so-many years ago has been accepted and continues to be accepted by millions of *Star Trek* fans throughout the world."

Following the formal ceremony, many in attendance remained to personally visit with Matt and discuss his career and plans for the future. Addressing the latter, Matt replied, "Mary Ann and I will continue to do what we most enjoy."

Indeed, what Matt and Mary Ann most enjoyed was their cozy home in the Hollywood Hills. Situated high on a steep hillside resplendent with lush vegetation, the location provides a quiet retreat from the bustling city. The site offers a panoramic vista of distant, tree-covered hills. Often during early morning hours, the hills are shrouded in fog, silently awaiting the rising sun to disperse the haze. A stand of towering eucalyptus trees lining a steep driveway

Producer Bob Justman and art director Matt Jefferies

Each year over a period of time, Matt crafted a Christmas tree ornament in the image of an elf. Working at various and sundry tasks to make Yuletide a happy occasion, they reflect Matt's artistry and his penchant for whimsical humor.

California License Plate Number- 35 Waco

provides shade and a sense of isolation. A profusion of flowering plants, lovingly tended by Mary Ann, border a broad patio encircling the ranch style house. A feeder, suspended from a branch of a sprawling Monterey pine, attracts colorful songbirds. Butterflies, bees, and hummingbirds feast on the inviting, nectar-laden blossoms. After sunset, wildlife, squirrels, raccoons, deer, foxes, coyotes, and an occasional bobcat, cross the patio in search of food and water. The interior of the house features an elongated living room with a fine-timbered, cathedral ceiling. Located on a lower level was Matt's studio, which contained his drawing board, art supplies, model airplane aviation history files, and reference library. The home provided Matt with a serene environment, one conducive to his continuing his art work and aviation research.

Holidays at the Jefferies's were festive occasions. Christmas decorations, artistically displayed, included Matt's cutout of a flickering candle atop the roof and a string of colored lights along the eaves. Each year, Matt added another of his hand-crafted elves to the Christmas tree. Guests spoke glowingly of the warm hospitality and gaiety attendant to the Yuletide celebrations. Matt took great pride in serving up his classic eggnog. Generous slices of smoked Smithfield ham evoked the praises of those who asked for seconds, "raised, aged, and cured in Virginia," he proudly stated.

"And, of course, these are Virginia peanuts?" someone asked.

"No doubt about it!" Matt replied.

"And this tasty cheese?"

"Monterey Jack!" Matt said.

Thanksgiving, Independence Day, birthdays, and other special occasions were similarly celebrated with family and friends gathered for partying and togetherness. Without exception, a prayer was recited before every meal. Matt's spirituality was rooted in his upbringing. Christian values were instilled in his consciousness from an early age. His faith was manifested in his relations with those he encountered each day. The Golden Rule and the Ten Commandments guided his actions. Raised as an Episcopalian, he readily accepted Catholic doctrine as an extension of his beliefs. His faith was absolute. One's religion, he believed, is private, allowing each of us to worship as we please. All who knew Matt and Mary Ann were cognizant of their faith as demonstrated by their wholesome persuasion.

Suffering from deteriorating health and a gradual loss of sight, Matt was resigned to remain at home in Hollywood and devote his time to working on many projects which were dear to his heart. His first priority was the formidable job of preparing his aviation archives for shipment to Wright State University. With the aid of powerful magnification, he was able to complete a few paintings for collectors of his art. His daily routine of "early-to-bed-early-to-rise" remained a constant as it had throughout his life.

Aviation archives—Matt's vast collection of photographs, prints, drawings, and manuals is estimated to exceed ten thousand in number. Starting with the few hundred given to him by aviation artist, William Heaslip in 1945, the collection eventually occupied a dozen file cabinets. Never without his camera, Matt searched for rare vintage aircraft. A visit to the basement of a New York City book store turned up dozens of photographs of the famed Ford Tri-motor cabin plane on the factory's production line. The owner of the store told Matt that he could have the entire lot free. Seems he needed the space.

⁜

Matt often quoted maxims from Ben Franklin's *Poor Richard's Almanac*. On the subject of his work ethic: *"Little strokes fell great oaks."* Regarding his Waco biplane: *"Old boys have their play-things as well as the young ones. The difference is only in the price."*

⁜

Matt's funeral mass—Among those attending were many who were associated with the motion picture and television studios, aviation artists and historians, pilots, friends, and family members. Mary Ann was presented an American Flag in recognition of Matt's service in the Air Force.

July 21, 2003, Matt was rushed to Sherman Oaks Hospital where he died of heart failure. A funeral Mass was held at St. Charles Borromco Catholic Church in North Hollywood. The celebrant, Reverend Jason Souza, spoke glowingly of Matt's eminence as a creative artist. I concluded my brother's eulogy with these words: *"So, Matt, you have left us . . . with O, so many fond memories. Rather than mourn the absence of your flame, let us celebrate how brightly it burned! We know where you are! And we know what you are doing! You are soaring with the angels . . . with God, as always, your navigator, in the copilot's seat."*

Burial service was conducted at Yeocomico Church in Virginia. Reverend Charles Sydnor Jr. concluded the solemn ceremony with this prayer: *"Rest eternal grant to him, O Lord. And let light perpetual shine upon him. May his soul and the souls of all the departed, through the mercy of God, rest in peace. AMEN."* Matt's ashes were laid to rest alongside his parents'.

Excerpts from Matt's eulogy—*"Matt returned home from the war, met and married the love of his life, Mary Ann, who has been a blessing to him for fifty-five years. Mary Ann, the love and support you provided Matt sustained him for those many years. God will reward you for your unselfish devotion. We are so grateful and truly love you."*

"We built model airplanes with balsa wood, glue, and tissue paper. Matt was always experimenting with ways to improve the performance of his aircraft . . . more elastic rubber bands and modified wing surfaces, rudders and props. He was a stickler for detail . . . particularly in the plane's markings. Once I asked Matt if he remembered the model he built of the Red Baron's plane with the German Maltese cross on the wings. He said that he didn't recall. 'Sure you do!' I said, 'You sent it down in flames!' 'Never happened!' he replied."

—Dick Jefferies

❋

MISSING MAN FORMATION

Five planes take to the air in a V formation. A lone wingman spirals off and heads west (into the sunset). The demonstration is a tribute to a fallen pilot. The origin of the tradition is unclear. However, it is believed to have been first performed by the British in World War I at the funeral of the German ace, Manfred von Richthofen, known as "The Red Baron."

Missing Man Formation

In October, Matt was remembered and honored at a "Celebration of Life" gathering at the Santa Paula Airport. The event was an opportunity for all to recall the many occasions when he was in their presence. Family, friends, fellow artists, and aviation buffs flocked to Matt's hangar and Logsdon's restaurant to celebrate his life. Jack addressed the hushed crowd and solemnly said: "My brother's life is best summed up by a reading of his eulogy." A reference to our father's employment by the Hershey Chocolate Company at the time of Matt's birth stated: *"The aroma of chocolate permeated our home and surroundings. Perhaps . . . just perhaps . . . that contributed to Matt's being such a sweet guy!"* Gerry Asher, president of the American Association of Aviation Artists rose and spoke glowingly of Matt's enormous contribution to aviation art.

At sundown, five planes flew over the airport in the traditional "missing man formation." It was a heartwarming and joyous, memorable occasion.

"In Memory of the High-Flying Spirit of Matt Jefferies"

TRIBUTES

"Matt was one of the most talented friends I ever had. We have chased a lot of clouds since we built, flew, and sold model airplanes in the '30s. I will sorely miss his telephone calls with the greeting, 'Hello Tiger!'"

—Neil November

Neilson J. November—For many years, Neil served his beloved city of Richmond, the state of Virginia, and the Jewish Community in positions of leadership for numerous organizations. Sparked by his lifelong interest in aviation, he held executive positions with the following:

Richmond Aviation Advisory Commission   Virginia Advisory Commission on Aviation

Capital Regional Airport Commission   Virginia Department of Aviation Board

Neil cofounded the Virginia Aeronautical Historical Society which, in turn, created the Virginia Aviation Museum in Richmond. In 1993, Neil was inducted in the Virginia Aviation Hall of Fame.

A hallmark of his achievements is the cofounding of the Virginia Holocaust Museum in Richmond. In recognition of his efforts at fostering understanding, Neil was recipient of an award from the National Conference of Christians and Jews.

"Matt Jefferies was a gracious gentleman from Virginia, always courteous, always soft-spoken, with a brilliant talent and a warm sense of humor. He was not only a wonderfully creative art director . . . from the stars of outer space to a little house on the prairie . . . but his talent as an aviation artist was outstanding and widely recognized. He loved to fly . . . and one of the projects closely followed by his friends was the restoration of his beloved Waco. He finally had to stop flying, but his heart was always in the sky. Now, he has truly reached out and touched the face of God."

—Dorothy Fontana, script writer

Dorothy Fontana—A script writer in Hollywood since the early 1960s, Dorothy wrote episodes for *The Waltons, Streets of San Francisco, Bonanza,* and *Ben Casey.* In 1963, Dorothy was hired by MGM as personal secretary to Gene Roddenberry, who was writing scripts for a Marine Corps television series titled *The Lieutenant.* Two years later, following the demise of *The Lieutenant,* Roddenberry retained Dorothy's services for a science fiction adventure series to be titled *Star Trek* and produced by Desilu Studios. As staff writer for the first television season, she edited Roddenberry's work and personally penned several of the episodes. For the second season of *Star Trek,* she was promoted to the position of story editor. Following the acquisition of Desilu by Paramount, Dorothy resigned and devoted her time to authoring several books. She returned to Paramount to assist with the animated series of *Star Trek* and *Star Trek: The Next Generation.*

"Matt Jefferies's interest in aviation history brought him to the American Aviation Historical Society. While serving as a director of the AAHS, he provided wise counsel. The society owes him a debt of gratitude. We will miss him but will not forget him."

—Jim Turner, Editor, *AAHS Journal*

"We are losing our aviation legends far too rapidly. Their names run to the very core of what aviation history is all about. Some were artists, others historians, and still others, writers and photographers. Matt Jefferies was all of the above."

—Mark Machat, editor, *Airpower Magazine.*

"We sadly mark the passing of one of *Trek's* founding fathers, Matt Jefferies. No matter how far back you trace your love of the *Trek* universe, it's a fact that this designer/illustrator . . . from that first phaser to the Starfleet bridge, to the original *Enterprise* . . . had so much to do with setting the *Trek* look and making it work for legions of eager fans."

—Larry Nemecek, managing editor, *Star Trek Communicator Magazine.*

"Matt Jefferies's precision carried over into his creative work on canvas and as a television and motion picture art director. Truly, Matt's has been a long, distinguished, and varied career."

—Ann Cooper, pilot, writer, and *Aero Brush* editor

"Matt was a gentle soul. He has put his stamp on everything we have done since his brilliant, classic *Enterprise*."

—Herb Zimmerman, *Star Trek* production designer.

"Throughout the numerous trials and tribulations that Matt and I underwent during the production of the series, he never once wavered. He was positive and supporting even when I came to him to cut our set construction budget, which was already minuscule. He'd just clear his throat a bit and think for a moment while his blue eyes would water up. 'I'll take a look, Tiger,' he'd declare, and with that I'd know he'd find a way to work his magic once again."

—Bob Justman, *Star Trek* producer.

"He was inspiring yet humble, his art and feel giving form to Gene's dream. So much of what made *Star Trek* beloved came from his pen . . . the look and dynamics of the show being timeless and futuristic and yet logical . . . and not in hindsight locked into the '60s like *Lost in Space*. It was just what Gene wanted: to be inspiring and yet believable . . . and, of course, on budget. Matt Jefferies will be sorely missed!"

—Majel Barrett Roddenberry

"Noted aviation artist, Matt Jefferies, who firmly established the Starfleet School of Design with his original designs of the U. S. S. *Enterprise* and her bridge, was one of the brightest lights we encountered in our research. Where so much television design is temporary and quickly dated, Matt's work has remained fresh and intriguing and still serves as daily inspiration to the new generation of Star Trek designers."

—Quotation from *The Art of Star Trek* by Judith and Garfield Reeves-Stevens

"I feel privileged to have known him. I watched every single *Star Trek* episode when I was young. What made the show so fascinating were the different places the Enterprise visited. It was his futuristic designs that made Matt so special."

—Janice Voss (PhD), astronaut, National Aeronautics and Space Administration.

"Matt, you were a very special brother-in-law! I'll miss you and your great sense of humor! Ed and I have fond memories of our good times together with you and Mary Ann."

—Doris Benson Ring

"Matt, a great human being! Great sense of humor, super artist, modest, and soft-spoken. An enjoyable brother-in-law for over fifty years!"

—Estelle Benson Rouse

"Walter 'Matt' Jefferies, the visionary designer of the original *Star Trek*, that guy who put standard divergent shapes together, saucer and nacelle, creating something that has remained supernaturally fresh for more than thirty-five years. Aviator, artist, historian, and wonderful, gentle human being. My mind boggles when I weigh the influence that he has had on my life as a designer and as a person."

—Doug Drexler, *Star Trek* Art Department, Paramount Pictures

"I very much admired Matt Jefferies. He was such a fantastically creative man, always so energetic and enthusiastic and a wonderful friend as well. I remember well the wonderful visits Louise and I had when we visited Matt and Mary Ann at their hangar in Santa Paula. In his honor I am only too pleased to contribute this pastel titled *In Memory of the High-Flying Spirit of Matt Jefferies*.

—Robert T. McCall, artist and author.

Robert McCall is a talented artist noted for his paintings of aircraft and space-related subjects. He was commissioned by NASA to chronicle the Mercury and Apollo Space Programs with his classic illustrations. Gracing the entrance of the National Air and Space Museum in Washington, D.C., is a McCall masterpiece: an immense painting titled: *The Space Mural, a Cosmic View*. Hollywood, recognizing McCall's talent for rendering conceptual paintings of outer space, acquired his services for poster artwork for the motion picture *2001—A Space Odyssey*. *Star Trek, the Motion Picture* used his paintings of galactic environments. One featured the Starship *Enterprise*, as originally designed by Matt Jefferies for the original series of *Star Trek*. Robert McCall is a founding member of the American Society of Aviation Artists.

"Matt Jefferies's quiet modesty was belied by the genius of his work which set the path for all of us who are lucky enough to follow in his very large footsteps. Today, nearly five decades later, Matt's original *Enterprise* still stands as a design classic."

—Michael Okuda, scenic art supervisor on the *Star Trek* spin-off series *Enterprise*.

Michael Okuda was the graphic art supervisor for *Star Trek: The Next Generation, Star Trek: Deep Space Nine, Star Trek: Voyager,* and *Star Trek: Enterprise.* He also served as a technical consultant to the writing staff of *Star Trek* and is coauthor of the *Star Trek: The Next Generation Technical Manual.* With his wife, Denise, he cowrote the *Star Trek Chronology* and the *Star Trek Encyclopedia.*

For NASA, Mike designed a commemorative emblem honoring the lost astronauts of *Apollo 1, Challenger,* and *Columbia.* The emblem hangs on the wall of Mission Control in *Houston.* To honor Matt for his contributions to aviation and science fiction, Mike designed this emblem illustrating the Waco flying "beyond the clouds."

"There was a time when, early on (before the first episode of *Star Trek* was shot) that Matt, having read the third or fourth script distributed to the production people, was compelled to tell me, 'If our starship has that many things go wrong with its engines every week, Kirk won't have his captaincy very long!' But for Matt, the *Enterprise* would never have survived its forty years in space.

     —John F. Black, executive story consultant and associate producer of the original series

"It's been said that 'Yiddish is the lingua franca of Hollywood.' There's a word from Yiddish— *mensch*. I've known few men who deserved to have 'sch' added to their gender description. The word means a man who is manly without being macho, whose behavior can be whimsical but never irrational, who can love people and be patient with them, who involves himself with work that he enjoys, and performs that work with imagination and dedication . . . Matt was truly a *mensch*!"

—Mary Black, screen writer

"Matt Jefferies was a quiet gentleman with a great gift. His *Enterprise* was spectacular!"

—Leonard Nimoy, actor, "Mr. Spock" in *Star Trek*

Postage Stamp—On September 17, 1999, the United States Postal Service issued a thirty-three-cent stamp featuring the U. S. S. *Enterprise* and the Starfleet insignia. Honoring famous people and events, the commemorative stamp is one of a 1960s series titled "*Celebrate the Century*," which has captured the imagination of millions of fans throughout the world. To have an image of the *Enterprise* appear on a United States postage stamp is likewise a momentous tribute to Matt, the designer.

Former (1952–1960) Postmaster General Arthur Sommerfield proclaimed: "The postage stamps of a nation are a picture gallery of its glories. They depict in miniature its famous men and women and the great events of its history."

Note: Throughout the years, Matt produced many paintings of the U. S. S. *Enterprise*. Other distinguished artists have also rendered paintings of the famous *Star Trek* space ship. The artist for the *Star Trek* postage stamp is Keith Birdsong. His art has graced the covers of over 300 books related to the *Star Trek* universe.

MATT'S FEATURE FILM
& TV CAREER

1956 **Towards the Unknown**. Warner Bros. feature film starring Willliam Holden, James Garner, and Lloyd Nolan. (Story of X-2 experimental, rocket-firing aircraft.)
Matt was a technical advisor.

1957 **Bombers B-52**. Warner Bros. feature film starring Karl Malden, Marsha Hunt, Natalie Wood, and Efrem Zimbalist Jr.
Matt was a set designer.

1958 **The Old Man and the Sea**. Warner Bros. feature film starring Spencer Tracy and Filipe Pazos. (Based on Ernest Hemingway's novella.)
Matt provided the technical illustrations for a twenty-foot mechanical shark.)

1959 **The Wreck of the Mary Deare**. Warner Bros. feature film starring Charlton Heston and Gary Cooper.
Matt was a set designer.

1960 **The Crowded Sky**. Warner Bros. feature aviation film starring Dana Andrews, Rhonda Fleming, Efrem Zimbalist Jr., and Anne Francis.
Matt was a set designer.

1960 **The Untouchables**. Desilu Studios/Paramount Pictures. Long-running television series (1959-1963) starring Robert Stack as Eliot Ness, a 1930s gang-buster and prohibition agent living in Chicago.
Matt was a set designer.

1963 **Ben Casey**. Desilu Studios. Long-running television series (1961–1966) starring Vince Edwards as Dr. Casey. A hospital drama.
Matt was a set designer.

1965 **Star Trek**. Desilu Studios/Paramount Pictures. Television series created by writer Gene Roddenberry. The original series (1965–1968), aired for three seasons (seventy-nine episodes).
Matt was set designer for two pilots, production designer for two episodes, and art director for the following (seventy-six) episodes.

1966   ***Mission Impossible***. Desilu Studios/Paramount Pictures. Long-running television series (1966–1973). Adventures of a team of government spies who received "impossible" assignments.

Matt was a set designer.

1969   ***Love, American Style***. Paramount Pictures. Long running television series (1969–1974). A comedic, one-hour weekly show comprising two or more romantic vignettes.

Matt was the art director.

1970   ***Catch 22***. Paramount Pictures. Feature film starring Alan Arkin, Jon Voight, Martin Sheen, and Orson Wells. About a WWII Air Force base in the Mediterranean.

Matt was set designer.

1974   ***Little House on the Prairie***. MGM. Long running television series (1974–1983), produced and directed by Michael Landon. Loosely based on Laura Ingalls Wilder's eight books.

Matt was art director for the entire series, comprising 183 episodes.

1981   ***Father Murphy***. MGM. Television series running two seasons (1981–1983) produced by Michael Landon.

Matt was art director.

1984   ***Dallas***. Lorimar Telepictures. Long-running television series which premiered in 1978. Fictional scoundrel J.R. Ewing, abused convention to expand his Ewing Oil Company empire. Larry Hagman played J.R. Ewing and Victoria Principal played his wife.

Matt was art director for two seasons (1984 and 1985).

1986   ***Riptide***. Stephen J. Cannell Productions. Television series aired for two seasons (1984–1986). Action-packed episodes relating the experiences of three Vietnam veterans who work as private eyes in southern California.

Matt was art director.

Note: Dates are those of release dates (feature films) and starting dates (television series).

JEFFERIES CLAN CREATES ITS OWN

"BROTHERHOOD OF ART DIRECTORS"

Butch Cassidy and the Sundance Kid, Star Trek, Matlock . . . at first glance, there's not a lot in common among the three. But a closer look turns up a curious coincidence: the art directors on all three, and on dozens of other TV shows and features, have a common last name: Jefferies. As improbable as it seems, three brothers, Matthews, Philip, and John Jefferies have not only made their mark in Hollywood, but all have done it in the same field. As art directors/production designers, and . . . in the years before reaching this stage . . . as illustrators, set designers and assistant art directors, they have each accumulated lists of credits that go back three and four decades.

—Daily Variety issue of January 16, 1987

Phil, John, and Matt

John and his 1958 Bellanca Cruise Master

For three decades, John designed sets for over forty feature television films and eight television one-hour series. His reputation as an accomplished designer led to his being selected as art director for *Matlock*, a courtroom drama starring Andy Griffith. Andy was best known for his leading role in the *Andy Griffith Show*, in which he played the sheriff of the mythical town of Mayberry. It aired for eight seasons, and the series attracted millions of fans.

Matlock was filmed in and around Wilmington, North Carolina. The popular series comprised 178 one-hour episodes (1986–94) and a televised, two-hour "Movie of the Week."

John returned to California with the intention of retiring. However, Paramount Studios urged him to remain in the business long enough to design sets for *JAG* (military jargon for Judge Advocate General), a drama series about the prosecution and defense of those accused of crime. After completing seven episodes, John retired to devote time to his love of flying and his family.

From his early years as an illustrator on feature films for Warner Bros., Philip's extraordinary talent as an artist did not go unnoticed by the producers. In 1954, he was named color consultant on *Young at Heart*, starring Frank Sinatra and Doris Day. The need for a consultant resulted from Eastman Kodak's introduction of color film. With the previous coloring process of *Technicolor*, the compatibility of various colors was firmly established. However, to insure that the colors on the new color film were sharp and pleasing to the eye, Phil inspected the costumes and sets and ran color tests before production began. "It was a great learning experience," he said, "one that exposed me to sides of the business that I didn't see from my drawing board." Philip progressed rapidly and received film credits on many motion pictures and television shows as art director and as production designer. He was nominated for an Academy Award for art direction on *Butch Cassidy and the Sundance Kid* in 1969 and *Tom Sawyer* in 1973. Phil died in 1987.

Phil on location

Walter Matthews Jefferies Sr. continued in his position as chief engineer for Merck & Company until his death on April 30, 1963, two months short of his sixty-fourth birthday. Over a period of several years, he worked weekends to build a lake home at Barnegat Pines near Toms River, New Jersey. It was there that Walter and Grace resided at the time of his untimely passing. Interment was at Yeocomico Church in Westmoreland County, Virginia. Chiseled into his grave marker are the words: "HERE LIES A MAN."

Grace Livingston (Sanford) Jefferies moved to Hollywood, California, in 1967 to be near Matt, Phil, Jack, and their families. She died in 1970 at the age of seventy-five and was buried alongside her beloved husband. Engraved on her grave marker are the words: "HIS LOVING WIFE."

Grace and Walter—Barnegat Pines, New Jersey

CONTRIBUTING ARTISTS

The author is grateful to the artists who contributed sketches for *Beyond the Clouds*. All have expressed their admiration and respect for Matt Jefferies, a fellow artist.

Wendell Dowling—Wendell studied commercial art at Ventura College in Santa Paula, CA. He was then employed by several firms as a draftsman and technical illustrator. Later, an advertising agency utilized his artistic services in their public relations department. The demise of the firm led to his decision to sell his art as a freelancer. He opened a sign shop and a studio located above a hangar at the Santa Paula Airport. Aircraft owners, aircraft services and suppliers, and the airport's management turned to Wendell for their art work. In 1996 he created an aviation comic strip titled "The Adventures of Nick Blade." The popular cartoon appeared in issues of *Aviation Illustrated* magazine. His art work also appears in *Wing Tips*, the Aviation Museum of Santa Paula's newsletter. Wendell's wife, Lynne, is the daughter of Sammy Mason, a former air show pilot and a retired test pilot for Lockheed Aircraft. Wendell and Lynne reside in Santa Paula.

John Amendola—John was born and raised in Queens, New York. As a boy he was an avid reader of "Buck Rogers" and "Flash Gordon." John also built model airplanes. His first model was a ten-cent balsa kit of Mr. Mulligan. John had an uncle who was a pilot and flew out of Floyd Bennett Field. He gave John his first plane ride. John's love of airplanes, his passion for flying, and his artistic talent culminated in his becoming a professional artist. His work has graced the covers and pages of numerous aviation books and magazines. Boeing, Grumman, Sikorsky, Republic, and Pacific Propeller commissioned John to execute paintings of their products. His renderings of history's first practical aircraft are featured in the Time-Life book, *The Epic of Flight*. John and his wife, Wendy, reside in Bellevue, Washington.

Daren Dochterman—Daren was born in New York City. He always had a love and aptitude for drawing. At an early age, Daren realized the nexus of his artistic skills could be found in the film industry. He attended the University of Southern California for two years and contributed to the production of student films. Striking out on his own, he worked as a model builder, prop maker, and graphic artist in Hollywood. His entry into movie production began when he worked for director, James Cameron, restoring props from the film *Aliens*. This led to his assignment as assistant to the art department for Cameron's film, *The Abyss*. Dochterman's work contributed to the success of *Dr. Seuss's How the Grinch Stole Christmas*. He was honored with a Video Premier Award for his work. He supervised the visual effects for Robert Wise's director's edition of *Star Trek: The Motion Picture*. Daren resides in Sherman Oaks, California.

Gerald Asher—Gerry is a third-generation aviator and self-taught artist. He has rendered works of aviation art since he was an Air Force jet aircraft mechanic. He is a contributing artist to the Air Force Art Program, through which his works hang in the Pentagon, the Air Force Academy, and other Air Force facilities around the country. Under the auspices of the program, he has traveled to military installations around the world and had the opportunity to fly training and combat profiles in a variety of aircraft ranging from the Lockheed T-33 to the F-16. Gerry is a charter member of the American Society of Aviation Artists and has served as president of the eminent association. He has created works for book covers, calendars, magazines, model kit "box art" illustration, and other aviation commissions. Gerry is employed by American Airlines. He and his wife, Meg, reside in Fort Worth, Texas.

Robert McCall—Renowned NASA artist Robert McCall's diverse visual canon varies in scale from his classic "Decade of Achievement" US Postage Stamp Series to the six-story mural, *The Space Mural, A Cosmic View*, in the National Air and Space Museum in Washington, D.C. In addition to a litany of famous murals on permanent exhibition at space and research centers nationwide, Bob has supplied conceptual paintings for the films *The Black Hole*, *2001: A Space Odyssey*, and *Star Trek*. His canvas entitled *The Prologue and the Promise* enjoys a commanding presence in the Horizons Pavilion at Walt Disney's Epcot Center in Orlando, Florida. Robert is a founding member of the American Society of Aviation Artists. Robert and his wife, Louise, reside in Paradise Valley, Arizona.

Michael O'Neal—Michael's paintings depict the earliest periods in aviation history from the dawn of flight to the end of WWI. Wood and fabric airplanes dominate his paintings. While still in high school, Michael compiled a list of WWI pilots who hailed from his home state of New Jersey. His interviews with several of these aging pilots served to focus his artistic energies on the World War period 1914–1918. Michael is a member of the

American Society of Aviation Artists. He states that his art instruction has come primarily through ASAA forums and its members. Several of his paintings have been judged the best of those exhibited at ASAA forums. Mike resides in North Brunswick, New Jersey.

Richard L. Jefferies Jr.—A freelance artist, "Ric" is a design engineer for fire protection systems—NICET certified. Ric and his wife, Vickie, reside in Arvada, Colorado.

Luther Gore—A life member of the American Society of Aviation Artists. In 1983, he sparked interest in forming an association among aviation artists when he staged a forum at the University of Virginia. He was a professor in the Division of Humanities of the School of Engineering and Applied Science at the university. He is a member of the Central Virginia Watercolor Guild. Luther has four paintings in the Air Force Collection, as well as works in several museums. He has published articles on aviation art in popular magazines. His main interests are in early flight and general aviation. Luther and his wife, Joan, reside in Charlottesville, Virginia.

Doug Drexler—Illustrator and graphic artist. Doug is an Academy Award-winning makeup artist. He did the graphics of all seven years of *Star Trek: Deep Space Nine*. Doug designed illustrations and diagrams for the *Star Trek Encyclopedia*. Doug and his wife, Dorothy, reside in Burbank California.

PHOTO INDEX

CHAPTER TEN

CHAPTER ELEVEN

BIBLIOGRAPHY

Berton, Pierre. *Picture Book of Niagara Falls*. Toronto: McClelland & Stewart Inc., 1993.

Blumberg, Lisa. "Toward the Little House." American Heritage Magazine, Apr 1997.

Caidin, Martin. *Flying Forts*. New York: Ballantine Books, 1969.
Construction of Boulder Dam. Department of the Interior Publication, 1936.

Day, Donald. *Will Rogers: A Biography*. New York: David McKay Co. Inc., 1962.

Engle, Joel. *Gene Roddenberry*. New York: Hyperion, 1997.

Garraty, James A. *The American Nation Since 1860*. New York: Harper & Row Publishers, 1966.

Muzzey, David S., and Arthur S. Link. *Our Country's History*. Boston: Ginn and Company, 1964.

Prendergast, Curtis. *The First Aviators*. Virginia: Time-Life Books, 1980.

Reeves, Judith, and Garfield Stevens. *The Art of Star Trek*. New York: Pocket Books, 1995.

Solow, Herb F., and Robert H. Justman. *Inside Star Trek*. New York: Pocket Books, 1996.

Solow, Herb F. and Yvonne Solow. *Star Trek Sketchbook*. New York: Pocket Books, 1968.

Stevens, Joseph E. *Hoover Dam*. Norman: University of Oklahoma Press, 1988.

Sulzberger, C. L. *The American Heritage Pictorial Heritage of World War II*. New York: American Heritage Press, 1966.

Trager, James. *The People's Chronology*. New York: Holt, Rinehart and Winston, 1979.

Whitfield, Stephen, and Gene Roddenberry. *The Making of Star Trek*. New York: Ballantine Books, 1997.